NEW WORLD ORDER

WORLDS IN COLLISION
AND THE REBIRTH OF LIBERTY

TERRY JAMES & PETE GARCIA

DEFENDER

CRANE

The New World Order: Worlds in Collision and the Rebirth of Liberty
by Terry James & Peter Garcia

Defender
Crane, MO 65633
©2024 by Terry James
All rights reserved. Published 2023.

Printed in the United States of America.
ISBN: 9781948014656

A CIP catalog record of this book is available from the Library of Congress.

Cover design by Jeffrey Mardis

ACKNOWLEDGMENTS

I would like to express my eternal gratitude to my lovely wife, who keeps me grounded and focused on not just the world to come, but also on the tasks at hand.

To my five wonderful children, who longingly wait for me to break away from the computer to get my "detention," or to play or dance: Your patience with my writing is approaching saint status.

To my mother, who for years helped shape my love for conversation over long breakfasts and morning coffees: Thank you for all your support and encouragement.

Mondo: Thank you for contributing your words and thoughts to this project.

To my fellow watchmen, who not only keep our collective spirits up in these, the twilight of days, but who also keep our irons sharp. Thank you for your prayers, support, and encouragement.

Lastly, to my Lord Jesus Christ, without whom all hope would be lost.

—Pete Garcia

My profound thanks to Pete Garcia for his tremendous work and spiritual insights presented in this book. I have learned much, as I know will the reader of his words on behalf of our Lord.

My love and thanks to my editor, Angie, who is like a daughter to me, and is the very best at what she does, in my estimation.

To the rest of my family, Margaret, Terry, Jr., Nathan, Kerry, Dana, Jeanie, and all "grandchildren," my absolute love and devotion.

To all at Defender Publishing, our gratitude for seeing in this volume a work worthy of publication, while together we try to accomplish God's work while there is yet time to do so.

To our Lord Jesus Christ, without whom all would be without merit.
—Terry James

CONTENTS

FOREWORD
by Mondo Gonzales

"YOU'RE A CONSPIRACY THEORIST!" Have you ever been called this when you are trying to share with someone the need for discernment? This is a well-known phrase intended to shame or distract someone from a real discussion based on evidence and reason. Officially, this is called an *ad hominem* fallacy that does not actually contribute to meaningful discussion, but does reflect our modern culture's tendency to be led by emotion, hype, and propaganda.

Sadly, I have experienced this too often when discussing prophecy and current events. We live in an age of censorship, virtue signaling, ostracism, and shunning, often followed by public and social media shaming. All of these can ultimately be summed up as "cancel culture." Who of us wants to be ridiculed? Shamed? Called names? It is human nature to want to avoid societal ostracization. Most of us have an innate desire to be liked or to receive approval by our peers. However, we should heed the warning found in the Bible that we are not to be seeking the approval of others, but instead, we should be seeking the approval of God (John 12:43; Galatians 1:10).

So, is it true that I am a conspiracy theorist? YES!

However, this does not mean I succumb to every possible conspiracy. Yet if you believe the Bible, then you must also believe in conspiracies... at least in some way.

At the same time, we need to define what "conspiracy theorist" really means. Wikipedia is a great source for getting what the *unbelieving* world thinks about a topic. Sometimes, the website's articles are helpful, but in other instances they reflect an ungodly and patently unbiblical perspective. Here is a comment made about those who engage in conspiracy theory:

> Psychologists usually attribute belief in conspiracy theories and finding a conspiracy where there is none to a number of psychopathological conditions such as paranoia, schizotypy, narcissism, and insecure attachment, or to a form of cognitive bias called "illusory pattern perception."

Do you notice the labeling in this description? Granted, there are some people who are extreme skeptics and see something sinister behind every bush, but are there genuine conspiracies?

Let's define "conspiracy." Wikipedia, in this instance, actually provides a helpful definition:

> A conspiracy, also known as a plot, is a secret plan or agreement between persons (called conspirers or conspirators) for an unlawful or harmful purpose, such as murder or treason, especially with political motivation, while keeping their agreement secret from the public or from other people affected by it.

It would be beneficial here to examine this definition from a biblical perspective. Can you think of anyone in the Bible who is working behind the scenes for harmful reasons (cf. John 10:10)? Do any of these plans involve murder (cf. John 8:44)? Does this secret effort involve political machinations (Revelation 13:1–4)? Will it have a wide-ranging effect on people (Revelation 13:5–8)? I hope you can see where I am going with this, but I must ask: Do you actually believe what the Bible says? I want to spend some time examining what the Bible teaches about conspiracy

and the master conspirator who has been working behind the scenes…
from the very first pages of God's Word.

When we study Genesis 1 and 2, we come away with a theology that
shows the beauty of God's newly created universe. The Bible reveals the
creating and forming of a universe that is suitable for humans to enjoy,
live in, and rule. We also observe that this creation is assessed by God
Himself and declared not just to be *good*, but "very good" (Genesis 1:31).
Have you ever wondered what your theology and worldview would be
like if you didn't have the first three chapters of Genesis? They give a
foundational understanding of God's goodness and also of how the world
became the way we see it today.

God wanted us to have this information to get a balanced understanding of how we evaluate our past, present, and future. As we read
chapters 1 and 2 of Genesis, we cannot help but feel uplifted, encouraged,
and excited for what God had in store for humanity. Then comes chapter
3, verse 1.

Immediately after a paradisiacal introduction, the Bible describes
a sinister character arriving on the scene. He is labeled as the craftiest
of all God's creations (Genesis 3:1; cf. Ezekiel 28:12) and deceives Eve
into rebelling against God's goodness (Genesis 3:13; 2 Corinthians 11:3;
1 Timothy 2:14). God then reveals the future for this insurgent spiritual
entity as being a lifelong opponent of humanity (the woman) and her
eventual heroic descendant who will one day destroy this renegade.

The Bible has much to say about the machinations of Satan as the
leader of an extensive wicked kingdom seeking to enslave and destroy
humanity (Matthew 12:26). There isn't enough room in this foreword to
be exhaustive, but if we take a bird's-eye view, we can gain some foundational truths about his activities in the past and as we approach the end
of the age.

Let's circle back for a moment. Do I believe in a master conspirator
who, from the beginning of time, has been working behind the scenes
to bring about a competing worldwide system of rulership? Absolutely.
We must embrace this if we believe how the Bible describes Satan. His

very name means "adversary" (Satan) and "slanderer" (Devil). Notice the importance of 1 John 5:19, which reads, "We know that we are from God, and the *whole world lies in the power of the evil one*" (emphasis added). Literally, the whole world "reclines under" the wicked one.

This makes great sense in that Satan is called the "god of this world" (2 Corinthians 4:4) and the "prince of the power of the air" who is working in and through all unbelievers (Ephesians 2:2) in order to deceive the nations (Revelation 12:9; 20:3, 8). His generals and lieutenants are described as "*rulers*, against the *authorities*, against the *cosmic powers* over this present darkness, against the *spiritual forces of evil* in the heavenly places" (Ephesians 6:12, emphasis added).

Jesus called Satan the "ruler of this world" (John 12:31; 14:30; 16:11) who seeks to steal, kill, and destroy (10:10). One of the most illuminating passages is when Satan began his temptations of Jesus immediately before the start of His ministry.

> And the devil took him up and showed him *all the kingdoms of the world* in a moment of time, and said to him, "To you I will give all this authority and their glory, *for it has been delivered to me, and I give it to whom I will.* If you, then, will worship me, it will all be yours." (Luke 4:5–7, emphasis added)

What can we learn from this passage? Satan has access to all the kingdoms of the world. He shows them to Jesus and offers them to Him if only He will defect from God and worship Satan. Jesus doesn't dispute Satan's claim. In fact, scholars recognize that the language used here from the Aramaic Syriac versions is technical language found in legal contracts. As we have seen, Jesus already acknowledged three times that Satan is the ruler (Greek: *arche*) of this world. The Greek word has the idea of administrative or ruling authority. It is the same word used to describe Satan as being the ruler (*arche*) of the demonic realm (Matthew 9:34).

We are looking at the forest here, but Terry and Pete are going to be delving into the trees. I am looking at the skeleton; they are going to be putting on the muscles and flesh. Satan has been active from the beginning of time. He has established his own parallel worldwide kingdom in direct opposition to God's sovereignty over this world. Make no mistake: God is the supreme owner of everything (Psalm 24:1). However, mankind is God's vice regent, and the entire sweeping story of redemption is God allowing this war between Satan and the woman (and her seed) to play itself out all the way until the end (Genesis 3:15).

Satan is crafty and is always seeking to influence individuals who, in turn, sway nations to his will. Satan also has tremendous help in accomplishing his behind-the-scenes manipulation of entire nations. When we examine the background of Daniel when he is praying in Babylon for the return of the Jews to Israel, we get insight into this secret war against God's plans.

> Then he said to me, "Fear not, Daniel, for from the first day that you set your heart to understand [three weeks earlier] and humbled yourself before your God, your words have been heard, and I have come because of your words. The *prince of the kingdom of Persia* withstood me twenty-one days, but Michael, one of the chief princes, came to help me, for I was left there with the kings of Persia, and came to make you understand what is to happen to your people in the latter days. For the vision is for days yet to come." (Daniel 10:12–14, emphasis added)

> Then he said, "Do you know why I have come to you? But now I will return to *fight against the prince of Persia*; and when I go out, behold, the *prince of Greece will come*. But I will tell you what is inscribed in the book of truth: there is none who contends by my side against these except Michael, your prince." (Daniel 10:20–21, emphasis added)

Daniel is praying for God's powerful hand to bring His people, Israel, back, but they are being opposed by evil princes. These aren't just minor demons, but extremely powerful beings who are principalities over entire nations (Persia and Greece). Michael serves as the chief prince of the nation of Israel. We get an insight into what scholars call the Divine Council.

Satan is the ring leader and the master conspirator who, along with his evil princes, are manipulating the nations of the world. This is not just relegated to times past, but is absolutely occurring in the present. Some of the characteristics Jesus uses to describe the end-of-the-age Tribulation are the following:

> And there will be signs in sun and moon and stars, and on the earth *distress of nations* in perplexity because of the roaring of the sea and the waves, people fainting with fear and with foreboding of what is coming on the world. For the powers of the heavens will be shaken. (Luke 21:25–26, emphasis added)

The nations of the world will be in chaos, not only because of God's supernatural cosmic judgments, but because Satan will be given permission to implement fully the plan he has been advancing from the beginning. This plan involves the nations aligning under Satan's complete and unmitigated power in order to bring him worship and to oppose the return of Jesus to establish God's righteous rule. This prophecy is revealed clearly in the book of Psalms.

> Why do the *nations rage* and the peoples plot in vain? The *kings of the earth* set themselves, and the rulers take counsel together, *against the LORD and against his Anointed,* saying, "Let us burst their bonds apart and cast away their cords from us." (Psalm 2:1–3, emphasis added)

This psalm has clear eschatological references. Psalm 2:9 is quoted in Revelation 2:27; 12:5; and 19:15 in reference to Jesus ruling with a rod of iron. Satan is constantly conspiring behind the scenes in the various countries of the world to position these nations to stand opposite God's plan for Jesus and the world. He has been doing this from time immemorial, but as we approach the end of the age, we see it coming to its culmination.

Satan knows the Bible very well (cf. Matthew 4:6) and looks forward to the time when God will grant him unlimited authority over humanity. He will also finally receive the opportunity to gain the worship he has so eagerly desired (Matthew 4:9; Isaiah 14:13–14).

> And I saw a beast rising out of the sea, with ten horns and seven heads, with ten diadems on its horns and blasphemous names on its heads. And the beast that I saw was like a leopard; its feet were like a bear's, and its mouth was like a lion's mouth. And to it the *dragon gave his power and his throne and great authority.* One of its heads seemed to have a mortal wound, but its mortal wound was healed, and *the whole earth marveled as they followed* the beast. And *they worshiped the dragon, for he had given his authority to the beast,* and they *worshiped* the beast, saying, "Who is like the beast, and who can fight against it?" And the beast was given a mouth uttering haughty and blasphemous words, and *it was allowed to exercise authority for forty-two months.* (Revelation 13:1–5, emphasis added)

As we approach the end game of this age, Satan is working overtime through his evil kingdom to establish his New World Order. He doesn't do this alone. In addition to his spiritual angelic and demonic collaborators, he finds willing human participants to fulfill his worldwide governmental system. In the same way Satan offered Jesus great glory and authority, he offers fame, riches, power, and sensual pleasures to those who will sell their soul to him. Satan is positioning these people in various strategic arenas so that when he gets the green light from God after the Rapture takes place, he will immediately begin to implement his New World Order. The Bible is not silent.

As for the ten horns, out of this kingdom ten kings will arise; and another will arise after them, and he will be different from the previous ones and will subdue three kings. (Daniel 7:24)

The ten horns which you saw are ten kings who *have not yet received a kingdom*, but they receive authority as kings with the beast for one hour. These have one purpose, and *they give their power and authority to the beast*. (Revelation 17:12, emphasis added)

From these two passages we learn several characteristics of these ten kings:

- The first is that the Greek word for king (*basileus*) in Revelation 17:12 can have a wider nuance than just what we understand in the word "king." One of the best Greek lexicons, BDAG [the Brill Dictionary of Ancient Greek], has the following as its second entry: **one who possesses unusual or transcendent power.** This meaning seems consistent with Revelation 17:12, where we are told that these ten figures do not have a ruling kingdom *as of yet*, but *will receive* authority to rule as royal kings for the final "hour" of Antichrist's (the Beast's) reign in the seven-year Tribulation period. We will call them ten "influencers" because they do have some valuable level of authority and power that the Antichrist would seek to leverage (17:13). In other words, they exhibit "unusual power" or influence, as BDAG mentions.
- They are not required to be in *governmental* or ruling positions at the time of their arrangement with the Antichrist. They receive this after their agreement with him.
- Additionally, when the time comes, they will give this influence or power over to the Beast and in return are given the ability to rule with him in his final kingdom (17:13).

Which nongovernmental figures are gaining authority, power, and influence in the present who could someday be handed over to the coming Antichrist in exchange for a share in his autocratic rule of the entire world?

Financial Oligarchs

We are witnessing in our day the super-rich not often sticking to the one industry that made them wealthy, but instead they're spreading their wealth into sometimes completely disparate technologies or fields of research. Think of Elon Musk, who began in web software, transitioned to financial services, then to SpaceX, Tesla, biomechanical engineering, and other industries.

Further, it's not rocket science to recognize that these same people, with staggering amounts of money, are capable of influencing on a worldwide scale. This certainly can include shaping the political landscape through outright bribes or the political lobby system. This level of indirect—but pervasive and massive—impact doesn't require them to be the ones in actual power or governmental positions. Instead, they wield their influence through proxies who have been purchased through the greed of politicians to stay in power. Why is Bill Gates so influential over many nations of the world?

Technological Oligarchs
(Technocrats)

When discussing the technological influence of these corporate giants, it would be good to give the definition of a "technocrat." A *technocrat* is a proponent of technocracy, which is defined as: "a theory and movement, prominent about 1932, advocating control of industrial resources, reform of financial institutions, and reorganization of the social system, based on the findings of technologists and engineers." Ultimately, technocrats seek to influence all areas of society and need not be the direct wielders of governmental power.

The World Economic Forum (WEF) is dedicated to seeing a complete reset of the way life on planet earth functions. They are unashamed in presenting their vision to be accomplished through technological advancement by the year 2030 (known as "Agenda 2030" and the "Great Reset"). Klaus Schwab wrote *The Fourth Industrial Revolution* in 2015, and in the appendix of that book he highlights the technological details that cover twenty-one up-and-coming technologies.[1]

Schwab writes:

> The World Economic Forum's Global Agenda Council on the Future of Software and Society conducted a survey of 800 executives to gauge when business leaders anticipate that these game-changing technologies would break into the public domain to a significant degree, and to understand fully the implications of these shifts to individuals, organizations, government and society.[2]

The following is his list of game-changing technologies:

1) Implantable technologies
2) Our digital presence
3) Vision as the new interface
4) Wearable Internet
5) Ubiquitous computing
6) A supercomputer in our pockets
7) Storage for all
8) The Internet of and for things
9) The connected home
10) Smart cities
11) Big data for decisions
12) Driverless cars
13) Artificial intelligence and decision-making

14) AI and white-collar jobs

15) Robotics and services

16) Bitcoin and the blockchain

17) The sharing economy

18) Governments and the blockchain

19) 3D printing and manufacturing

20) 3D printing and human health

21) 3D printing and consumer products

We could add some ancillary technologies that are connected with all the above, including nanotechnology, quantum computing, biotechnology, the Internet of Things, the industrial Internet of things, decentralized consensus, fifth-generation wireless technologies, and satellite Internet technology for worldwide distribution.

These ungodly financial oligarchs and technocrats are conspirators working behind the scenes who will one day give their influence to their leader, the master conspirator, Satan. Even before the latest extreme increases in wealth, secret societies and individuals have been corrupting, extorting, threatening, and enriching political leaders in order to weaponize and militarize intelligence communities for the coming New World Order. The Bilderbergers, the Rockefellers, the Council on Foreign Relations (CFR), the United Nations, and the Trilateral Commission, etc., are just some of the groups that are solidifying the groundwork for its arrival.

Do you believe in a master conspirator seeking to establish a one-world system? If you believe the Bible, you must. He is relentless and his kingdom is arriving very soon. Thankfully, this is not the end of the story.

And then the lawless one will be revealed, whom the Lord Jesus will kill with the breath of His mouth and bring to nothing by the appearance of His coming. (2 Thessalonians 2:8)

Mondo Gonzales
Prophecy Watchers

PROLOGUE

"PROLOGUE" IS DEFINED by one dictionary as "an event or action that leads to another event or situation." Nothing could more appropriately frame what the people of the world face today.

God's Word lays out the greatest story ever foretold. The Bible does so in much, but not minute, detail. There is, however, more than enough detail to say with profound certainty the course mankind is on, in terms of trajectory and destination.

In one sense, that course is tragic, even horrendous. In another sense, that ultimate destination is glorious.

We strive with this book to present that course, trajectory, and destination—employing issues, events, and a degree of offered thoughts on history yet future—all through the prism of Bible prophecy.

It is our view that humanity has now entered the last of the last days. That is, we see the hour-by-hour, day-by-day developments in every aspect of human life as preparation for fulfillment of Bible prophecy leading to Christ's return and beyond.

All in this regard is a prologue to "things to come," as the title of the great work by Dr. J. Dwight Pentecost would have it.[3]

New World Order: Worlds in Collision and the Rebirth of Liberty covers, in-depth, the unfolding actions, reactions, and interactions of humankind within the realms of the physical, geophysical, and spiritual. In order to begin looking at future prophecies and their prospects for fulfillment, we look at when, where, and why things have developed to this point.

The Garden

Most all of us know the story of the Garden of Eden. Many, particularly those in the worlds of academic, medical, scientific, and other disciplines, speak of the narrative as myth. We—the authors—believe the account of the Garden of Eden and the Fall of man to be absolutely true, as presented in the book of Genesis.

When the first woman, then the first man partook of the forbidden fruit from the tree of the knowledge of good and evil, the world order as they knew it came crashing down. They were removed from the Garden and were forbidden to be near the tree of life, which would have kept them from aging toward life-ending pronouncement upon sin. Such an eternal state of moving farther from their Creator would have, it is thought, produced monstrous degeneration that is unfathomable.

This is the story of the First World Order, told from the very mind of God through Moses.

The term "New World Order" in most Internet searches will turn up articles declaring the matters involving conspiracy theories entertained by religious fanatics. This is to be expected from sources attuned in every way to the god of this world and the prince of the power of the air. Those so attuned cannot see truth and have no desire to do so, because truth is spiritually discerned.

That First World Order degenerated because of sin infection that brought death upon everyone in it except for Noah, his family, and Enoch, who "walked with God, and was not, for God took him" (Genesis 5:24).

God told Adam that in the day he ate of the tree of the knowledge of good and evil, he would surely die. Looking at this forewarning in the sense of God saying that a day is like a thousand years and a thousand years are as a day (2 Peter 3:8), God's Word again proves infallibly true.

No man or woman reached that thousand-year mark in age—Methuselah being the oldest, at 969.

People, apart from the God who created us, have proven to become increasingly worse. The First World Order so alienated from the Creator became, to this point in human history, the vilest world order of all.

Genesis tells us that every thought of humankind was "only on evil continually" (6:5). That First World Order was filled with violence; the order became total disorder. It became so wicked and corrupt that the Lord said He was sorry He had made the human race (Genesis 6:6). What a statement!

While we are sure there is much more than we can possibly know wrapped up in the meaning of God's declaration in that regard, the antediluvian world order, if Scripture is to be believed—and it is—was demonstratively shown to be the most rebellious of human history. God, Himself, proved it by destroying all but the eight souls who went into the ark the day the deluge began.

Tower of Babel

When people again began to repopulate the earth, the rebellious spirit returned with a vengeance. Influence by fallen angelic activity doubtless plagued the generations after the ark alighted on the mountain of Ararat. There came from among that demonic influence, many scholars believe, the leader named Nimrod.

As there were myths and legends of giants and demigods that arose from the fallen angelic activity during the pre-Flood generations, so too, following the Flood, other beings that seemed to have demonic powers determined to again establish a world order. These beings, wanting no part of Heaven's influence, corrupted fallen humankind at the time of Babel (see Genesis 11:1–9).

The people were basically of one mind, thinking they would build a tower that would reach into the heavens. By this, we take it, they had determined to usurp the very throne of the Creator. Again, they wanted no deity to rule over them, although they had chosen, in effect, the god of this world—Satan—to do so.

God, of course, looked down and told us the people had begun to build that tower, and that, because they were created in His image, they would eventually be able to do whatever they determined to do. Again, there is almost certainly much more wrapped up in that statement than our finite minds can comprehend.

God brought this second attempt at world-order-building to an end by His heavenly forces coming to earth and disrupting the tower construction. He scattered the people throughout the earth, first confusing their communication by giving them different languages.

Since that Heaven-sent disruption, fallen humanity has been determined to incessantly try to rebuild that tower. It is not a physical structure they endeavor to build, but a spiritual construct, led by the same nucleus of fallen angelic activity as during antediluvian and tower of Babel times.

Satan and his minions still use people as "useful idiots," like Vladimir Lenin, who was thought to have coined the phrase, did in his use of the dupes within the proletariat (common people) in constructing the communist model.

The Bible puts it in the following terms for times leading up to the establishment of the Final World Order:

> For we wrestle not against flesh and blood, but against principalities, against powers, against the rulers of the darkness of this world, against spiritual wickedness in high places. (Ephesians 6:12)

New World Order looks in-depth at the neo-tower builders who are not only present among us today, but are stepping up their efforts exponentially to bring in one world order. A primary indication of where things stand now can be found in the New World Order blueprint document/program termed "Agenda 21."

Agenda 21

Agenda 21 policies date back to the 1970s, but the plan got its real start in 1992 at the Earth Summit in Rio de Janeiro when President George H. W. Bush signed onto it. President Bill Clinton signed it later and continued the program in the United States.

This United Nations-spawned document lays out the neo-tower of Babel builders' strategy for resetting the world order. It is the same old plot, disguised as a plan to "save Mother Earth."

The gist is that it intends to remove 95 percent of earth's human population. At last report, they intend to accomplish this by 2030. In this way, the earth will be made "sustainable" so that all other life—wildlife, the environment, the trees, waters, etc.—can live/exist in pollution-free symbiosis.

Human interaction is, the Agenda 21 planners believe, destructive to the planet, thus global warming (now called "climate change") must be dealt with, even by draconian measures, when necessary.

These globalists want to remove all private property owners' rights to make decisions on the lands. Only the governing body—presumably the elite UN officials—knows how best to handle such matters.

They believe people don't have the ability to be good stewards of the land. They must therefore take control of lands, move most of the populations left after the paring-down by 95 percent into cities, and let the rest of the lands return to a natural state.

So, external threats from diabolists like UN would-be masters and aggressor-dictatorships such as Russia and China, as well as internal threats by administrative state wickedness, persistently eat away God-guaranteed rights. Again, we have witnessed this result, from the seismic shift in morality within our nation to the economic reset declared by the internationalist tyrants of globalist reconstructionists bent on instituting the New World Order.

But to think of liberty-ending threats to America and freedom throughout the world in terms of political ideologies is to miss what is happening in actuality. It is not the tyrannical, geopolitical enslavement mentality that is the great threat. It isn't the national, liberal political ideology versus the conservative—not Democrats versus Republicans—that represents the greatest threat. It is Satan and his minions versus God in Heaven—evil versus good—that is most deadly. It is, again, the titanic struggle against the "wickedness in high places" of Ephesians 6:12.

Of course, at the heart of this blueprint is Satan's hatred of God and of His creation of the human race. The serpent's plan has always been to destroy as much of God's creation as he can. God's absolute love for people particularly brings that old serpent's fangs to bare—fangs with which he has injected the sin-venom that brought death into the world.

Globalists Go after America

While the powers and principalities of Ephesians 6:12 are intent on bringing the entire world under their rule, it is the United States of America they consider a priority. This is because America is the apex nation in all of human history in terms of material blessings (wealth and technology). These enemies of the US ravenously desire to have our assets for building their supposed Utopia.

America is the primary holdup to their goal of getting rid of all national sovereignty.

America was founded upon Judeo-Christian concepts, its Constitution a document that itself seems miraculously bestowed through the founding fathers and their recognition of God's preeminence over human affairs. Sadly, and tragically, we have watched Heaven's influence over this great experiment in liberty being assaulted in every philosophical, ideological, and, particularly, spiritual way.

Prayer and Bible-reading in public-school classrooms were forbidden through judicial fiat, and the killing of babies in the wombs of their mothers was instituted through the same extraconstitutional way, and we now come to the time of national insanity through LGBTQ (lesbian, gay, bisexual, transsexual, and queer or questioning) and other wickedness.

The "reprobate mind" of Romans 1:28 and following is where we stand, rather than "in God we trust."

Satan has had his way, and America is being led into his coming Antichrist regime one cultural and societal act of national suicide at a time.

The New World Order machinery has its own gravity that becomes stronger the deeper we move into the end of the age. It will ultimately draw all into its quagmire. It will result in seven years of Hell on earth.

Liberty's Rebirth!

The satanic tug of the humanistic drive to separate man from the Creator is powerful. We see what it has done to history's most profound national experiment in liberty. Removal of prayer and Bible reading in classrooms has devastated a nation, in that it started a decline that has now become practically a freefall into the abyss of sin enslavement.

But the final chapter, as they say, has not been written. That wicked regime of a one-world, satanic New World Order is on track to collide with God's World Order. It will indeed be a collision! The collision will be more titanic in impact than anything produced throughout all the ages.

From the collision of those opposing worlds will come a time of peace and prosperity like in the time before all of this hellish rebellion, destruction, and death began—like in the pre-sin time in the Garden of Eden.

Read *New World Order: Worlds in Collision and the Rebirth of Liberty* with assurance from the Word of God on high: All will be well. There is coming a rebirth of freedom that can only be endowed by the Savior of the world and the King of all kings—the Lord Jesus Christ, the Creator of all things.

ONE

THE FIRST CONSPIRACY

We are the representatives of the cosmos; we are an example of
what hydrogen atoms can do, given 15 billion years of cosmic
evolution.[4]

CARL SAGAN

WHILE WE CAN'T BE ABSOLUTELY CERTAIN, the year 2033 should mark
somewhere close to the six-thousandth year since Creation. We know
that because the same year marks the two-thousand-year anniversary
since Jesus walked the earth. Abraham lived two thousand years before
Him, and Adam, two thousand before him.

The Bible is quite clear that, in the beginning, everything was good—
not just according to human standards, but good according to God's
perfect standard. That should tell you just how pristine and beautiful
the earth used to be. But it wasn't just the earth and the universe that
were good; the first man and woman were also included in this worthy
standard.

God made man out of the dust of the earth and woman out of the
man's side. They were created in the image of God to be His image-bear-
ers upon the earth and to govern the new creation on His behalf. The first
man, Adam, was given this authority when God gave him dominion over
not just the earth, but over the newly created creatures as well (Genesis
1:26). Although we can't be dogmatic about how long Adam and Eve
lived in this state of perfect innocence, we know it wasn't long enough
before another would come to ruin God's good work.

Before God created the earth, He put into place the immeasurable angelic order. These were spirit beings of immense power who were to serve as God's messengers, oracles, guardians, and worshippers, and were to carry out countless other roles in the heavens. In this angelic order, there was one angel, Lucifer, who had been created above them all. The angels, which included the cherubim, seraphim, archangels, and presumably numerous other types, were eyewitnesses to all of God's creative acts in bringing the universe into existence during Creation week (Job 38:4–7).

Prior to Adam, Lucifer was the pinnacle of God's created order. God described this angel as being "perfect" in his "ways...till iniquity was found in" him (Ezekiel 28:15). However, instead of rejecting a darkened and prideful thought, Lucifer embraced it and allowed it to fester in his mind until he was convinced he could overthrow God. In the process, he convinced a third of the angelic host to follow him, and in the rebellion, they were cast out of Heaven and condemned to eternal judgment in the age to come (Revelation 12:4; Luke 10:18; Ezekiel 28:16). Adding insult to injury, the newly created man, Adam the image-bearer of God, took this position, displacing Lucifer. It was at this point that another darkened thought entered his corrupted mind. He would destroy humanity if it was the last thing he ever did.

The Garden Conspiracy

Now the serpent was more cunning than any beast of the field which the Lord God had made. And he said to the woman, "Has God indeed said, 'You shall not eat of every tree of the garden'?" And the woman said to the serpent, "We may eat the fruit of the trees of the garden; but of the fruit of the tree which is in the midst of the garden, God has said, 'You shall not eat it, nor shall you touch it, lest you die.'" Then the serpent said to the woman, *"You will not surely die. For God knows that in the day you eat of it your eyes will be opened, and you will be like God, knowing good and evil."* (Genesis 3:1–5, emphasis added)

If we were so inclined as to receive our history on the origins of humankind from the secular, westernized public education system, or perhaps from any number of higher academic institutions, leading scientific research groups, or even pop culture, we would be uncompromisingly led to believe that life began not an act of divine providence, but rather, of cosmic coincidence.

We would be taught that the origin of life was an accidental combination of a chain of events spanning millions of years. We would be inculcated with the belief that the earth is hundreds of millions of years old, and that the universe can be dated back into the billions. We would be shown, through impressive modeling data, how the big bang erupted (out of nothing) and produced (out of nothing) all the necessary planetary and celestial material necessary to create both the light and the planetary conditions necessary for evolutionary life to begin. Again, we would be taught that life was, *in fact*, not an act of divine providence, but rather the result of spontaneous, unmitigated willpower.

Truth be told, the only fact in all of this is that the teachings presented in the previous paragraph have been the standard model of public education dating back to the 1930s here in the United States.

Nevertheless, for the godless, life spontaneously erupted from nonliving material into a single-celled organism that, miraculously, contained all the genetic material for all future living matter. Then, over the course of millions of years, those unbelievable organisms began to evolve into something akin to tadpoles. Much later, our *tadpolian* forefathers decided they'd had enough of the primordial goo and decided to try out land for a change.

However, don't ask where land, plants, or the atmosphere came from—or which came first. Better yet, don't ask any questions at all; just accept it all on blind faith.

For them, all of life boils down to a simple phrase captured in the epic twentieth-century mockumentary, *Jurassic Park*, in saying, "Life finds a way." Thus, through the act of sheer willpower, simple life—somehow, some way—continued to defy the laws of thermodynamics by evolving into increasingly complex organisms that eventually produced what pale-ontologists would later come to believe was our great, great, great, great, great, great, great, great, great, great, great, great, great, great, great (*ad infinitum*) ancestor: the caveman.

The experts, so-called, of our day believe early primeval man and woman (not sure about the other 406 gender identities) lived nothing more than short, rudimentary lives consisting of hunting woolly mammoths, doodling on cave walls, and clubbing each other over the head with large sticks. To these same supposed learned and esteemed scientists and scholars, ancient history was primitive, brutal, and short.

But was it really?

Does science show how life can come from nonlife? Does science show in what order our *tadpolian* forefathers evolved? Was it the eyes and the arms first, or the mouth and feet? What about stomachs or digestive systems? Where did the land and atmosphere come from? Where else does science show us that simple organisms can continually evolve into increasingly complex organisms without any new genetic information added? Who provided the impossibly complex genetic information anyway? Does science show that humankind is increasingly evolving?

Or are we de-evolving?

Which makes more sense—that humankind is physically evolving through natural selection, or that we are de-evolving as we increasingly inherit genetic deficiencies from our ancestors?

What about the Neanderthal model the godless want us to believe in that early primal people were ape-like, impossibly simple-minded, and incapable of higher intellect?

If that were true, what do we do with the massive megalithic stone structures that both defy ancient construction capabilities (e.g., Bronze Age tools cutting hardened stone) and litter our planet thousands of years later? Never mind the fact that today we still can't figure out how they accomplished these feats, or why.

But somehow we're expected to take it on faith that we are the evolved and they are the primitive?

If you hadn't picked up on the sarcasm bleeding through the previous dialogue, our apologies.

Yes, we are making fun of the so-called experts who have somehow managed to control the narrative of our origin story since Charles Darwin first plagiarized his ideas on "natural selection" from his grandfather, Erasmus Darwin.[5]

The truth is, since before Adam and Eve took their first steps on planet earth nearly six thousand years ago, a malevolent agenda was already afoot. That previously mentioned angelic being of extreme beauty and unparalleled intelligence, Lucifer, had already been cast out of Heaven for his failed *coup d'état*. Angry at God and resentful of humankind, he made it his mission to not just *destroy* creation, but to *defile* in every way possible this new pinnacle of God's creation. Therefore, being our chief adversary, Lucifer must have taken great pleasure in convincing man he was not, in fact, God's image-bearer; rather, he was a monkey's uncle.

In a more pragmatic sense, this conspiracy of origins dates back to the 1800s, when science itself was still in its embryonic stage. Since then, research has increasingly demonstrated that the existence of natural order and humans could not be accidental, due to our impossibly complex genetic structure. In light of this dawning realization, Lucifer (Satan) made it one of his primary missions to keep humankind confused as to who they are and where they came from. So long as folks remained uncertain on these two points, Lucifer, the Devil, could continue to wreak havoc upon the human race.

But why bring all this up in a book about the New World Order?

Well, because it's foundational to the worldviews of the men and women leading this globalist agenda. If there is no God, then there is no creation. If there is no creation, then we are here as some type of cosmic accident, thus, natural selection (survival of the fittest) is applicable. And the globalists firmly believe they are the fittest. The only other option (apart from God creating us) is that there is some benign, yet detached, all-powerful force working through the cosmos.

Either way, the globalists believe they should inherit the earth, and we (those living in the economy-class section of the world) should make it happen.

This reeks of elitism. It also reeks of paradox.

You see, if what they believe is true—primeval man's life was simple, brutish, and short—why would they invoke ancient gods and beliefs to bring the world back to the way it was? We see in invocations at places such as CERN (European Organization for Nuclear Research) and the United Nations this desire to slather the occult and pagan on all these globalist efforts, yet they insist we evolved from simple life to masters of destiny. If that is true, then why invoke the ancient past? Why try to get back to an age of myth and magic?

It is inconsistency at its finest.

The simple truth is that they (the global elite) will invoke any god, any belief system, and any occult practice, so long as it is not of the one true God of the Holy Bible. It makes sense if Lucifer is behind the scenes pulling all the strings.

Lucifer doesn't care who we are or what we believe, provided it's not of God or of the Holy Bible.

Thus, the agenda behind obscuring our true history: In blinding us to our past, Satan can dictate our future.

Now, according to Scripture, the Antediluvian Age (roughly one to two thousand years or so from Adam to Noah's Flood) wasn't filled with knuckle-dragging cavemen, but with folks who were, in fact, quite advanced. Not only that, but they were—physically speaking—far superior to us today. This thought is far more scientific than anything Darwin or his pro-evolutionist protégés could claim.[6]

For example, if Adam was the perfect man and Eve the perfect woman, both handmade by God Almighty Himself, it makes sense that they should be the most perfect physical specimens to ever live. And, after their Fall, once sin (the corrupting agent) was introduced into the human genome, it also makes sense that their offspring (successively) would inherit that corrosive sin nature. This would, to an increasingly diminishing degree, breed out through subsequent generations that original level of perfection (just as copies of copies increasingly degrade in quality with each succeeding copy). As time passed and subsequent generations came and went, humankind's level of genetic and physical perfection would continue on its entropic decline toward where we are today.

Scientifically speaking, this is what makes the most sense as explained to us by the law of increasing entropy (i.e., the second law of thermodynamics), which states that, as time passes, moving energy creates unusable energy that is lost forever. Translated into our own world, it means, given enough time, things break down and fall apart. This includes humankind.

Evolutionary scientists teach the opposite: Things begin in complete disarray and somehow, miraculously, become more organized and complex over time. Therefore, what evolutionists propose is quite the opposite of what *natural law* actually does. So what is natural law? The Roman lawyer Cicero, in *De Republica*, wrote:

> True law is right reason in agreement with nature. It is applied universally and is unchanging and everlasting...there will be no different laws in Rome and in Athens, or different laws now and in the future, but one eternal and unchangeable law valid for all nations and all times.[7]

Decades later, and inspired by the Holy Spirit, the Apostle Paul said very much the same thing:

> (...or when Gentiles, who do not have the law, by nature do the things in the law, these, although not having the law, are a law to themselves, who show the work of the law written in their hearts, their conscience also bearing witness, and between themselves their thoughts accusing or else excusing them) in the day when God will judge the secrets of men by Jesus Christ, according to my gospel. (Romans 2:14–16)

It is in this rejection of what God has ordained as the natural law that has perverted their understanding of it. Through this perversion comes a blinding. What is the culmination of this blinding but the divine process of judgment wherein people are being *given over* to a reprobate mind (Romans 1:18–31)? That's where we are today. Not only are these globalists elite being given over to these corrupt ways of thinking, but now they're unable to come to the knowledge of the truth.

This wouldn't be so bad if they were just Internet trolls living in their parents' basements spewing their nonsensical gibberish to an uncaring world. But they aren't. These are the movers and shakers in our world today. They are the politicians and technocrats dictating how our nations are to function. And if they are given over to this degenerate mindset, then we must suffer unnecessarily under the tutelage of their godless, logic-less, secular humanism.

So what does the modern-day godless, secular, humanist education illogically promote?

1) Life is accidental. (If that were true, we shouldn't know it.)
2) Life can come from nonliving things. (If this were true, why isn't that principle demonstrated anywhere else in nature?)
3) Life evolves from simple to complex without new information. (Again, the laws of nature disprove this via the law of entropy.)

All three of these tenets directly contradict not only the teachings found in Bible, but the natural law as well!

Again, the reason we're bringing this up in a book on the New World Order is that this belief the godless have is foundational to everything they are trying to do in the here and now. The continued propaganda of human evolution is essential to their godless eschatology. It is why they are fighting so hard to promote global depopulation, transhumanism, and moral relativism. You must understand, dear reader, that the people promoting and championing this idea of a New World Order don't believe in the God of the Bible. As such, they don't believe in the true history of the origin of humanity. Therefore, if they are confused on where we came from, you can bet your bottom dollar they are confused on where we are headed.

Origin of Hidden Knowledge

Let's revisit for a moment when Adam and Eve rebelled against their Creator in the garden paradise of Eden and followed the advice of a slimy serpent (possessed by Lucifer). This part is critical, because it is something the New World Order types, who are Luciferians, need to believe in order to remain Luciferians.

The moment Adam and Eve ate from the forbidden fruit, they realized they were naked. Now, according to the Bible, being aware of their nakedness was not a sin, but it directly correlated to their sin. The sin was eating what they had been told not to eat. In fact, God had specifically warned: "In the day ye eat of it [the fruit of the tree], ye shall die" (Genesis 2:17). However, modern Luciferians would like us to believe that what Lucifer actually did by possessing the snake and tricking Adam and Eve into eating the fruit was freeing humankind from the clutches of an authoritarian God. For them, this was the moment people became enlightened and realized that self-deification was in the realm of possibility. As silly as this idea sounds, it has spawned countless religions and inspired numerous secret societies to search for an elusive truth that doesn't exist.

Scripture teaches that while Eve was deceived, Adam ate willfully (1 Timothy 2:13–14), and the consequences of their actions were immediate. Here are the three noticeable changes in the first couple's situation:

1. **Fear of the consequences of their action:** They were suddenly cognizant of their dire situation. An example of this we can relate to in the twenty-first century is in those dawning seconds when you realize the phone call or email you just responded to, believing it was legitimate (thus you gave the caller or sender all your correct information), is really a scam. At that moment, your emotions

range from panic and anger to disbelief (you can't believe you fell for it) and fear of the consequences. Now, multiply that by infinity and make the consequences of said scam perpetual and successive (i.e., something your children, grandchildren, etc., will inherit), and you get an inkling of the gravitas of that moment of supposed *enlightenment* Adam and Eve experienced.

2. **Awareness of their nakedness:** Prior to eating, the couple's nakedness was actually covered by a kind of shimmer (some say it was the *Shekinah* glory, a visible indication of God's presence) that covered their bodies but was removed after their disobedience. Another example of this would be to get dressed up and go out to some upscale restaurant or event and realize you have a giant red stain on your backside. Before you notice it (or are made aware of it), you just act normally. But after you know about it, you feel awkward and ashamed.

3. **A combination of both of the above:** The moment Adam and Eve partook of the fruit of the tree, they became awkwardly aware that they were, in fact, both naked *and* afraid.

The Bible goes on to describe their immediate actions following their fleeting moments of rebellion:

> So when the woman saw that the tree was good for food, that it was pleasant to the eyes, and a tree desirable to make one wise, she took of its fruit and ate. She also gave to her husband with her, and he ate. Then the eyes of both of them were opened, and they knew that they were naked; and they sewed fig leaves together and made themselves coverings.
>
> And they heard the sound of the Lord God walking in the garden in the cool of the day, and Adam and his wife hid themselves from the presence of the Lord God among the trees of the garden. (Genesis 3:6–8)

That's when they realized they had been duped. As for Lucifer's big lie about becoming like God, we are willing to bet that, in that second, they realized there is only one God, and He doesn't share His role as *the Almighty* with anyone. Adam and Eve did gain a knowledge of good and evil; however, what they lost in the process was both their immortality and their innocence.

This is the most effective strategy Lucifer employs, and it set a precedent going forward in everything he does. His most effective ploy is to mix lies into truth. This is why the Apostle Paul wrote that we should be forgiving to others, "lest Satan should take advantage of us; for we are not ignorant of his devices" (2 Corinthians 2:11). This is the same strategy adopted and embraced by the godless elite: Mix lies into truth to obfuscate the true agenda.

After the divine chastisement and punishment, God made tunics out of animal skins (Genesis 3:22), also establishing the fact that innocent blood must be shed in order to atone for wrongdoing (sin). Thus, after providing the couple with clothes from the skin of a slain animal, God removed them from the Garden and shut the way back in, stationing cherubim at the entrance to stand guard with a flaming sword. God had to remove Adam and Eve because, had they eaten from the *tree of life* in their now corrupted state, they would have regained immortality in a corrupted state...always dying, but never being able to die.

Nevertheless, from Adam to Noah, the generations of humans spanned some one to two thousand years (estimate, depending on whether you use the Septuagint or Masoretic Text). During that time, there were no written Scriptures and no Gospel message. There weren't even (from what we can ascertain) organized religions. Everyone did what was right in their own eyes. And, due to the genetic perfection subsequent generations inherited from Adam and Eve, the couple's descendants still lived for centuries. Even secular scientists today do not dispute the fact that the human body is capable of living that long.

Not only were lifespans significantly longer during this ancient time, but the gateway between the spiritual domain and our physical one lay wide open. There was no barrier between the two at this point, and it is because of this that fallen angels (those who had rebelled with Lucifer) took advantage of the open door in one of the greatest conspiracies of all: the premediated destruction of the human race through genetic contamination.

It wasn't through calamity or violence they intended to do this (although the world of their day was quite violent), but through genetic corruption. If we go back to the moment right after they sinned, when Lucifer was disguised as the snake, God confronted Adam, Eve, and the serpent, and gave them what Christian theologians call the "protoevangelium." This was the first prophecy ever given in the Bible, and it forecast the Gospel in a way that terrified Lucifer and gave hope to Adam and Eve. Here, God said to the serpent (Lucifer/Satan):

> And I will put enmity between you and the woman, and between your offspring and hers; he will crush your head, and you will strike his heel. (Genesis 3:15, NIV)

Now, we don't often quote Scripture using the New International Version (NIV), but we think this captures the sentiment much more appropriately than do other translations. This was when Satan knew his destruction wouldn't come directly from God or other angels, but that someone from the human race would one day destroy him. Thus, this spiritual-physical conundrum set the stage for the very plight we call the human drama. It is the greatest of stories, one that encompasses the struggle for our physical survival as well as for our eternal destinies. This epic is breathtaking in scope, sweeping in tragedy, and yet unrivaled in both love and hope.

The story of humankind has been a grand struggle ever since, a perpetual struggle between two forces—the Creator God and a rebellious fallen angel who happens to be the second-most-powerful being in all of creation. Despite God's unlimited and matchless power and omnipotence, He has chosen to allow members of the human race to exercise their free will as to which eternal destiny they will follow. And thus it has been ever since.

But it will not always be this way.

As epic and sweeping as this story has been, we are but in the opening chapters of God's *magnum opus*. These chapters, which have been accounts of human history up until this point, shall soon find their foretold culmination concluding accordingly and opening the pathway to grander and loftier tales in eternity future. In fact, the book we are in has no ending, and, as fascinating as it has all been thus far, we are simply the comma or the ellipsis between what was and what will be. Therefore, we still have all of eternity future ahead of us—and even that has no end.

Nevertheless, back to the serpent.

It is their predetermined date with the lake of fire that Lucifer and his fallen, unholy angels are desperately trying to avoid. They will say anything and try everything to keep from going there. They tried tempting Eve and succeeded. They got Cain to kill Abel (whose lineage they thought the Messiah would come through) and succeeded. They made an effort to corrupt all humankind genetically (and they very nearly succeeded). They tried wiping out the genetic line (of Abraham) through which the human Messiah would one day come; they actually came close several times (via Pharaoh, Haman, and Herod). But now we are in the end game. We're in the final moments of the fourth quarter, when Lucifer is hoping against hope he can pull off some miraculous half-court shot.

But it will never happen.

Try as he might, Lucifer will succumb to the preordained ending that was determined for him the moment he first conceived the plot to overthrow God before Creation. His attempt to do so is even more foolish and less likely to succeed than would be the effort of a child attempting to destroy Mount Everest by pounding on the ground with his fists near its foothills. In other words, the child has more of a chance of crumbling Mount Everest than Lucifer does in succeeding.

Regardless of the hopelessness of Lucifer's plight, we can at the very least conclude that he hasn't yet given up. He is the roaring lion seeking whom he may devour. He is the *father of lies* and the very author of confusion. He will say and/or do anything to anyone to get them to separate from God. To date, he has been very successful in this endeavor. In finding this success, he uses conspiracy to obfuscate the truth and conceal his true agenda, blinding the minds of humans with secrecy and shadow. This is his domain.

Thus, in the opening chapters of the Bible, we're introduced to this wicked character who emerges with the conflicting question to Eve, inserting doubt and poisoning the well. That's what Lucifer does: He sows confusion into our minds to nurture distrust, uncertainty, skepticism, and ultimately, antagonism against our Creator. He traffics in confusion, not just in the minds of individuals, but in the worldview of generations. This is the power of conspiracy.

Distinctions

Regarding humankind's comings and goings on this earth, we must recognize two immutable facts: 1) God never changes; He is the same yesterday, today, and forever (Hebrews 13:8); and 2) the way He has dealt with humans has, at various times, changed. Just as a good father doesn't treat his toddler the same way he would his teenager, or vice versa, God has interacted with us according to our dispensational environment. For example, He no longer requires us to walk around naked and avoid eating the fruit of certain trees. He doesn't instruct us to build our own arks to avoid a coming watery judgment. Further, Christians aren't required to keep the 613 laws He gave Moses.

Therefore, to acknowledge these differences, there is a hermeneutical discipline called "dispensationalism" (Greek: *oikonomia*). A "dispensation" is the same thing as an economy or an administration. It is how one runs a particular time and place that is operating under the same parameters of existence. If we go back to the former example, a father wouldn't treat his seventeen-year-old child the same way as he would his three-year old. The reason he won't is that there is a maturity difference. There is an experiential difference. There is a physical difference in size and strength. Yet, the father offers the same amount of love and care for his kids regardless of their age.

Seven unique dispensations are identified in Scripture: Innocence, Conscience, Human Government, Promise, Law, Church, and Millennial Kingdom. Adam and Eve began in the first dispensation (Innocence), but quickly moved to the dispensation of Conscience when they transgressed against God. This period existed during the antediluvian (or pre-Flood world) for about one to two thousand years, until the Flood of Noah's day. At the conclusion of the Flood, a new dispensation began: the dispensation of Human Government. It is here that God introduced some major changes to the natural order. Listed below are just a few of the major changes found from Genesis 8:22–9:17:

1. Seed time and harvest, cold and heat, winter and summer, and day and night would not cease.
2. Wild animals would fear mankind.
3. The rainbow would be the sign He would never flood the world again.
4. Humans could eat whatever they want, so long as it doesn't contain its lifeblood.

Now, murder would not go unpunished. If one man took another's life, his own life was then forfeited. The dispensations of Promise and the Law are exclusively focused on the physical and ethnic people (and nation) of the Israelites. We see this reflected in the pages of Scripture, where Genesis chapters 1 through 12 speak of humankind in an overly broad fashion. God is dealing with everyone as Gentiles. However, in chapter 12, we see that He begins to single out one man, through whom the Messiah (from the protoevangelium) would one day come. Thus, from Genesis 12 through the Gospel of Matthew, we see almost exclusive attention paid to the Jewish people. The Gentiles (non-Jews) are only mentioned insofar as how they interact with the Israelites/Hebrews/Jews.

The dispensation of the Church is, for obvious reasons, focused on the post-Resurrection time when Christ begins building His Body of believers (corporately made up of both Jews and Gentiles) to create a new type of people, the Church (Matthew 16:18–19). Now, Jews and Gentiles are only mentioned regarding how they interact with the Church.

The last (or seventh) dispensation is the Millennial Reign, the thousand-year Kingdom in which Christ rules on the earth from His throne in Jerusalem. For the purposes of this book, we will be primarily focused on two dispensations—Human Government and the Kingdom, and the tensions therein.

It is the kingdoms of the world versus the *Kingdom to come*. Satan and his human minions are committed to either creating a world wholly given over to his control, or, at the least, to keeping the status quo indefinitely. However, this Luciferian agenda, no matter how dark and devious it may be, is still on God's timeline. This means everything—Satan, his kingdom of darkness, the empires of the earth, and everything else—is on a divine conveyor belt that is relentlessly moving forward every single day toward the end of all things. Satan knows this and is becoming increasingly desperate as time continues to wind down. He will do anything to avoid the fate awaiting him, and, in his final act of defiance, he will attempt to co-opt all of God's creation into committing mutiny against the Creator.

TWO

PARADISE LOST

If we want to live in paradise, we will have to engineer it ourselves.
If we want eternal life, then we'll need to rewrite our bug-ridden
genetic code and become god-like…only hi-tech solutions can ever
eradicate suffering from the world. Compassion alone is not enough.

DAVID PEARCE, *HUMANITY+*[8]

Then the Lord God said, "Behold, the man has become like one
of Us, to know good and evil. And now, lest he put out his hand
and take also of the tree of life, and eat, and live forever"—therefore the Lord God sent him out of the garden of Eden to till the
ground from which he was taken. So He drove out the man; and
He placed cherubim at the east of the garden of Eden, and a flaming
sword which turned every way, to guard the way to the tree of life.

GENESIS 3:22–24

NEARLY SIX THOUSAND YEARS AGO, the first man and woman were cast
out of the Garden of Eden, or Paradise, for rebelling against their Creator.
Their crime? They listened to the subtle and deceptive reasoning of a
serpent promising them forbidden knowledge if only they ate from the
tree of the knowledge of good and evil. Then, walking out of Eden, they
looked back to see that the entrance had been closed and was guarded by
a mighty angel. From that point on, they would succumb to the consequences of their actions, knowing their days were now numbered.

Within a generation, humankind had begun to proliferate upon the earth. Given the proximity to the first two perfect humans and the still-idyllic natural environment, people lived for centuries. Their numbers began to swell, and numerous generations began to overlap. The terrain was, at this point, fairly flat, and its land masses were joined together in a giant supercontinent that scientists now call "Rodinia" (Genesis 1:26).[9] With the temperate climate and a lack of any natural barriers to separate the people, the world began quickly filling up.

Although people had inherited a sin curse from the first humans, the genetic ramifications of that curse had not yet become noticeable. The animal kingdom remained docile and unafraid of people, and the environment's abundance reduced the need for the earth's inhabitants to engage in perpetual labor. In short, the world was as perfect as it ever would be. Paradoxically, this is described in the book of Acts as the "times of ignorance," when men and women blindly walked in the darkness and were guided only by their fallen consciousness (Acts 17:30).

Even though the pagan world did not subscribe to a biblical antediluvian period, it is this same stretch of time they would later refer to as "the Golden Age." There were no written Scriptures at this point. Neither were there organized religions (that we know of), and the gateway between the physical and spiritual domains remained open. Everyone did what was right in their own eyes, and before long, the world became exceedingly wicked. In this wickedness, dark thoughts began to seed the minds of men and women, and they were encouraged to rebel against their Creator. Lucifer knew it was time to strike.

For his part in the first conspiracy, Lucifer had been told by God that someone coming out of the race of humans would be his destroyer. God didn't say who; He only said that the one who would defeat him (Lucifer) would come from the "seed" of a woman. Hindered but not deterred, Lucifer once again conspired in his heart to thwart God's plans. He had managed to corrupt the human race once before with Adam and Eve, severing their intimate relationship with God; now he set out to do it again. In derailing the first couple, he had also managed to contaminate them physically, stealing away their immortality and introducing sin and death into the human condition. Now, Lucifer would corrupt them genetically so this human Messiah could never come. But Lucifer couldn't do it alone, so he enlisted help.

As previously mentioned, when Lucifer rebelled, he convinced a third of the angelic host (the sons of God) to join him. Seeing as angels are more numerous than the stars in Heaven, one-third of that number is an imposing number—in the billions. Out of this group, Lucifer hand-picked hundreds of his elite unholy angels, and they began to make physical trips to the earth with the sole mission of seducing human women, impregnating them, and causing them to give birth to beings who were neither fully human nor fully angel.

> Now it came to pass, when men began to multiply on the face of the earth, and daughters were born to them, that the sons of God saw the daughters of men, that they were beautiful; and they took wives for themselves of all whom they chose.
>
> And the Lord said, "My Spirit shall not strive with man forever, for he is indeed flesh; yet his days shall be one hundred and twenty years." There were giants on the earth in those days, and also afterward, when the sons of God came in to the daughters of men and they bore children to them. Those were the mighty men who were of old, men of renown. (Genesis 6:1–4)

You might be wondering how angels could impregnate women.

Even though angels are spirit beings (their normal state), they can take on a physical form, as demonstrated throughout the Bible (Hebrews 13:2). People, for their part, despite their closeness to the Creation event itself, and having all the advantages they would ever have (long life, super strength, and keen intelligence), began to give themselves over to their basest natures. Guided only by their God-given conscience, and having no rule of law or other normative constructs we take for granted today, the antediluvian population became exceedingly violent and vicious. They took advantage of the animals' submissive nature with extravagant cruelty. In their corruptness, they gave themselves over to fallen angels. Both the Apostle Peter and Jude confirm that these ancient peoples began to go after "strange flesh," which is to say "fallen angels" (2 Peter 2:4–5; Jude 1:6–7). From these unnatural unions between the "sons of God" and the "daughters of men" came forth the Nephilim, the men of old, the men of renown.

According to tradition, in addition to being very large and strong, the Nephilim had enormous psychic abilities. They performed out-of-body experiences, levitation, mind control, time travel, mind reading, and remote viewing. They had the power of pronouncing and removing curses and diseases, and had ways of knowing and predicting the future. Having aligned themselves with Satan, the source of their powers, they controlled and enslaved mankind, perverting God's creation almost to the point that it was beyond redemption.

The Nephilim were also extremely intelligent. They knew all about science, architecture, and engineering. Some believe they combined these skills with their powers of levitation to build the Great Pyramid and other great monuments around the pre-Flood world. And they were not just in Mesopotamia. Nephilim may have sacrificed human beings all over the planet in temples and pyramids they built in Central and South America, the Far East, the British Isles, Egypt, and other places. They drank blood and slaughtered our babies, and were almost certainly tampering with both human and animal gene pools to pervert the creation and make redemption impossible. They were the heroes of old, the mighty men of renown, memorialized in every mythology; they were the primary reason God had to destroy the world and all its inhabitants with the Great Flood."[10]

As mentioned earlier, the pre-Flood world was, at one point, joined together in a supercontinent. We know this because God indicated on day three of Creation that the waters would be gathered "to one place" (Genesis 1:9). The pre-Flood world was encased in a crystalline water canopy (Genesis 1:6–8), which would have provided numerous atmospheric and geological advantages (the conditions would be similar to a greenhouse) in producing a temperate, oxygen-rich climate with minimal-to-no changing weather patterns. This climate's effect on the humans and animals living then (along with their proximity to Creation) would have promoted gigantism in size and longevity in age.

After the Flood, the earth's climate, geography, and atmosphere were radically changed. With the atmosphere no longer protected by the water canopy above the earth as it once was, the northern and southern poles began to freeze over, drawing back the waters to form shoreline boundaries similar to what we see today. The unnaturally long life spans people enjoyed before the Flood diminished to what we consider today as normal. The physical size and strength of the survivors of the deluge likewise decreased. The knowledge people had accumulated before the Flood was literally wiped away.

In regards to pre-Flood infrastructure and architecture, those were washed away as well. However, what remained were the memory and knowledge of how to build the sophisticated cyclopean architecture that would be echoed later in the post-Flood world beginning at Babel. Due to their size and precision, examples of megalithic structures stump modern historians and archeologists to this day. We see examples of these structures in Giza with the Great Pyramid and the Sphinx; the Easter Island structures; Göbekli Tepe in Turkey; Gunung Padang in Indonesia; the Knossos Palace in Crete; Baalbek in Lebanon; and the Cusco, Sacsayhuaman, Ollantaytambo, and Machu Picchu sites in Peru. Clearly, these megalithic sites demonstrate at least two things: 1) A profound knowledge about and understanding of building incredibly complex and mathematically superior architecture once existed; and 2) Our limited historical understanding of how and why they built these structures demonstrates that early people were not primitive brutes.

After the Flood, the human race started over with eight people in a new world order wherein the continents were now separated by vast oceans and imposing mountain ranges. If the pre-Flood world's population reached into the billions (which the natural advantages and long life spans seem to indicate), now people would have a much tougher time of repopulating the planet given the harsher conditions. In other words, God put more barriers to our capacity to become overwhelmingly wicked.

This explains, in part, why God instructed Noah's sons to disperse after the Flood. When people congregate in large numbers, wickedness abounds. To prove this, we need only to map out the majority of crime and violence in the world today, and we will see they are mainly centered in large, urban areas. In spite of God's instructions to spread out across the land, however, humankind did not scatter, but instead spent the next four hundred years congregating on the plains of Shinar under the leadership of Noah's great-grandson, Nimrod (whom some identify as Sargon of Akkad).[11]

FROM BABEL WITH LOVE

Now it was Nimrod who excited them to such an affront and contempt of God. He was the grandson of Ham, the son of Noah, a bold man, and of great strength of hand. He persuaded them not to ascribe to God as if it was through his means they were happy, but to believe that was their own courage which procured that happiness. He also gradually changed the government into tyranny, seeing no other way of turning men from the fear of God, but to bring them into a constant dependence upon his power. He also said he would be revenged on God, if he should have a mind to drown the world again; for that he would build a tower too high for the waters to be able to reach and that he would avenge himself on God for destroying their forefathers.

JOSEPHUS, *ANTIQUITIES OF THE JEWS*, VOL. 2[12]

But the Lord came down to see the city and the tower which the sons of men had built. And the Lord said, "Indeed the people are one and they all have one language, and this is what they begin to do; now nothing that they propose to do will be withheld from them. Come, let Us go down and there confuse their language, that they may not understand one another's speech." So the Lord scattered them abroad from there over the face of all the earth, and they ceased building the city. Therefore its name is called Babel, because there the Lord confused the language of all the earth; and from there the Lord scattered them abroad over the face of all the earth.

GENESIS 11:5–9

AFTER THE FLOOD, God had told Noah and his sons atop Mt. Ararat that they should spread out and repopulate the earth. We know this as part of the Noahic Covenant (Genesis 6:18; 9:1–17), which, interestingly, is the first time we see the word "covenant" used in the Bible. We also know, as discussed in chapter 2, that their descendants did *not* spread out, but rather, gathered on the plains of Shinar and planted small cities. This is where they attempted to build the tower at Babel, which was probably closer to ancient Nineveh (Micah 5:6) in the north (in the Khabur River Triangle), rather than in the traditionally cited location in the southern, marshy area of Iraq, later known as "Ur of the Chaldees."

> It is unknown as to why the human race didn't initially separate, but given the harsher environment (much harsher than the pre-flood world), it would seem they banded together to survive. If these post-flood descendants maintained a birthrate of least a 3.2%, their population over four-hundred years, they would be somewhere in the neighborhood of 2.3 million people.[13]

If humanity would not separate of their own accord, God would do it for them. Not only did He divide the people by language, but presumably, by genetics as well. He confused their languages so they could no longer understand each other, and it is our belief that He physically relocated them as well.

This is likely why vastly different cultures (Aboriginals, Chinese, Middle Eastern, Indigenous Americans, etc.) share similar folklore surrounding a global flood story, because the only possible explanation for this is that they came from the same source: Noah and his family. The sole surviving record of the pre-Flood world would have been the accounts of family members who survived the catastrophe. Their stories were recorded and passed down by Noah's sons Shem, Ham, and Japheth to their respective descendants. It was through Shem—whose lineage would include the patriarchs like Abraham, Isaac, and Jacob—that the narrative was passed on down to Moses, who recorded the words which would later come to be known as the book of Genesis nearly a thousand years later.

The Archetype

We often wonder why God supernaturally (rather, "naturally" for Him) scattered mankind after they began to construct the tower. What was their motivation for building it in the first place? According to Scripture, it all began with one of Ham's grandsons, Nimrod (grandson of Ham, great-grandson of Noah).

> Cush begot Nimrod; he began to be a mighty one on the earth.
> He was a mighty hunter before the Lord; therefore it is said, "Like
> Nimrod the mighty hunter before the Lord." And the beginning
> of his kingdom was Babel, Erech, Accad, and Calneh, in the land
> of Shinar. From that land he went to Assyria and built Nineveh,
> Rehoboth Ir, Calah, and Resen between Nineveh and Calah (that
> is the principal city). (Genesis 11:8–12)

Although the phrasing Moses used doesn't necessarily lead to the clearest understanding, the gist is that Nimrod's agenda was anti-God. It doesn't appear that He began building the tower solely to escape from some future flood, as it was common knowledge via the Noahic Covenant that God had already decreed He would never again destroy the world with a flood (Genesis 9:11). We believe Nimrod was attempting to regain something lost in the deluge.

Since the catastrophe had radically altered the face of the earth, the former pathways to the spiritual portals had all been washed away. We believe Noah's descendants, then, were attempting to recreate those pathways, which is why they began building the same type of mega-lithic structures (e.g., the tower) as the antediluvians had constructed. In addition to making a name for themselves as a great kingdom, they were busy invoking the same dark spiritual forces to grant them "demigod" powers similar to those the pre-Flood "men of renown" once enjoyed: super strength, unnaturally long lives, and super intelligence. This is a reasonable assumption, since humankind has been seeking to regain these characteristics ever since.

So it was that, after the Flood, the *New World Order* wasn't just a major change in humanity, but a major change in the earth's geology and climatology as well. The world that was destroyed with water was dramatically different than the world that emerged afterwards. That's because, during the year the earth was submerged, it was being terraformed by God as He broke apart the continents, causing mountain ranges and canyons to form. The old world, along with its secrets and mysteries, was washed away and buried under tons of mud and rock.

Some believe Nimrod was part of the earlier-noted hybrid race angel/human race known as "Nephilim." As Tim Chaffey points out in his book, *Fallen: The Sons of God and the Nephilim*, while all Nephilim were *gibborim* ("mighty men of old," "men of renown"), not all *gibborim* were Nephilim.[14] As previously discussed, Nephilim were designated in the Septuagint (LXX) as *gigantes* or *gigantas*, the Greek word for "giants."[15] The Septuagint was the earliest Greek rendering (or translation) of the Hebrew Old Testament by seventy Hebrew scholars under the reign of the Greek pharaoh of Egypt, Ptolemy II Philadelphus. Nimrod could have been a Nephilim, but he was most certainly a *gibborim*. Either way, he was the first to begin to publicly raise his fist against God in defiance, and perhaps he sought to once again open the portal to the spiritual domain that was seemingly closed at the Flood. Satan then urged Nimrod to take advantage of their waning superhuman status in an effort to reopen the interdimensional pathways.[16]

This knowledge of "what was" is critical to the foundation of the New World Order mantra: If Paradise (and all its trappings) can be lost, it can be regained.

Presumably angered by the loss of their proximity to immortality, Nimrod sought to do this through the construction of the tower at Babel in order to bring back access to the fallen angels and the old ways. Quot-

ing from Pete Garcia's portion of the book *Lawless*, the modern draw
to the ante- and post-diluvium world is likened to an addiction modern people cannot let go of. Nevertheless, this forgotten age is one that
humans have been trying to get back to ever since.

> To the pagan, the period before the Flood was an idyllic time of
> monsters and magic. It was a time of heroes and mythological
> tales of lore so fantastical that, even to this day, teases our deep-
> est desires. It was a time so far back that even the ancient Greeks
> referred to it as "ancient history."
> It was a "Golden Age" of humankind's greatest accomplish-
> ments. While modern science has worked tirelessly to promote
> the idea that we evolved from lower, ape-like cavemen to where
> we are today, the truth is, if anything, we have regressed.[17]

Aside from his own personal vanity, why would Nimrod want to
build a giant tower at Babel?

While we can't conclusively say, we can, based on an understanding of human nature, render some potential scenarios. First, this new,
post-Flood realm was not only vastly different from the old, antediluvian
world, but there were also new natural constraints that had not previously
existed. These are what we believe to be the second- and third-order reasons for building a tower at Babel:

1. Before the Flood, humankind had experienced routine physical
interactions with the spiritual domain. Afterward, the spiritual gateway
was closed to the physical realm.

2. The long life spans people enjoyed before the Flood had, afterward, shrunk to the normal age expectancies we see today (due to the
collapsed ice canopy over the earth).

3. The world's atmosphere before the Flood was temperate and without cyclical weather patterns (i.e., it never rained pre-Flood). Afterward,
the climate was harsher, and changing weather patterns and seasons were
becoming part of the normal cycle of life.

Before he scattered the tower builders, Lucifer/Satan was able to inject a storyline into that prototypical Shinar community. This is not just why so many cultures draw on the same antediluvian world as the source of their own mythologies, but it is also why they draw on the same false religious ideas regarding a mother/son deity (see appendix B). In other words, Babel became the fountainhead of all false religions moving forward.

But it wasn't just the source of false religions.

Nimrod became the archetypal ruler for all future kings, warlords, emperors, and dictators to emulate. In truth, he was the only world ruler to control nearly 100 percent of the entire human population. Granted, the number of people living on earth a century after the Flood was still miniscule as compared to today; nevertheless, Nimrod's insatiable desire to control everything—thus the desire for global domination—became the standard trait amongst all future potentates.

But why build there—on the plains of Shinar?

Given what we've seen in recent times with places like the Large Hadron Collider (LHC) at CERN under the Franco-Swiss border, both Babel's location and its existence were presumably multipurpose in nature. It was likely that Nimrod sought to build the tower at this specific location due to the demonic spiritual influences present there, but he justified its construction by indicating that it would provide a safe haven should God choose to flood the world again (which God said He wouldn't do).

However, the tower's real purpose was shrouded in secrecy. Nimrod desired to bring back some access to the old world and its age of magic. He sought to use the tower as a means to reopen a portal or a star gate to the spiritual domain. Although Scripture doesn't state the specifics about the goal of the project, given the passage below, the above reason seems plausible:

And the Lord said, "Indeed the people are one and they all have one language, and this is what they begin to do; *now nothing that they propose to do will be withheld from them.*" (Genesis 11:6, emphasis added)

Think about that for a second: Nothing will be withheld from humankind when they are united in one purpose and in one language. Given the proper amount of time, resources, and knowhow, we *could* colonize Mars. We *could* figure out interdimensional teleportation. We *could* create a technological Singularity. We *could* figure out how to genetically (or via some cyber-physical scheme) extend the average life span beyond one hundred years.

However, God *will not allow* things to go that far.

We see in the last book of the Bible, Revelation, how advanced technology will be used to aid the Antichrist and the False Prophet in subjugating the entire world. While the technology itself is not specified, its capabilities are. So when we see the current crop of industrialists, tech entrepreneurs, and scientists pushing beyond the boundaries as laid out in Revelation, we must understand that those things will not come to pass.

After all, this is why God blocked the entrance to the Garden of Eden after Adam and Eve sinned (Genesis 3:22–24). This is why God flooded the earth during Noah's day (Genesis 6:5–7) and stopped construction of the tower of Babel before it was finished (Genesis 11:6). God didn't do those things because He is afraid of tall buildings, or even of their purpose, but that the building itself (as well as the situations in Eden and with Noah) would have permanently and disastrously altered the course of human history moving forward.

We are seeing these types of agendas and motivations resurfacing in our own day. Only this time, we have the ways (knowledge) and the means (technology) to accomplish them.

Not only that, but we also have the ability now to minimize the linguistic differences among people groups through both human and computer translators; we even have an almost universal language in the form of English. For the first time since the antediluvian era, we have enough of an understanding of the human genome, quantum physics, and particle physics to begin monkeying with the fabric of our existence. We are closing in quite rapidly on what Jesus described as "the days of Noah," which is a frightening prospect (Luke 17:26). For if God purged the earth in a watery judgment for the evil the folks of Noah's day engaged in, how much worse will it have to get before conditions require Him to purge the earth with fire?

In regards to the tower, we are witnessing a similar effort today with the likes of secret societies, CERN, artificial intelligence, Singularity, and dozens of other earth-shattering initiatives.

"Out of this door might come something, or we might send something through it," said Sergio Bertolucci, then director of CERN's research and scientific computing back in 2009.[18]

CERN is the largest man-made machine in the world and sits miles underground at the Franco-Swiss border. Its creators claim it was designed to discover what the universe is made of. It was intended to operate in the name of scientific discovery, and to some degree that might be true. However, it also appears to have been designed to search for dimensional portals much like those at Babel had tried to do many thousands of years earlier. Eventually, they will succeed in doing so if God does not intervene (see Genesis 11:6). Aside from its seemingly bifurcated existence, why does a multinational endeavor (said to be purely scientific) cling so vociferously to occult imagery in its many public facets? For example, it clearly uses three sixes in its official logo.

It proudly displays the Indian government's gift of the "Dancing Shiva" (destroyer of worlds) outside its headquarters, and includes disturbing Wiccan/pagan pageantry at certain public ceremonies.

Does it seem like opening dimensional gateways is absurd?

Maybe it would have been considered bizarre a hundred years ago—or even fifty years ago. However, it's not hard to believe it's possible to open dimensional gateways these days, given our already rapid advancements in just about every sector of technology and science, from genetics to quantum physics.

It just goes to show that this desire to restore Paradise goes back millennia. The unregenerate people of the earth are always trying to find an alternative path to immortality that avoids God's desired plan for spiritual restoration first. God deliberately closed the veil between the physical and spiritual dimensions at the Flood to prevent those kinds of unnatural unions from corrupting the human race again. Nevertheless, many are determined to reopen said portals, and at some future point (inside the Seventieth Week of Daniel), they will succeed. Then the supernatural will once again return to earth in full force (2 Thessalonians 2:9–12; Revelation 11:4–6; 13:13–15). Humanity's unrelenting desire to return to the "Golden Age" will result in the most horrific time the earth has ever seen (Matthew 24:21–22).

FOUR

THE TIMES OF THE GENTILES

You, O king, were watching; and behold, a great image! This great image, whose splendor was excellent, stood before you; and its form was awesome. This image's head was of fine gold, its chest and arms of silver, its belly and thighs of bronze, its legs of iron, its feet partly of iron and partly of clay. You watched while a stone was cut out without hands, which struck the image on its feet of iron and clay, and broke them in pieces. Then the iron, the clay, the bronze, the silver, and the gold were crushed together, and became like chaff from the summer threshing floors; the wind carried them away so that no trace of them was found. And the stone that struck the image became a great mountain and filled the whole earth.

DANIEL 2:31–35

TO THWART GOD'S divine prophetic proclamation of Genesis 3:15, Satan's effort to genetically contaminate the human race failed when God flooded the world. At this point, Satan was forced to turn to an alternative plan to take control of the population: He placed them under a single Babel government headed by Nimrod. Upon seeing this feeble attempt, God then divided the post-Flood population into seventy families speaking seventy different languages and dialects, then scattered them over the face of the newly terraformed earth. So, once again, Satan was back to square one. Now, all he had left to do was to attempt to raise up empire after empire, hoping to use one of them to conquer the rest of the world the old-fashioned way—by force.

Babylonian King Nebuchadnezzar dreamed of a statue built with many different metals, which the Hebrew prophet Daniel would later reveal (with God's help) as representing kingdoms, with Babylon as the head of gold. Although they're not mentioned as being represented in the statue (since they preceded Babylon's ascent to power), Satan enjoyed limited regional success in places like Egypt and Assyria. However, it wasn't until Alexander the Great (the Greeks) did the potential for global governance finally become a reality again.

With Alexander conquering much of the known world at that time, the rest of the global regions (the Americas, the Pacific islands, northern Europe, southern Africa, and the Arctic Circle territories) largely remained either undiscovered or sparsely populated. But Alexander's untimely death caused his once-mighty empire to fracture into four kingdoms (the Ptolemaic, Seleucid, Cassandri, and Lysimachi).

It wouldn't be until the Romans rose to power two centuries later under Caesar Augustus that they would be begin to capitalize on all the groundwork the Greeks had laid in the process of Hellenizing the world. It would be through the Romans that Satan's full aspirations for global domination would be fully realized. We know this because he has never let go of this model of worldwide governance.

The Roman Empire began as a monarchy with the semi-mythological seven kings between 753–510 BC. In 509 BC, it became a republic and remained one until a dictator finally took power some four centuries later. The rest of the Western Roman Empire is marked by the rule of the Caesars. The empire then split in two in the third century AD, and while one side collapsed (Western Rome), the other continued for another thousand years (the Byzantine Empire). But long before the Byzantine Empire was conquered by the Turkish Ottomans in 1453, Satan had used the former (Western Rome) to create a Holy Roman Empire in central Europe (modern-day France-Germany). This would later morph into competing colonial powers all bent on conquering the world both militarily and economically. However, all those centuries of infighting would prove useful as Europeans finally got to the point that they wanted to reunite again under a single authority. And after two world wars (largely based in Europe), they've done (and are doing) it now *vis a vis* the European Union.

Considering Rome's long and storied pagan history, it makes sense that Satan would use it as the *vehicle* by which he would later corrupt the flourishing Christian population around the Mediterranean. In AD 313, Emperor Constantine converted to Christianity and legalized it across the empire. In the process of doing this, pagan temples and priests began converting to Christian churches and clergy. Although this was seen as progress by Christians then, what ended up happening was that instead of the Church going out into the world, the world came into the Church, fulfilling Jesus' prophetic statement in the parable of the mustard seed:

> Another parable He put forth to them, saying: "The kingdom of heaven is like a mustard seed, which a man took and sowed in his field, which indeed is the least of all the seeds; but when it is grown it is greater than the herbs and becomes a tree, so that the birds of the air come and nest in its branches." (Matthew 13:31–32)

Given the negative context of the use of birds in all of Jesus' parables, "birds" that will "nest" in the "branches" as indicated in this passage signal varying degrees of corruption. It is this ecumenical prototype Satan would successfully use for the next two thousand years during the dispensation of the Church. Where he couldn't stamp out the Church through the use of persecution, he would use subtle corruption. Thus, the merging of paganism into Christianity became the Luciferian model that would become a mainstay through 99 percent of the subsequent kingdoms that would rise and fall over the next two millennia. Furthermore, the Romans' ecumenical approach to religion would come to foreshadow what the future Beast Kingdom will emulate, in accepting every belief system as equals (religious relativism) so long as the state continued to provide the requisite degree of control over messaging.

In *The Decline and Fall of the Roman Empire*, Edward Gibbon said:

> The policy of the emperors and the senate, as far as it concerned religion, was happily seconded by the reflections of the enlightened, and by the habits of the superstitious, part of their subjects. The various modes of worship, which prevailed in the Roman world, were all considered by the people, as equally true; by the philosopher, as equally false; and by the magistrate, as equally useful. And thus toleration produced not only mutual indulgence, but even religious concord.[19]

The Roman Model

As history has borne out, the Roman Empire collapsed in stages, with the Western leg (Rome) beginning to fall apart from AD 430–476. The Eastern leg, however, continued on as the Byzantine Empire for another thousand years until it was undone by the rising Muslim force of the Ottoman Turks sometime in the fifteenth century. Even still, the Western leg's collapse morphed into a Holy Roman Empire by the eighth century under Charlemagne, and was very much considered the Second Roman Empire or, as the Germans saw it, the First Reich.

If we step back for a moment and look at what Satan has spent the majority of his time focusing upon, we see that it is overwhelmingly in and around the Mediterranean and Mesopotamian regions. In particular, he has spent an enormous amount of time (3, 345 years, to be exact) on one particular kingdom: Rome. So if we think back to the stages of the

Roman Empire, we can see its evolution over more than three millennia. Satan is not going to abandon this structure/system he already has in place.

Furthermore, consider the correlation between the Third Reich's historical claims to the Holy Roman Empire (the First Reich) and where we are today. We think, in a way, that the Third Reich may have been Satan's test run for this final kingdom. We also know, according to Scripture (Daniel 9:26), that the Antichrist will come from somewhere within the boundaries of the Imperial Roman Empire (since that is the period when Jerusalem was besieged and the Temple was destroyed). This future Antichrist will subdue three of the coming ten kings, then claim authority over the entire earth. Since the Nazis' concept of a "Third Reich" presupposes that there were "First" and "Second Reichs," it behooves us to know what they believed this was before moving forward:

> **Third Reich**, official Nazi designation for the regime in Germany from January 1933 to May 1945, as the presumed successor of the medieval and early modern Holy Roman Empire of 800 to 1806 (the First Reich) and the German Empire of 1871 to 1918 (the Second Reich).[20]

Not to rehash a thousand-plus years of European history (see the following image for that), let's just say that Germany did in fact play a central role in the entirety of the Holy Roman Empire. It began when Pope Leo III crowned the Frankish King Charlemagne as the Holy Roman Emperor on December 25, AD 800. The Holy Roman Empire itself was the product of the imperial pairing by the Roman Catholic Church, which was attempting to consolidate its control over the varying (and often warring) factions in central Europe, as well as revive the Western Roman Empire, which had effectively ended around AD 476. Thus, the title claim (Third Reich) by Herr Hitler and company is at least historically accurate, if not tragically misguided.

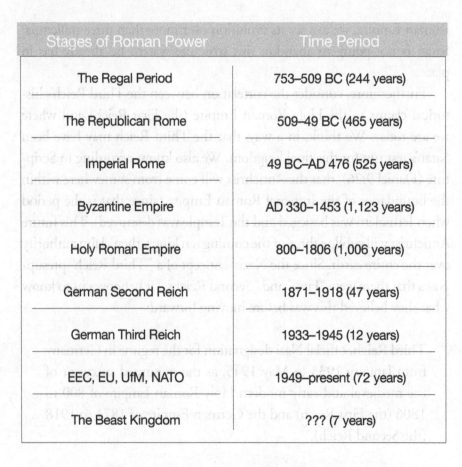

Stages of Roman Power	Time Period
The Regal Period	753–509 BC (244 years)
The Republican Rome	509–49 BC (465 years)
Imperial Rome	49 BC–AD 476 (525 years)
Byzantine Empire	AD 330–1453 (1,123 years)
Holy Roman Empire	800–1806 (1,006 years)
German Second Reich	1871–1918 (47 years)
German Third Reich	1933–1945 (12 years)
EEC, EU, UfM, NATO	1949–present (72 years)
The Beast Kingdom	??? (7 years)

Coming Together

The present statehood of Israel is a powerful indication of the ending of the age. The Ecumenical Movement is another. Perhaps equal to either of these is the European Common Market with its many implications…it is an economic community, a breaking down of national barriers, a getting together on certain common bases. The whole idea is to reshape the face of Europe. This was attempted by Caesar, by Napoleon, and by Hitler, but their means to this end were not subtle or as work-able as those proposed by the Common Market. They used ammunition; today's promoters use bread. And let it be said that the reshaping of the face of Europe approximates the kingdom to arise out of the old Roman Empire—the last Gentile power.[21]

Since Europe has been reunited now for seventy-two years (since 1950), its leadership has finally come full circle in their post-World Wars' pacifism. They are recognizing that, without military might, they will always be viewed as nothing but *paper tigers*. They see that, no matter how powerful they become economically and politically, without the military strength to match, they will never be taken seriously as a global super-power. But in these past seventy-plus years, they haven't had the need. America was strong. America funded and carried NATO. America was always there…until the forty-sixth US presidential administration came to power. Now it seems like one misstep after another, and the Europeans are waking up to the reality that America is not always going to be able to come to their defense (for example, the Afghanistan withdrawal, Ukraine war). Take note of this *Gatestone* article about the call to arms regarding the desire to create a new European Defense Force:

This is from EU [European Union] observer Dave Keating [who] noted: "The Brussels buzzword is now 'strategic autonomy,' an effort to wrestle the word 'sovereignty' away from nationalists and make the case that only a strong EU can make Europeans truly sovereign in relation to Russia, China, and the United States." European federalists increasingly have called for building an autonomous EU military force:

March 8, 2015. In an interview with the German newspaper Welt am Sonntag, Jean-Claude Juncker, then the president of the European Commission, the EU's administrative arm, declared that the European Union needed its own army because it was not "taken entirely seriously" on the international stage. The proposal was flatly rejected by the British government, which at the time was still an EU member: "Our position is crystal clear that defense is a national—not an EU—responsibility and that there is no prospect of that position changing and no prospect of a European army."

September 26, 2017. President [Emmanual] Macron [president of France], in a major speech at Sorbonne University, called for a joint EU defense force as part of his vision for the future of the bloc: "Europe needs to establish a common intervention force, a common defense budget and a common doctrine for action."

November 6, 2018. Macron, marking the centenary of the armistice that ended World War 1, warned that Europe cannot be protected without a "true, European army." He added: "We have to protect ourselves with respect to China, Russia and even the United States of America."

November 13, 2018. German Chancellor Angela Merkel echoed Macron's calls for a European army: "The times when we could rely on others are over. This means nothing less than for us Europeans to take our destiny in our own hands if we want to survive as a Union.... We have to create a European intervention unit with which Europe can act on the ground where necessary. We have taken major steps in the field of military cooperation; this is good and largely supported in this house. But I also have to say, seeing the developments of the recent years that we have to work on a vision to establish a real European army one day."

September 10, 2019. During her first press conference as the new president of the European Commission, Ursula von der Leyen, who has long called for a "United States of Europe," said that she will lead a "geopolitical Commission" aimed at boosting the EU's role on the world stage. She did not offer many details other than a vaguely worded pledge that the European Union would "be the guardian of multilateralism."

November 7, 2019. President Macron, in an interview with the London-based magazine, The Economist, declared that NATO was "brain dead" and warned that European countries can no longer rely on the United States for defense. Europe, he said, stands on "the edge of a precipice" and needs to start thinking of itself strategically as a geopolitical power and regain "military sovereignty" or otherwise "we will no longer be in control of our destiny." Macron criticized U.S. President Donald J. Trump because he "doesn't share our idea of the European project." Chancellor Merkel said Macron "used drastic words — that is not my view of co-operation in NATO."

November 26, 2019. France and Germany announced the "Conference on the Future of Europe," a two-year post-Brexit soul-searching exercise aimed at reforming the EU to make it "more united and sovereign."

June 17, 2020. The European Council tasked the EU's foreign policy chief, Josep Borrell, with drafting a written "Strategic Compass." The document should have three main purposes: 1) to formulate the EU's first common threat analysis; 2) to strengthen the EU's security and defense role; and 3) to offer political guidance for future military planning processes. The Strategic Compass, aimed at harmonizing the perception of threats and risks within the EU, is to be presented in November 2021, debated by EU leaders in December 2021, and approved in March 2022.

December 3, 2020. EU foreign policy chief Josep Borrell, in the blog post, "Why European Strategic Autonomy Matters," wrote: "It is difficult to claim to be a 'political union' able to act as a 'global player' and as a 'geopolitical Commission' without being 'autonomous.'" He described "strategic autonomy" as a long-term process intended to ensure that Europeans "increasingly take charge of themselves."

May 5, 2021. Fourteen EU countries—Austria, Belgium, Cyprus, Czech Republic, Germany, Greece, France, Ireland, Italy, Luxembourg, the Netherlands, Portugal, Slovenia and Spain—called for the creation of a so-called EU First Entry Force consisting of 5,000 troops with air, land and sea capabilities.

August 29, 2021. In an interview with the Italian newspaper Corriere della Sera, Borrell, the EU's foreign policy chief, said that the moment had come to establish an EU expeditionary force—a "First Entry Force"—to compensate for U.S. "disengagement" from international affairs. A senior EU diplomat, speaking to the Guardian newspaper, asked: "We have been here before—which leader is going to allow their nationals to be killed in the name of the EU? What problem is this reaction force meant to solve? Does Borrell seriously entertain the idea the EU would be able to step into the void the US left?"

September 15, 2021. In her annual State of the Union speech delivered to the European Parliament in Strasbourg, von der Leyen urged greater military independence from the United States. "Europe can—and clearly should—be able and willing to do more on its own," she said. She called for a "European Defense Union" but admitted the "lack of political will" to "build the foundation for collective decision-making."

October 2, 2021. European Council President Charles Michel, speaking at an award ceremony of the International Charlemagne Prize, declared that "2022 will be the year of European defense."

October 5–6, 2021. At an EU Summit in Slovenia, EU member states were so divided on the issue of strategic autonomy that the topic was not even included in the summit's final declaration. To create the illusion of consensus, Michel issued an "oral conclusion" of the summit: "To become more effective and assertive on the international stage, the European Union needs to increase its capacity to act autonomously."[22]

Where we part ways with the EU "experts" at Gatestone and elsewhere is where they're convinced the EU cannot put a cohesive, multinational army together serving under the banner of the European Union. We would agree that a German, Dutch, Italian, French, and/or Polish army would not fight effectively in a bureaucracy, which is what the EU represents. However, they would fight to the death were the EU to rebrand itself as the "New Roman Empire," the "Fourth Reich," or some other name reminiscent of Europe's glory days. Seeing as how most of human history has had Europe at the center stage of world power in one degree or another, it has a lot of options to choose from.

The problem with most of today's international affairs specialists and think tanks is that they refuse to accept the prophetic narrative for where the Bible says the world will end up. And because they don't, all they can do instead is offer up utterly unrealistic and naïve futuristic visions of a socialist utopia where people are content to own nothing, eat less meat, and have every inch of their lives micromanaged by some "benign" bureaucratic government. Conversely, the other half of these so-called experts are stuck in neutral and can't seem to stop wanting to fight the last war. The reason the US military and political leaders are *just now* starting to panic regarding China's military potential is the same reason they won't see the truly terrifying potential the EU represents.

These "experts" keep thinking of the EU twenty years ago. Back then, it was just a bureaucratic paper tiger perpetually gridlocked by infighting and incompetence. However, given the recent and utterly chaotic Afghanistan departure by the US military, as well as the Russian invasion of Ukraine, we're fairly certain that EU and NATO leaders no longer trust the United States to defend them against a future Russian invasion. And, under this administration and senior military leadership, we don't blame them. If they weren't convinced before, they are absolutely convinced now that the time is right to build their own army and take charge of their own continental defense.

So, to summarize and perhaps clarify this theory thus far is that the EU/UfM/NATO will become one of the ten regions the world realigns into after the Rapture. We know, at some level, the demonic forces (those territorial princes) are anticipating this and are feverishly pushing world leaders into laying the groundwork for this totalitarian state to arise (courtesy of the UN's Agenda 2030, the Great Reset, etc.). These demonic princes know the moment the Rapture happens, it will decimate the US politically, economically, militarily, and societally. They also know that when the US goes under, it will quickly drag the global economy down with it, and it will be that much harder to regain order. It also stands to reason that, after the Rapture, the EU would be in position to take control of the vast US military arsenal we've been posturing in Europe for decades during the Cold War.

FIVE

E PLURIBUS UNUM

America is the only country ever founded on an idea. The only country that is not founded on race or even common history. It's founded on an idea and the idea is liberty. That is probably the rarest phenomena in the political history of the world; this has never happened before. And not only has it happened, but it's worked. We are the most flourishing, the most powerful, most influential country on Earth with this system, invented by the greatest political geniuses probably in human history.

CHARLES KRAUTHAMMER,
THE CASE FOR AMERICAN EXCEPTIONALISM[23]

THE MAGNA CARTA (Runnymeade, England, 1215) was the first modern effort to *free* mankind from the unchecked tyranny of monarchial rule. While its original aims were limited to the landowners in medieval England, it became the first "constitution" of sorts that Europe ever had. Since Europe was still the center of world power at that time (and had been since the days of Alexander the Great), the idea of personal rights began to be transported throughout the world by way of European colonialism. Most notably, this idea took root in the British colonies of the New World—which, as we know, would later become the United States of America.

By 1776, the colonists of the thirteen colonies had endured enough of the abuses and taxation without representation from King George III of

England. Thus, the leaders (America's founders) of this revolution leaned heavily upon the past to create what would become the most important document in modern history. They borrowed from the philosophies of the Greeks, the ideals of governance from the Romans, and morality and ethics from the Bible. Then, with the Magna Carta as a model, they created the Charters of Liberty.

The Charters of Liberty included the Declaration of Independence, the Constitution, and the Bill of Rights. These documents were the foundation for creating the greatest constitutional republic the world had ever known. Their overarching theme was designed around limiting the government's power by acknowledging that human rights and freedoms are both inherent and God-given. It also prevented the consolidation of power within the government by dividing it amongst the three branches: executive, legislative, and judicial. Furthermore, power that was not assigned to the federal government was to be automatically delegated to the states. In essence, these writings became the epitome of perfection regarding human government. In a sense, they completed what was begun centuries earlier in 1215. So, for the next two and a half centuries, the United States became that "shining city on a hill."

The "shine" was so bright, in fact, that we became a beacon that drew peoples from all around the world who fled here to escape oppression or to seek out better lives than the ones they were living in whatever darkened corners of the world they came from. What caused this so-called shining? For one thing, the US was a land of religious freedom and opportunity the likes of which the world had never before seen. It also became a beacon of stability in the sense that, while empires and nations were in a state of constant flux, the US remained...thus, "the shining city on a hill."

Pax Americana

We can trace the origins of our current world order (with the US at the helm) back to the smoldering ash heaps of Europe at the end of World War II. As the Allied troops begin their final push into Nazi Germany (circa 1944–45), the world bankers and Allied politicians were already busily conspiring on ways to best shape this New World Order. During the war, Europe (the Old World) had gone into serious debt to the Americans, who had been financing numerous fronts across the European theater. From the 1950s–2000s, that same money and wealth slowly (then quickly) began to transfer back across the Atlantic from whence it came. History notwithstanding, American thinkers and politicians began to see this reversal of fortunes as not only probable, but inevitable. They began maneuvering and then implementing several initiatives to keep this newfound wealth and power centered in the New World. These seven US-led initiatives/events have largely come to shape our world order (for better or worse) over the past seventy-four years:

1. **The Bretton Woods Agreement:** This was an attempt to stabilize the postwar markets by creating an agreement (there were 730 delegates there at Bretton Woods, New Hampshire) to use the gold standard as a means to fix the currency exchange rates. This, in turn, created a new international monetary system that lasted from the mid-1940s until the early 1970s. This agreement pegged the value of other nations' currencies to the US dollar, which, in turn, was attached to the price of gold—fixed at $35 an ounce at the time. But by the 1970s, the Bretton Woods Agreement was on the verge of collapse, allowing countries to choose other ways to set the value of their currencies.[24]

2. **The Petrol Dollar:** By the late 1960s and early 1970s, the impending collapse of Bretton Woods was on the horizon. After this came the ingenious way American financiers sought to extend the preeminence of the US dollar. Instead of linking it to gold (a system that was already strained due to Lyndon B. Johnson's Great Society Initiative and the Vietnam War), the US dollar would be tied to the sale of oil *vis a vis* the Organization of the Petroleum Exporting Countries (OPEC). Therefore, if a nation wanted to buy oil from the largest oil producer (OPEC), it would have to

be done in US dollars, thus requiring every nation to keep ample supplies of US currency on hand in reserves.

3. **The United Nations:** Having already attempted instituting a League of Nations at the conclusion of World War I and failing miserably (i.e., the Third Reich), the twentieth-century globalists took advantage of the crisis created by World War II (WWII) to attempt to implement another system of global governance. With the full backing of the United States (land, money, resources, and governance), they succeeded. One of their first major accomplishments was to vote to allow for the portioning of the former Ottoman territory known as Palestine (Palestine Partition Resolution 181). While fairly toothless at present, the UN has ironically grown into a largely anti-American and anti-Israel organization.

4. **The Marshall Plan:** Named after its primary driver, US Secretary of State George Marshall, this plan was designed to "aid in the economic recovery of nations after WWII and to reduce the influence of Communist parties within them". Having learned this lesson the hard way after WWI (Versailles Treaty), the US was determined not to repeat this mistake by allowing the conditions to occur and potentially create another Adolf Hitler.[25]

5. **Cold War/NATO:** With both the West (US, Western Europe, Australia, Canada, etc.) and the East (Russia, China) having fought and won against the Third Reich and the Japanese Imperialists, the end brought the dividing of the spoils of war. With clear and irreparable divisions on governance and economics, for both the West (capitalist democracies) and the East (communist regimes), the fragile war-time alliance had ended. This created the need for Western Europe to form an alliance with the North Atlantic Treaty Organization (NATO) to protect them from further Eastern encroachment. This geopolitical tension created a forty-year Cold War between East and West, which lasted from the 1948–49 Berlin Blockade until the collapse of

the Soviet Union in 1991. The creation of NATO in 1949 was designed as a preemptive strike against any Russian aggression or intentions. However, after Russia invaded and annexed parts of Georgia (2008) and later Crimea (2014) without any Western military response, many have wondered what good NATO actually does. The role of NATO seemed to be further deteriorating with the 2016 election of President Donald Trump, whose public insistence that the EU take a more proactive role (financially and physically) in providing for their own self-defense seemed to be highly offensive to the Europeans.

6. **The Nuclear Arms/Space Race:** Beginning with the highly secretive Manhattan Project, the world's race toward a weapon of mass destruction finally ended with the American's use of two atom bombs on the Japanese cities of Nagasaki and Hiroshima in the summer of 1945. For four brief years, the US enjoyed atomic supremacy, but this was soon dashed with the Soviet Union's first successful test of their own atomic weapon in 1949. Not to be outdone, both the US and USSR began a several-decades initiative to create even more devastating weapons. Relating to this was the race to space, which the Russians initially won. However, the US was the first nation (and only nation as of yet) to put a man on the moon.

7. **The Rebirth of Israel:** From AD 70 until 1948, the nation of Israel existed only in the history books. But, due to the defeat of the Ottoman Turks (1918) and the Nazi Holocaust (1933–1945), there was both opportunity (the land) and support (sympathy/determination) for and by the Jewish people to return to their ancient homeland *en masse*. Despite intense internal opposition to supporting Israel from within US President Harry Truman's own administration, the US became the first nation to recognize the newly formed state on May 14, 1948. Since then, the Middle East has been a hotbed of anti-Semitism, violence, and war in the Muslims' repeated attempts (1948, 1956, 1967, 1973, etc.) to destroy the world's only Jewish nation.

Thus, as in the case with most of history, war changes things...and quickly. The bigger the war, the bigger the change. Even greater and more pronounced than World War II was the forty-year Cold War, which, as mentioned earlier, lasted from approximately 1945 to 1991 and spanned the entire globe. During this time we saw the dramatic increase in the rise of new powerful intelligence agencies and the beginning of information warfare. But when the Soviet Union suddenly collapsed in December 1991, it ended, and these new titans of informational warfare had no threats to warrant their continued and expensive existence. As it turns out, there was a threat, but one that needed a little rattling to shake up the hornets' nest...the radical Islamists. Thus, ten years later, the Western intelligentsia had a new *casus belli* ("reason for war")—the War on Terror.

The Postmodern Error

Our Constitution was made only for a moral and religious people. It is wholly inadequate for the government of any other.[26]
—President John Adams

It has been 243 years since 1776, and we have fallen very far from what our forefathers could have ever imagined. This occidental decline is not accidental, but rather, intentional. After a century of infusing cultural Marxism into every educational and entertainment medium possible, we have become not only amoral (and immoral), but also exceedingly ignorant and lazy. There has been a massive dumbing down of the masses—so much so that the average person probably could not tell you what the Bill of Rights is or where to find Washington, DC, on a map. Bred into this newfound ignorance is the foolish notion of uniformitarianism. That is, most people alive today think the way things are now is the way they have always been and will always be.

This line of reasoning is also a form of "normalcy bias," by which people judge tomorrow by the persistent presence of the present. Most people fail to realize that this experiment in human liberty (the United States) was only ever the exception to the rule, not the norm. There are now multiple generations of folks who either don't know or don't care about our exceptionalism, and so they have begun handing over their God-given liberties in exchange for the promise of free handouts and security.

President Ronald Reagan said:

> Freedom is never more than one generation away from extinction. We didn't pass it to our children in the bloodstream. It must be fought for, protected, and handed on for them to do the same, or one day we will spend our sunset years telling our children and our children's children what it was once like in the United States where men were free.[27]

With a growing number of Democrats and Millennials these days militantly demanding that we turn to socialism to solve our current problems of social inequality, we are at the tipping point for this nation's survival. We say "tipping point" because these aspiring communists only used to make up the outer fringes of society. Now, they are found in most universities (as faculty and students), among a growing number of elected officials, and even among giants within the tech industry. These groups are now demanding that socialism be instituted everywhere regardless of its economic and political ramifications.

This is the fruit of more than a century of socialist propaganda being foisted upon us through academia, the media, politics, and pop culture. Since these socialists could not dismantle the Constitution and the Bill of Rights to their speed and liking, they have turned to corrupt the institutions. For example, since Hillary Clinton lost the 2016 election, there is a growing call to remove the Electoral College and go to a purely popular vote to determine presidential winners. Furthermore, whichever party instituted it would virtually guarantee its own supremacy into perpetuity. This would spell the end of the American experiment.

On the other side of the coin is the *perceived* need by both Republicans and Democrats to expand the powers of intelligence and law enforcement agencies. This is due to the emerging diversity of threats (such as via cybercrimes, mass shootings, and weapons of mass destruction) that face the nation. Additionally, the vast advancements tech companies have made in genetics, micro technology, artificial intelligence, unmanned autonomous systems, and surveillance have become downright Orwellian.

While most of this seems innocuous to normal, law-abiding citizens today, the creation of all that power in the hands of a nation in a moral and spiritual freefall should be frightening. Imagine what things would be like if radical socialists and communists should ever gain control of all three branches of government.

In our current two-party political system, one party has seemingly steered so hard to the left that it has become the single greatest threat to our own national existence. While the Republicans (mainstream GOP types) think power can be shared and we should all play nice, the Democrats are out for blood. For them, there is no "live and let live" anymore; it is "win by whatever means necessary and punish the losers mercilessly." Make no mistake, the Democratic Party of 2022 is not the Democratic Party of 1990, 1980, or earlier. The Democrats' platform of 2022 centered on three things: enacting abortion on demand at any stage of pregnancy (even post-birth); promoting anything anti-Israel and anti-Christian; and putting forward socialism (or Socialist ideals).

Very few leaders have the foresight or moral backbone to stand against the growing tide of immorality. It is easy to caution against issues like out-of-control spending or our ballooning national debt. Nevertheless, when we stand against immorality, we make it personal for the wicked, and we will reap the whirlwind. It is only when it concerns evil that these godless Marxists will ever cling to the Bill of Rights. Yet, their understanding of liberty has become perverted. They believe, for example, in abandoning the Second Amendment but keeping the First Amendment, not realizing they cannot have the First without the Second.

Mene, Mene, Tekel, Upharsin
("Weighed and Judged")

Belshazzar the king made a great feast for a thousand of his lords, and drank wine in the presence of the thousand. While he tasted the wine, Belshazzar gave the command to bring the gold and silver vessels which his father Nebuchadnezzar had taken from the temple which had been in Jerusalem, that the king and his lords, his wives, and his concubines might drink from them. Then they brought the gold vessels that had been taken from the temple of the house of God which had been in Jerusalem; and the king and his lords, his wives, and his concubines drank from them. They drank wine, and praised the gods of gold and silver, bronze and iron, wood and stone.

In the same hour the fingers of a man's hand appeared and wrote opposite the lampstand on the plaster of the wall of the king's palace; and the king saw the part of the hand that wrote. Then the king's countenance changed, and his thoughts troubled him, so that the joints of his hips were loosened and his knees knocked against each other. (Daniel 5:1–6)

Since the 1960s, our nation has embarked upon a descent into godless immorality with frightening rapidity. This has all but assured our demise. This is not our own subjective reasoning, but a historical fact that has played out repeatedly. Acts such as embracing infanticide or deviant lifestyles have never boded well for a country. The depraved in America have now begun openly targeting children in the name of abortion, gender confusion, transgender story times, unisex bathrooms, and homosexual adoptions. As was the case with Belshazzar's party, by the time the writing is on the wall, it is already too late.

1. America's first "writing on the wall" moment was on April 19, 1995, with the terrorist bombing of the Alfred P. Murrah Federal

Building in Oklahoma City. This was the first major "homegrown" terror event within the United States. Although it came on the heels of the Democrat-led effort to pass the Orwellian 1995 Omnibus Homeland Terror Bill (later renamed the Patriot Act), it would come to serve as a perpetual reminder for the need of such a bill.

2. America's second warning came on September 11, 2001, when nineteen Muslim terrorists hijacked four planes and crashed them into the Twin Towers in New York City; the Pentagon; and a field in Shanksville, Pennsylvania. This exposed America's soft underbelly (our mobility) by hitting us where we were most vulnerable. With the massive increases in security required following the tragedies, it had the subsequent effect of making transportation virtually unbearable ever since. Adding insult to injury, these were the events that triggered the need for the previously mentioned Patriot Act.

3. America's third warning came in 2007 with the subprime mortgage crises. Since 1992, the government had been subsidizing "affordable" housing and adjustable-rate mortgage (ARM) loans to people who could not afford them. As early as 2003, this began spiraling out of control by creating a fake real-estate bubble. After three massive bank bailout loans, fifteen years later we are still suffering the repercussions of this event.[28]

4. America's fourth warning came in 2008–16 with the election of Barack Hussein Obama (aka Barry Sotero). As president, he did more in eight years to destabilize our nation (morally, economically, and geopolitically) than did all the previous presidents put together. As of 2022, he was still instrumental in controlling the Joe Biden regime since the same people have littered both administrations.

5. America's fifth warning came with the planned 2020 pandemic (designed in part to weaken and destabilize the Trump administration and the United States), as well as the resultant stolen

2020 election through coordinated, multi-state election fraud, implanting the most incompetent man in the world, Joe Biden, into the highest office of the land. (See point # 4.)

The End of Pax Americana

Decadence is a moral and spiritual disease, resulting from too long a period of wealth and power, producing cynicism, decline of religion, pessimism and frivolity. The citizens of such a nation will no longer make an effort to save themselves, because they are not convinced that anything in life is worth saving.[29]

—John Bagot Glubb, *The Fate of Empires and Search for Survival*

We should take serious note of the lack of US representation in the coming Gog-Magog war, as well as biblical end-times prophecies altogether. If we were to go back and read eyewitness testimonies from those who lived to see their world destroyed in previous calamities, they often say there was almost an inescapable sense of dread just prior to it happening. In fact, many have said they were haunted by the things they were witnessing (deterioration of an ethical culture, vast indebtedness, insecure borders, increased lawlessness, etc.) in the days, weeks, and months leading up to their demise. With that said, and understanding the calamities and challenges of the past two hundred years, it is neither lip service nor hyperbole to say we are now living in the last stages of the United States.

With the end of the American dream on the horizon comes the inevitable rise of some new form of global government to fill the vacuum left behind. That outcome is as assured as the rising of the sun in the east or its setting in the west. So what has prevented this new global order from emerging thus far? God is the one who "preappointed the times and boundaries of the nations" (Acts 17:26–27). If this is true (it is), then the United States was put in this specific time and place to serve as a final restraint of sorts to prevent a global, one-world government from forming before its appointed time.

The United States was the world's only true superpower over most of the twentieth century for a reason. However, that restraining purpose appears to be at its end, and try as we might, there is no undoing or redirecting God's plan for the trajectory of this nation. A nation that once operated as a constitutional republic, under God, has abandoned those values and is now coming apart at the seams. As the "melting pot" made up of every tribe, tongue, and peoples, it seems a fitting picture to show the United States' collapse as signaling the coming end to the times of the Gentiles. The once-mighty republic whose very existence prevents it from subordinating itself to any other political entity will soon become beholden to all.

In summary, from the days of Alexander the Great (circa 300 BC) until 2022, world power (economic, military, and political) has largely remained centered in the West. We know the Babylonians (under Nebuchadnezzar's grandson) were conquered by the Medo-Persians. The Greeks conquered the Persians. The Romans conquered the Greeks. The Roman Empire split in two after four hundred years of Empire rule. From Rome (the Western leg) geopolitical power moved to the north through the succeeding European barbarian hordes.

However, the barbarians were only able to conquer the Romans because they were already in a state of widespread decline (morally, economically, and militarily) and had become vulnerable on too many fronts. Sound familiar?

In the absence of *Pax Americana*, Europe will once again rise victorious and ascendant. In closing, and with regard to the fate of the United States, remember these six things:

1. The United States (or anything resembling the US) does not appear to be in the biblical prophetic picture at all.
2. The last Gentile power on planet earth will be the Beast, whose power seems to be centered in both Europe and the Middle East (Daniel 9:26; Revelation 13:1–2).

3. The Beast appears to be a regional power (or confederacy) at first, then becomes the global authority through the aid of technology and the supernatural demonic forces consolidating and centralizing its power into two men (Revelation 17:12–13).
4. The entire world is given over to the Beast (Revelation 13:7).
5. The kings of the East will challenge the Beast's power toward the end of the seven years (Revelation 16:12).
6. The Beast will make one last attempt at crushing the nation of Israel (the people; Revelation 12:13–17)

SIX

THE GREAT ILLUSION

War has no longer the justification that it makes for the survival
of the fittest; it involves the survival of the less fit. The idea that
the struggle between nations is a part of the evolutionary law of
man's advance involves a profound misreading of the biological
analogy. The warlike nations do not inherit the earth; they represent the decaying human element.

NORMAN ANGELL, *THE GREAT ILLUSION*, CIRCA 1910[30]

IN 1910, Norman Angell wrote a book titled *The Great Illusion*. In it,
he stated that industrialization, modernization, and capitalism disincen-
tivized war between modern Western nation-states. He reasoned that
because the cost of war is too high, thus unprofitable, it was unlikely to
ever happen again. Even the periodical of note at that time, *The Economist*, was smitten. In 1913, it heralded: "War Becomes Impossible in
Civilized World."

However, by June of 1914, the world would be engulfed in its First
World War.

The theory championed then by Angell was similar to the one we
hear being bantered around today: *There has never been a war between
two countries with a McDonald's in them.* Nonsense. As a matter of record,
there are 60 McDonald's franchises in Ukraine, and 847 in Russia. There
are 3,500 McDonalds in China, and 413 in Taiwan. Somehow, the sway
of the "Golden Arches" was not enough to quell the expansionist desires
of one Vladimir Putin any more than a single McNugget would appease

the hunger of a ravenous bear. Apologies up front for the excerpt's length, but we need to set the context by quoting from an amazing 2014 article titled, "World War One: First War Was Impossible, Then Inevitable."

The real "Great Illusion," of course, turned out to be the idea that economic self-interest made wars obsolete. Yet a variant of this naïve materialism has returned. It underlies, for example, the Western foreign policy that presents economic sanctions on Russia or Iran as a substitute for political compromise or military intervention.

The truth, as the world discovered in 1914 and is re-discovering today in Ukraine, the Middle East and the China seas, is that economic interests are swept aside once the genie of nationalist or religious militarism is released.... Russia has in past conflicts withstood economic losses unimaginable to politicians and diplomats in the Western world—and the same is true of Iran and China.

Though historians continue to debate World War One's proximate causes, two key destabilizing features of early 20th-century geopolitics created the necessary conditions for the sudden spiral into all-consuming conflict: *the rise and fall of great powers, and the over-zealous observance of mutual-defense treaties*. These features are now returning to destabilize geopolitics a century later....

Today, Russia is a declining power and China is rising, while the United States is trying to maintain the 20th-century balance of power, with Europe and Japan as junior partners. Under these conditions, both rising and declining powers often conflict with nations currently in control....

Rising and declining powers naturally tend to unite against the status quo leaders. In 1914, for example, Germany, Austria-Hungary, and the Ottoman Empire did this against France, Britain, and Russia; today it is logical for China and Russia to collaborate against the United States, the European Union, and Japan....

Which brings us to the clearest lesson from 1914: the pernicious nexus of treaties and alliances that commit great powers to fight on behalf of other countries. This turned localized conflicts into regional or global wars—and did so with terrifying speed and unpredictability....

Consider this statement by General Sir Richard Shirreff, formerly NATO's second most senior military officer at a debate about Russia: "Everyone surely agrees that we would be ready to go to war to defend Britain's borders. Well, as a NATO member, Britain's borders are now in Latvia."

It may seem almost impossible that Washington would go to war against Beijing to defend some uninhabited Japanese islands. Or against Moscow over some decrepit mining towns in Donbas, if Ukraine ever joined NATO. In early 1914, though, it seemed almost impossible that Britain and France would go to war with Germany to defend Russia against Austria-Hungary over a dispute with Serbia. Yet by June 28, war moved straight from impossible to inevitable—without ever passing through improbable. Four years later, 10 million people had died.[31] (Emphasis added)

A century ago (to the year) after the Bolsheviks officially cut ties with their Tsarist past, a dying Vladimir Lenin handpicked Josef Stalin to be the new secretary-general of the Bolshevik Party. He would go onto become one of the greatest tyrants of the twentieth century. Under his iron fist, nearly forty million Russians, Ukrainians, Jews, and others died in gulags, starvation, and by violence.

A century later, we are seeing the shadowy façades coming off another Vladimir (Putin) as he removes any pretenses of going along to get along. The era of coexistence between the East (Russia and China) and the increasingly globalist West is over. Vladimir Putin and Xi Jinping see the West as collectively trying to impose their own Westernized version of a New World Order upon them, and they are having none of it. The problem for the West is that both China and Russia face serious existential issues. Russia faces a rapidly declining population due to high death rates and low birth rates. China faces a significantly skewed male-to-female ratio, as well as an increasingly aging population.

China's population is growing old at a faster rate than almost all other countries. The effects of China's 36-year one-child policy, combined with dramatic improvements in health care, have contributed to increases in life expectancy and decreases in China's birth rate. During the years that the one-child policy was in effect, life expectancy in China improved from 67 to 75 and fertility rate decreased from 2.8 to 1.7. China's looming demographic shift presents considerable social and economic challenges.[32]

On top of that, they're facing challenges and repercussions due to:

a) Their construction and property markets being wobblier than a two-legged chair (i.e., *Evergrande's* recent debt default).
b) Their aggressive manipulation of their currency (the yuan) being called out by numerous other nations who are tired of it .
c) The origin of the COVID-19 release, whether accidental or intentional, as well as the subsequent cover-up, accelerating the increasing number of nations that are withdrawing their expansion into Chinese markets.

Both Russia and China face serious existential threats to their long-term prospects as global powers. This makes them even more dangerous than ever, because they realize if they don't act now, they won't get the chance later.

Macro View

Even more than the above-mentioned motivations is the question of global dominance between nationalist entities like Russia and China and

Western-minded globalists. The West is eager to usher in the Great Reset and the United Nation's Agenda 2030, but Russia and China are having none of it. This is why George Soros recently turned against China in a very public way, and why the World Economic Forum (WEF) is solidly standing behind Ukraine and its WEF-backed President Volodymyr Zelenskyy.

There are two visions for the way ahead, according to the current world order: either the coming Westernized global government or the multi-polar super-states with Russia and China at the helm. At least, that is the way men like Vladimir Putin and Xi Jinping see it. For them, this is the World War I moment, except they have all the momentum behind them. They see the US-EU status quo in decline and are beginning to make their moves to accelerate that decline.

They know the US dollar (the world's current global reserve currency) is on the outs, and they are trying to stay ahead of the curve. They are minimizing their ties and debt to the US dollar and are ready to bring online their own Central Bank Digital Currencies (CBDC) to take the place as the global reserve currency.

The great illusion in all this isn't that thriving economies drive peace, or that the US is in control (it isn't and we aren't). The great illusion is not even economical or geopolitical. It's the biblically derived conclusion that unredeemed people think they are running world affairs. Regardless of whether you are an Egyptian pharaoh, a Babylonian king, a Roman Caesar, a US president, or a global potentate, humans don't control anything; God does. He, not we mere mortals, sets the boundaries and the times for which nations rise and fall.

> And He has made from one blood every nation of men to dwell on all the face of the earth, and has determined their preappointed times and the boundaries of their dwellings. (Acts 17:26)

According to Scripture, there are still two major global conflicts yet to happen. The first is the Gog-Magog war, and the second, the Armageddon campaign. These authors firmly believe the players and actors in the Gog-Magog war include Rosh (Russia) and Magog (the nations formerly aligned under the Soviet Union), as well as the African, Turkish, Persian, and Asian cohorts who join in on the invasion of Israel. When these nations begin to march, no other nation(s) can stop them. The Armageddon campaign will happen when all the nations march against Israel. Both conflicts will be ended by divine force, not by geopolitical actions. This means that, in either scenario, the United States, as the world superpower, is not in the picture.

Nevertheless, we can figure out rather easily why the Armageddon campaign will happen. It is Satan's last-ditch effort to thwart God's prophetic plan by prematurely destroying Israel. But it begs the question as to why the Gog-Magog War happens. Why do Turkey, Iran, Libya, Sudan, Russia and its *Magogian* hordes decide to come against tiny Israel?

There have been recent rumors that Israel is set to discover massive amounts of gold, silver, and precious stones that had been acquired under the reign of King Solomon, but were lost to the annals of time. Simultaneous to this has been the Eastern Mediterranean pipeline project (EastMed) that was launched at the discovery of massive natural gas fields off the coast in the Israeli Levant. The project has been in the works for years now as Israel has sought to connect those gargantuan natural gas reserves off their coast through Cyprus, into Greece, and into the rest of Europe.

Although EastMed was suspended for a brief time, it has now been revived and is being expedited to secure the EU's divorce from Russian energy. This pipeline project will replace the Russian Nordstream pipelines, and will certainly be enough cause to turn Russia's ire toward the south. Why else would they be so vested in pumping billions of rubles into a failed state like Syria?

It seems the excuse for wanting a warm-water port at Tartarus is a façade for assuring Israel's enemies they have a great northern ally. In so doing, the Russians will find no shortage of Israeli enemies who will join their fracas only to find out they are no match for God's divine providence.

It appears that a convergence of geopolitical events is happening before our eyes, as Europe, which has long been wedded—by its energy dependence—to Russia, finally seeks a divorce. Given the recent Russian invasion of Ukraine, the West's shunning and boycotting of Russia, and China's laser-focused intent on unifying Taiwan back with the mainland, a geopolitical storm of epic proportions is brewing on the horizon. Just as it did in the days leading up to World War I, it appears this clash of civilizations has nowhere to go but ballistic.

The people of the great nations of the past seem normally to have imagined that their pre-eminence would last forever. Rome appeared to its citizens to be destined to be for all time the mistress of the world. The Abbasid Khalifs of Baghdad declared that God had appointed them to rule mankind until the day of judgement. Seventy years ago, many people in Britain believed that the empire would endure forever. Although Hitler failed to achieve his objective, he declared that Germany would rule the world for a thousand years. That sentiments like these could be publicly expressed without evoking derision shows that, in all ages, the regular rise and fall of great nations has passed unperceived. The simplest statistics prove the steady rotation of one nation after another at regular intervals.[33]

SEVEN

THE LUCIFERIAN AGENDA

Lest we forget at least an over-the-shoulder acknowledgment to the very first radical: from all our legends, mythology, and history (and who is to know where mythology leaves off and history begins—or which is which), the first radical known to man who rebelled against the establishment and did it so effectively that he at least won his own kingdom—Lucifer.

SAUL ALINSKY, *RULES FOR RADICALS*[34]

TWO UNDERCURRENTS are presently channeling this increased obsession with globalism in our world today. The first is the spirit of Antichrist (Luciferianism) that has stirred up an increasingly frenzied state of wickedness. Now, we should cast aside any notions that Luciferians are only those black-robed Satanists wearing inverted crosses and dancing strangely around their midnight bonfires.

Luciferianism, in actuality, is a belief system that venerates Lucifer as the "morning star" or "light bearer" and regards him as either the hero or the antihero in the human drama. Proponents of the system believe Lucifer originally set out to free humanity from the bondage of a totalitarian God by opening the eyes of Adam and Eve through the fruit of the tree of the knowledge of good and evil. Thus, knowledge—particularly secret knowledge—is prized as the key to enlightenment.[35]

The modern Luciferian is many things, but anonymity has become its adherents' new black robe, and, subtlety, their midnight dance. They specialize in cloaking their true intentions with ideas like tolerance, ecumenicalism, inclusivity, intersectionality, postmodernism, cultural relativism, and subjectivism (all sly forms of confusion), all the while shrouding their language in doublespeak and nonsensical political correctness. The new Luciferian still hates the Gospel of Jesus Christ and still loathes the Bible, but does so in such a way that most of us would never know.

Humanism: "Ye Shall Be as Gods"

A today's form of Luciferianism is secular humanism. Humanism rejects the supernatural view of reality (which primarily means Christianity) and defines humans as the be-all and end-all in this present age ("ye shall be as gods"). With the meteoric rise of developments in technology and science over the past two centuries, humanism has thrived in government, academia, and the corporate arenas as the dominant "nonreligious" belief system. For the purposes of this book, we shall simply call this convergence of humanism, technology, and science "modernism."

Thus, modernism has enabled the legal rejection of biblical Christianity, Judeo-Christian morality and ethics, as well as Bible-based academics from the public arena of ideas on such grounds as "separation of church and state"—in addition to the aforementioned Luciferian principles.

While Luciferianism and humanism might seem like odd bedfellows, they share at least three things in common: They are antichrist in nature (denying true biblical Christianity); they view knowledge as the path to "redemption" (self-deification); and they share the common source—Satan himself. The truth is, any worldview, philosophy, or religion that denies the deity of Jesus Christ is of the "spirit of antichrist" (1 John 4:3). At the end of the day, it matters not how it disguises itself; if it (the worldview, religion, philosophy, policy, etc.) denies either the deity of Christ or His humanity, its origins are from the very pit of Hell.

Within the broad spectrum of Luciferianism, we are acknowledging the many-faceted approach to its unique modification in our present age, as opposed to those in the near and distant past. Our world is supposed to be sophisticated and evolved, thus considers religion an antiquated idea that should be extinct. However, there is still a growing realization that the natural world is not all there is. Furthermore, secular humanism can only lead to nihilism ("everything is meaningless"), which is akin to the ouroboros tail-eating snake that soon runs out of itself to eat. This is one of the greatest detriments to pure humanism, because so much is now beginning to happen that can no longer be explained by science or reason that humanists are often left empty-handed.

Supernaturalism

This is where supernaturalism comes in to fill the vacuum created by humanism, while aiding and abetting the Luciferian agenda. But first, a basic definition.

"Supernaturalism" subscribes to the belief of an existence beyond what we perceive as the physical reality. Although it's most often associated with religion, supernaturalism can also extend to the belief in nonreligious ideas like monsters, spirits, extraterrestrial life forms, and otherworldly dimensions.

Even though the fascination with the mysterious past began many centuries ago, it has come screaming back into the forefront of news, academia, archeology, and pop culture with the recent (relatively speaking) discoveries of the ancient Egyptian pyramids, as well as numerous other megalithic sites in the late nineteenth and early twentieth centuries. Since then, Western civilization has become enamored with the mythos of the ancient pagan world through the likes of books, movies, and television (The History Channel, National Geographic, etc.).

Since then, comic books—and later, other pop-culture media—began borrowing heavily from ancient mythology in order to provide a hero-starved society with the likes of the "mighty men of old." In addition to creating vast new pantheons of superheroes, pop culture has introduced the ideas of mirror dimensions, intergalactic civilizations, lost worlds, and the multiverse to explain how all of these characters could coexist.

This curiosity about the paranormal has since transformed into a global obsession, which many have since capitalized on by creating billion-dollar industries from these modern-day mythos (including Marvel and DC Comics, the Harry Potter and Star Wars franchises, etc.). Sadly, the process of creating books, television shows, video games, and movies is an attempt to fill the void left by the rejection of Christianity, as well as a way to desensitize the masses to the realm of the occult in general.

As the real world continues to de-evolve into barbarism and wickedness, so too have these stories become darker and grittier, many of which have been dedicated to uncovering and rediscovering the glories of the ancient pagan "histories." The once-secret tales of lore, at one time (from the Renaissance to the Enlightenment) highly guarded mysteries amongst the secret societies like the Rosicrucians, the Golden Dawn, and Theosophists are now broadcast by every medium known to exist.

The result, as previously noted, has been an explosion of interest in all things supernatural, paranormal, and occult. This revival has also helped bring ancient paganism and mythology out from the shadowy fringe and back into the mainstream of societal conscience. Given the often sparse information available about many of these ancient belief systems, the details are often exaggerated (or reimagined altogether) by their advocates and romanticized into pop culture. Sadly, the teachings and beliefs then become the truth to many who are ignorant of ancient history, whether willfully or not.

The general historical illiteracy of the common man has been one of Satan's greatest assets throughout the ages. It has allowed him to recycle these fables countless times, often only changing the names. Given the antiquity of many of these pagan origin stories, modern secularist historians, archeologists, and anthropologists frequently give greater credence and gravitas to them since they often predate Christianity by many centuries. Be that as it may, these pagan myths do not predate Judaism—from which, of course, comes Christianity.

In contrast to supernaturalism, which tends to focus on the more sensational and unexplainable entities and events within our reality, Luciferianism and human secularism directs its laser beams on knowledge—

hidden knowledge, to be exact. For the Luciferian, knowledge is the key to immortality and the path to godhood. However, both complement each other, with supernaturalism drawing in the crowds with signs and wonders and Luciferianism baptizing them in the occult practices that invoke dark spirits.

Ironically, Luciferianism claims to offer enlightenment, yet the "enlightened" only know about Lucifer from the same Bible that unapologetically pronounces Satan as the "father of lies." The same can be said for the so-called forbidden knowledge that secret groups claim to want so desperately, when in fact they have had the truth right in front of them the whole time.

As for the globalists' modern connection with Luciferianism, the roots trace back to Madame Helena Blavatsky, who was a Theosophist in the late 1800s. Her esoteric and mysticism-based teachings went on to influence the likes of Alice and Foster Bailey. These two went on to found the Lucifer Trust (later shortened to Lucis Trust), which would become the primary publishing house for the newly formed United Nations. Alice Bailey's teachings would go on to be used in the founding of the United Nations, which has maintained its ecumenical underpinnings ever since.

Here is the Baileys' history (taken from the Lucis Trust website;www. lucistrust.org), in which they proudly proclaim their esoteric heritage.

> The Lucis Trust was established by Alice and Foster Bailey as a vehicle to foster recognition of the universal spiritual principles at the heart of all work to build right relations. The Trust was incorporated in the State of New Jersey, USA, on April 5, 1922. A separate limited company, Lucis Trust Ltd. was established as an educational charity and incorporated in the United Kingdom in 1935. And in 1951 Lucis Trust was established as a legal entity in Switzerland, with an office in Geneva.
>
> A publishing company, initially named Lucifer Publishing Company, was established by Alice and Foster Bailey in the State of New Jersey, USA, in May 1922 to publish the book, Initiation

Human and Solar. The ancient myth of Lucifer refers to the angel who brought light to the world, and it is assumed that the name was applied to the publishing company in honour of a journal, which had been edited for a number of years by theosophical founder, HP Blavatsky. It soon became clear to the Bailey's that some Christian groups have traditionally mistakenly identified Lucifer with Satan, and for this reason the company's name was changed in 1924 to Lucis Publishing Company.[36]

The truth is that Luciferianism, humanism, and supernaturalism will come together in a renewed way the world hasn't seen since the days before the Flood. However, in the moments immediately following the Rapture of the Church, it will be the merger of realized enlightenment (via forbidden knowledge) with the clearly evidenced physical expression of the supernatural (lying signs and wonders). This is why the Apostle Paul wrote the following:

The coming of the lawless one is according to the working of Satan, *with all power, signs, and lying wonders*, and with all unrighteous deception among those who perish, because they did not receive the love of the truth, that they might be saved. (2 Thessalonians 2:9–10, emphasis added)

Universalism

Again, when we speak of the growing Luciferian zeitgeist ("zeitgeist" meaning "the spirit of the age") sweeping through the world, it's not going to sound overtly demonic at first, because Luciferianism (despite its name) rarely goes by its name. Rarely will we find anyone who claims to be Luciferian specifically, unless they are a practicing Satanist or Wiccan. However, we will find, with surprising ease, those who espouse the ideas of Luciferianism because it specializes in subtlety and operates with absolute tolerance and inclusivity. Most of the ideals within Luciferianism consist of self-deification, sexual debauchery, a rejection of accepted truths, and knowledge above all.

All of these points (and more) are things that governments are normalizing with increased intensity. The world is being primed to receive (and be deceived) by the return of magic and the occult through scientific efforts, pop culture, and even politics! This is just another harbinger pointing to the times that Jesus Himself described as being like the days of Noah (Luke 17:26–29). This Luciferian new order is the growing convergence of reinserting religious paganism into the global body politic and disguising it as enlightenment through advanced knowledge and supernatural power.

In 1994, a *World Goodwill* newsletter reported the creation of a UN Interfaith Organization called the Temple of Understanding, its goal being to create a "spiritual UN."

Its supporters, in fact, were not small fries, but people like Eleanor Roosevelt and Anwar Sadat, indicating that this organization has top-level approval. Two other facts stand out verifying that the UN's purpose far exceeds just the legal and political realms.

Founded in 1995, the United Religious Organization was founded under the UN's watchful eye, stressing a unification of all religions. According to UN documents, the organization fell into place by 2000 and became fully operational by 2005.

> Do not worry if not all religions will join the United Religious Organization. Many nations did not join the UN at the beginning but later regretted it. It was the same with the European communities and it will be the case with the world's religions because whoever stays out and aloof will sooner or later regret it.[37]

Furthermore, this Luciferian new order will have one more ace up its sleeve in uniting all the world's remaining religions: artificial intelligence.

> What you try to do a thousand years ago with the priest preaching
> from the pulpit you will be able to do in a far more invasive way
> in 10 or 15 years with all kinds of brain-computer interfaces and
> direct biological interventions.[38] —Yuval Noah Harari, *Homo Deus*

At present, there are seven major belief systems in the world today: Christianity, Islam, Hinduism, Buddhism, Judaism, paganism, and humanism. Underneath these major categories, there are between four thousand and ten thousand subsects/groups. Since Babel, Satan has had to shift his plans from establishing global universalism to that of "divide and conquer." Now that the end of the age has come, he is once again attempting to bring it all back together under one roof.

As has been noted by numerous biblical scholars and teachers, the coming Antichrist's Beast kingdom will have three legs to its political structure: economic, military, and religious. However, we believe this coming system will have a fourth leg that seemingly enables (or super-charges) the other three: the supernatural.

According to Scripture, the Beast will begin as a ten-nation/region imperial power that rises up at a time of great global crisis, then imposes its political will over the entire earth. It's not a stretch to see how this power will then extend into its economic authority to control all buying and selling everywhere. Militarily, the Beast will incorporate the latest and greatest technology information, surveillance, and deterrence weapons to enforce its iron-fisted political control over both people and economies.

> We do not want another committee. We have too many already.
> What we want is a man of sufficient stature to hold the allegiance
> of all people, and to lift us out of the economic morass in which
> we are sinking. Send us such a man and, be he God or the devil,
> we will receive him.[39]

The religious component of the Beast system will be called "the whore." It's called that because it mandates a state-sanctioned church that tolerates all religious views as equally true, which, of course, is not only ludicrous but blasphemous. This "Mystery Babylon" will become the de facto religious force on the planet after the Rapture of the Church removes the role of the Holy Spirit's Restrainer from the earth. However, this system will not simply be an organized religion filled with oddly dressed clergy spouting tenets of relativism. It will be filled with magic and supernatural lying signs and wonders, and its clergy will be empowered to exercise these gifts to deceive the world into following the Beast.

This final kingdom of earth's inhabitants will be hailed as the long-awaited arrival of the new "Golden Age" (or "Age of Aquarius"), along with the accompanying cosmic signs in the heavens (UFOs, extraterrestrials, etc.), reopened dimensional doorways, and the demonic forces (masquerading as enlightened beings) who will once again flood the earth.

But this isn't going to happen overnight.

There is a process.

This process is called "desensitization," which we are undergoing presently through the aforementioned fascinations and obsessions with the strange, dark, and mysterious. Like a dog that has been deprived of cooked steak it can smell but can't eat, the world's populations will jump on this new global religious system once it demonstrates it has actual supernatural power.

Think about it this way: This global church will capitalize on the more than two centuries of frustrations of living in a world where the universities, scientists, and governments have operated largely in an atheistic way, ignoring the reality of the supernatural as if it either doesn't exist or isn't relevant. This is why pop culture has profited so greatly from the sci-fi, fantasy, superhero, and occult genres…because people want to believe there is something more to our world than just what they can see and hear. The spiritual component is ingrained in people, because we are as much spiritual beings as we are physical beings. And when the so-called experts operate in absolute nihilism, it depresses the human spirit to a point of desperation akin to starvation. So trust the Bible when it says that, when a politician finally comes on the scene who can actually do signs and wonders (lying or not), he will sway and enthrall the masses into complete, messianic obedience.

> Then I stood on the sand of the sea. And I saw a beast rising up out of the sea, having seven heads and ten horns, and on his horns ten crowns, and on his heads a blasphemous name. Now the beast which I saw was like a leopard, his feet were like the feet of a bear, and his mouth like the mouth of a lion. The dragon gave him his power, his throne, and great authority. And I saw one of his heads as if it had been mortally wounded, and his deadly wound was healed. And all the world marveled and followed the beast. So they worshiped the dragon who gave authority to the beast; and they worshiped the beast, saying, "Who is like the beast? Who is able to make war with him?" (Revelation 13:1–4)

EIGHT

THE ILLUSION OF MODERNITY

> But you, Daniel, shut up the words, and seal the book until the
> time of the end; many shall run to and fro, and knowledge shall
> increase.
>
> DANIEL 12:4

LIKE LUCIFERIANISM, one of the most deceptive and, admittedly, effective methods of Satan's stranglehold on modern humanity is the rise of—and our inevitable dependence upon—technological advancements. In fact, it would be impossible to discuss the coming Beast kingdom without addressing the technology that enables it. This is not to say technology in and of itself is satanic (it's not), but it will most certainly be used in a way to enslave humanity to such a degree that there will not only be nowhere to hide, but no way to resist the coming kingdom of the Beast.

From the time of Noah's Flood (circa 2800 BC) until the 1800s, people were limited to traveling at the speed of horses. But around the time of America's founding, miraculously, it seemed like wave after wave of technological advancements began to come upon the earth like another kind of flood. And to this day, the tsunami of innovations has neither slowed nor weakened.

When the Apostle John was given the book of Revelation (circa AD 95), the technology suggested in it was unheard of at the time. In fact, how many of the future scenarios would be played out remained a mystery for the next two millennia. Specific tech developments, of course, weren't mentioned in the book, but their capabilities were described. The two most obvious ones are found in chapters 11 and 13. In Revelation 11:9–10, we see a future scene wherein the entire world can see the bodies of the Two Witnesses (presumably Moses and Elijah) lying dead on a street of Jerusalem. Clearly, this is speaking to the real-time, live-streaming capabilities we possess today through satellite and/or Internet-based advancements that didn't exist until the 1990s.

The second example is the implementation of the mark of the Beast, which is implanted into either the hand or forehead of the Christ-rejecting earth dwellers to control all buying and selling in the world (Revelation 13:16–18). Now, no world leader, regardless of how powerful, has ever been able to do this. In fact, this technology didn't even exist until the 2000s. It could be argued that Radio Frequency Identification (RFID) technology had existed since the 1970s, but there was little to no supporting infrastructure for practical use anywhere in the world. Nevertheless, both of these examples of technology demonstrate capabilities far beyond anything any previous generation has ever had.

Yet, a curious thing has occurred in our day.

Whereas in decades and centuries past, the technological capabilities just mentioned stumped theologians and skeptics alike, today we are baffled about the things not mentioned. This is because we are quickly entering a time when the advanced developments around us are outpacing those alluded to in Scripture. This can lead to only two possible explanations.

1. The world continues to advance, but only the aforementioned capabilities in Revelation are suggested.

2. Our generation comes to an abrupt end courtesy of the Rapture of the Church.

Given God's history of prematurely stopping mankind when necessary (i.e., the Flood, the tower of Babel, Acts 17:26, etc.), it seems the latter is more likely than the former. Moreover, while we are racing to colonize Mars and the Moon by the end of this decade, God's warnings to "those who dwell upon the earth" increasingly seem to ring empty should mankind achieve this, as those warnings wouldn't apply to anyone *not* dwelling on the earth. Thus, beyond-earth colonization seems to be pushing the boundary of the farthest distance God will let us go, leaving possibility #2 as the only logical option.

Another aspect of this illusion of modernity is the "normalcy bias" that creates an artificial barrier between people and the unrelenting nature of this fallen planet. As we have progressed technologically, particularly in the past century, we have become farther removed from the elements (dark forests, oceans, weather events, etc.) that used to invoke so much fear; thus, we've become numbed by a false sense of control. Our natural state of mind is on normalcy bias cruise control until some event momentarily shakes us from our slumber. Even then, most believe the latest advancements can save us from whatever calamity nature throws at us...until it can't. These brief lapses into reality brought on by sudden catastrophes fade in memory just as quickly, and we go back to the normal state of mind by forgetting the past.

This is why dystopian and apocalyptic movies like *Mad Max* and *The Walking Dead* are so popular in the West. This idea of absolute societal collapse seems impossibly strange and foreign to us here in the United States because it's never happened since our founding in 1776. Thus, the normalcy bias mindset of, "Since it's not happened yet, it could never happen here," sets in. Besides, all the experts say, the possibility of societal collapse is so remote that its sole purpose is to be fictionalized into stories and sold for entertainment. However, it's only impossible until it happens. Then, after it does, we look back and see how inevitable it was all along and wonder why nobody saw it coming.

Another illustration of this illusion regards humanity's false sense of bravado. Being so removed from nature, we (at least in the Westernized world) have lost almost all sense of fear and respect for how fragile we really are. For example, most people these days don't often interact with larger wildlife, apart from seeing a deer cross the road or taking an occasional trip to the zoo. Looking at a caged and docile animal has removed the natural caution that should exist, but has been numbed by subdued threat. However, if you actually ran into a full-grown wolf or bear in the wild, we can guarantee you will instantly be reacquainted with that primal fear to which you've grown numb.

The final component to this illusion is the coming trap of modernity. It's the reality that technology itself will become part of the coming terror. After the Rapture of the Church, the Holy Spirit ministry of restraining evil will be removed from the earth, thus there will be no one curbing wickedness anywhere. The demonic realm will seek to possess earth's remaining inhabitants and compel them to commit the most vile and heinous acts of evil, and they will also pursue power and control of systems as well. This marriage between the supernatural and technology may be expressed in the form of artificial intelligence or of outright demonic sovereignty. It will become the method of demonic-cyber control that will be used to clamp down on everyone, everywhere, making it next to impossible to hide from—or even fight—the Beast kingdom. The only relief or sanctuary to come will be for those whom God provides it directly.

It was granted to him to make war with the saints and to overcome them. And authority was given him over every tribe, tongue, and nation. All who dwell on the earth will worship him, whose names have not been written in the Book of Life of the Lamb slain from the foundation of the world. (Revelation 13:7–8)

End State: Globalism

We will have a world government whether you like it or not. The only question is whether that government will be achieved by conquest or consent. —James Paul Warburg[40]

The obvious conclusion of Luciferianism, perpetuated by the illusion of modernity (human evolution) is globalism. Satan's goal, from the beginning, has been total control of planet earth. He tried it in Noah's day, and God washed the world away in a flood. He tried again at Babel, and

God divided up the population linguistically, culturally, and genetically. Since then, Satan has been attempting to militarily impose his will over the world through varying empires. Each time, God has raised up other nations, which has, to date, thwarted Satan's efforts.

However, by the time Satan arrived at the time of the Greeks and Romans, a new formula was in play. This was the combination of cultural, linguistic, military, economic, and religious conquest. When you defeated a nation, it wasn't just militarily; you absorbed its culture and blended it with yours. You didn't make the newly subjugated peoples assimilate to your culture; you blended it with yours. Before long, people couldn't tell where they began or when things changed. This is the success of Hellenization: It changed every aspect of a culture. Thus, from the Greeks moving forward, this seem to be the "standard" model for global conquest, which we see culminating now with the Great Reset.

How to achieve the Great Reset has been the long pole in the tent. Before our recent times, the technology wasn't there to deliver the lofty utopian ideals of the aforementioned globalists. But now they see the time is ripe to strike. They've been afforded the ability to control everywhere at once with just a push of a button. Now they can see everything, track everything, and regulate who does anything with such ease that every tyrant from history is likely looking up longingly from the pit of Hell wishing they had these tools in their own day.

While they didn't, their master, Lucifer, does. He has used countless tyrants and empires to perfect his schemes and machinations for just how to control the world. He will hand this coming global empire over to his hand-selected agent of destruction, the Man of Sin.

NINE

WORLDS IN COLLISION

To understand the Great Reset, then, we must recognize that the project represents the completion of a decades-long and ongoing attempt to destroy classical liberalism (the free market, free speech, and liberal democracy), American constitutionalism, and national sovereignty. The idea of resetting capitalism suggests that capitalism had previously been pure. But the Great Reset is the culmination of a much longer collectivization process and democratic socialist project, with their corresponding growth of the state.

MICHAEL RECTENWALD, *THE GREAT RESET*[41]

ROYALS VS. COMMONERS. Nationalists vs. imperialists. Free-market capitalism vs. the varying shades of socialism. Anarchy vs. conservatism. Catholic vs. Protestant. After the countless revolutions and wars that plagued Europe for the better part of a turbulent five centuries, the global elite finally had enough. By the mid 1800s, they—who, at the time, largely consisted of disaffected wealthy Europeans—were convinced that the time was at hand for them to make their moves. They wanted a New World Order that consisted of an all-powerful, stable world government...with themselves positioned comfortably at the helm. They believed, given the right motivations, they could unify the nations of the world underneath them politically, economically, and militarily and raise the standards of living for everyone. They were convinced that a fractured and nationalistic world would never become the utopian paradise they thought it could be.

At the present day I become a member of the Masonic order I see the wealth and power they possess the influence they hold and I think over their ceremonies and I wonder that a large body of men can devote themselves to what at times appear the most ridiculous and absurd rites without an object and without an end....Why should we not form a secret society with but one object, the furtherance of the British Empire and the bringing of the whole world under British rule, for the recovery of the United States, for making the Anglo Saxon race but one Empire? What a dream, but yet it is probable; it is possible. —Cecil Rhodes, *Confessions of Faith*, 1877[42]

This idea of empire building went beyond simply acquiring wealth and lands to something far greater: legacy (generational wealth and power). The Spanish had it, but couldn't keep it. The French and Germans wanted it. The English were getting it. The Americans would soon come to discover it. Yet, as antiquated and odious as colonialization appears to us here in the enlightened twenty-first century, the same irresistible compulsion remains the same, just under different pretenses. Instead of claiming lands for king and country, they are now using vague concepts like "sustainable development," "climate change," and "social justice" to justify their enormous power grabs.

By the mid-twentieth century, the United States, due to a combination of variables, began to dominate global geopolitics. Whether these factors included some or all of the things like abundant natural resources, a pro-liberty Constitution, a growing economy, hard-working and patriotic citizenry, and a seeming divine favor from on high is debatable. However you slice it, though, by the end of World War II, the US became the undisputed world superpower. In fact, America was so sure of its own military, political, and economic strength that it agreed to host an entirely separate, supranational, and often anti-American government (the United Nations) within the boundaries of its own borders.

The US dominance in global affairs from 1945–present has always been a problem for the global elite who envisioned a one-world government under the auspices of the United Nations. So long as the US remained on top, the world government they'd so long dreamed of would never come to fruition. America was firmly bound to its Constitution, Declaration of Independence, Bill of Rights, and separation of powers, which forbade subservience to any foreign entity. Yet, that was exactly what the Western globalists wanted: a powerful, yet subservient United States, serving as both wallet and muscle for all the geopolitical terraforming they needed to do. But, if they couldn't get the US to play along, they would need to cut her legs out from under her. This required a plan.

So they devised two strategies: the long and short game. For obvious reasons, the long game will take decades to fully mature, but will produce the requisite amount of systemic internal rot necessary to topple the American giant from the inside out. The short game (or sprints) is used from time to time to inject momentary crises (real or contrived) into the narrative in order to expedite this planned destruction when lagging on their projected timelines. Of course, these schedules have to be adjusted from time to time (i.e., Agenda 21 to Agenda 2030) due to unforeseen developments. Likewise, the threats have to be updated as time passes (if the crises fail to materialize), but other than that, the push towards global governance has marched steadily onward.

The long game consists of four major enterprises:

1. Imploding the US economic/financial markets and currency
2. Corrupting educational and academic institutions
3. Bureaucratizing the government
4. Eroding American military power

Now, given the unrecoverable $31 trillion in debt our nation has accrued, with the majority of all educational institutions drowning in cultural Marxist ideology (e.g., critical race theory, political correctness, social-justice initiatives, LGBTQ agendas, etc.), the impossibly bureaucratic nature of our present government (and shadow government) finds itself in, and geopolitical challenges rising up from every corner of the planet to challenge our weakening dominance, we could say they have been exceedingly successful in all their endeavors.

The Long Game

From about 1913 onward, nobody paid much mind to the creeping, but steady, pace at which government bureaucracies were growing during the twentieth century—but grow they've done. Like mold spreading in a darkened corner, these grifters soon became the rust on the underbelly of the American engine, grinding it to a halt. Before we knew it, these usurpers had infiltrated virtually every organization from large to small across the federal government. If there was an issue, you better believe there was a vastly over-bloated federal agency to deal with it…but not fix it. If these bureaucracies fixed all the problems they exist for, they'd be out of business.

Speaking of grift, the responsible thing the US government should do is start shuttering agencies that have long outlived their original purpose (e.g., the Natural Resource Conservation Service, Rural Electrification Administration, US Geological Survey, Rural Housing Development Service, Small Business Administration, Public Health Service Corps, Economic Development Administration, Corporation for Public Broadcasting, etc.). Yet these agencies continue to live on. Simply closing down these offices could save the US hundreds of billions of dollars each year. Instead, they become breeding grounds for powerful and permanent, statist hives we've since come to call "the swamp." And, just as mold hates the light and rust fears the steel brush, so, too, do these New-World-Order types hate having their deeds uncovered.[43]

- These were the powerbrokers whose names President Woodrow Wilson feared to say aloud in 1913.
- These were the military industrial-complex types that, in his final address to America in 1961, President Dwight D. Eisenhower warned us would come.

- These became the "monolithic and ruthless conspiracy" President John F. Kennedy bravely tried to shine the light upon that same year.
- And these were the same "overwhelming presence[s] that [break] down democracies" that Reagan warned us about in 1982.

The grifters are the elitists from every nationality and political stripe. They have either inherited their wealth or acquired it through capitalistic or political means. They have arrived at the pinnacle of life's pyramid and feel they are entitled to more.

As Proverbs 30:16 states:

There are three things that are never satisfied, four that never say, "Enough!": the grave, the barren womb, land, which is never satisfied with water, and fire, which never says, "Enough!"

If we might be as bold as to add a fifth category, the rich and powerful are never satisfied with enough. They are never satisfied with the status quo. In fact, the world itself is not enough for them. If they could conquer the sun, moon, and Mars, they would.

As the old saying goes, "With great power comes the irresistible urge to abuse it."

Hence, the takeover.

What has been in the planning stages since Adam Weishaupt's first Illuminati meeting in the Holy Roman Empire-era Germany has now come to its inevitable and inescapable conclusion: action. To what do we owe this climax?

Well, it seems that technology has finally reached the appropriate Orwellian degree as to give the elite appropriate leverage against the colossal proletariat chattel class. Everyone beneath them is a "thing" to be used up and then discarded. Although few are bold enough to say aloud what they really think, their actions belie their intentions. They believe 90 percent of the global population is comprised of "useless eaters" destined to live out our days riding in the cramped economy-class railcars with the final destinations to places like Auschwitz, Dachau, and Treblinka.

Sound like hyperbole?

Enter the Great Reset/Agenda 2030/Fourth Industrial Revolution (4IR)/Green New Deal/pandemic mandates, etc.

Although given different and official-sounding names, these agendas all seem to address some fundamental crisis threatening the world today. What they don't tell us is that these plans are essentially the same: to install a global totalitarian oligarchy. They also never disclose that they are the cause of most of the "crises" that are now reaching critical stages.

This oligarchy will place the whole world under the control of a ruling elite with themselves at the top. And, although we might have known about the ends, or what they intended, we never understood the *ways* and *means*. What we mean to say is that, for all their elaborate-sounding schemes, none were designed to actually work.

Common sense could tell us that much.

These plans were meant to create just enough chaos to justify using the government's newfound technological superpowers to install the global totalitarian system they've been preparing all these years.

That's why we're witnessing the populist uprisings in the United States, Canada, Sri Lanka, the Netherlands, the United Kingdom, and France, among other places. In fact, you can find these populist revolts anywhere these leftist governments are trying to impose these ridiculous economic policies.

The people are rebelling because these ideological political agendas are dangerous and don't work. These WEF-backed policies were crushing their economies, promoting famine and scarcity, and legislating lawlessness and immoral debaucheries of every stripe. If that is the case, then why are globalists pushing all these failed policies? It's because they know if they can push populations to the breaking point, they can break that society (or nation). This will trigger a civil war, a regime change, or some other tumultuous societal collapse. Whatever it becomes, the tumult is designed to encourage and foster chaos, which makes said society/city/

nation all the weaker and primed for taking over. That is why they (glo-balists) are almost always pushing for armed conflict and war. Any war.

These elite know one irrefutable fact about both history and human nature: Warfare is the only proven strategy for creating change quickly and establishing a New World Order. Just consider how the world has changed after each of the following events:

- The Revolutionary War
- The Civil War
- World War I
- World War II
- The Cold War
- The War on Terror

Globalists know that any time you can slap the label "war" on an issue, they get carte blanche to do whatever they want, and they have the supposed justification they need to back their wicked machinations. These elitists are not as dumb as we think. They didn't get to where they are today without being masters in scheming and plotting. Furthermore, they're not opposed to breaking as many eggs as necessary in order to get the utopian omelet they've always wanted. Thus, if you remember nothing else from what we just said, remember this—we are the eggs.

Pre-Gaming the New World Order

Many of the policies advocated by the council have been damag-ing to the cause of freedom and particularly to the United States. But this is not because the members are communists or commu-nist sympathizers. This explanation of our foreign policy reversals is too pat, too simplistic.

I believe that the Council on Foreign Relations and its ancil-lary elitist groups are indifferent to communism. They have no ideological anchors. In their pursuit of a new world order, they are prepared to deal without prejudice with a communist state, a socialist state, a democratic state, a monarchy, an oligarchy - it's all the same to them.

Their goal is to impose a benign stability on the quarreling family of nations through merger and consolidation. They see the elimination of national boundaries, the suppression of racial and ethnic loyalties, as the most expeditious avenue to world peace. They believe economic competition is the root cause of international tension.

Perhaps if the council's vision of the future were realized, it would reduce wars, lessen poverty and bring about a more efficient utilization of the world's resources. To my mind, this would inevitably be accompanied by a loss in personal freedom of choice and re-establishment of the restraints that provoked the American Revolution.[44] —Sen. Barry Goldwater, 1979

In its summarized form, the theory of generational dynamics posits that a major geopolitical reset happens roughly every eighty years (plus or minus ten years). At least in regards to American history, this seems to have been accurate. Eighty-four years from our nation's founding was the American Civil War. Eighty years from the Civil War was World War II. Eighty years from the WWII window is where we are now. While we are still in this position for another few years, and if history holds true, then we should expect some major change nationally or internationally as a global realignment shifts the balance of power away from the United States. Another way to look at it is that it has been 161 years since our last Civil War. It has been 81 years since the start of World War II. Either way you figure it, we are long overdue for one or the other.

Whether or not we admit it, both of these events represent and result in their own kind of Great Resets. The Civil War reset us from "*these*" United States to "*the*" United States. World Wars I and II geopolitically transformed the global landscape away from empires and colonies to the fractured world we live in today, littered with independent *sovereign* nation-states. However, most of those can't really govern themselves and are in constant need of support from other, more-established nations. In so doing, these nations then serve as "proxy" states to some greater nation (the US, Russia, China, etc.).

The Great Reset (which is supposed to happen by 2030) wants to terraform us even more, removing the sovereignty from these individual nation-states and putting everyone under worldwide governance—a global empire, if you will.

Today no war has been declared—and however fierce the struggle may be, it may never be declared in the traditional fashion. Our way of life is under attack. Those who make themselves our enemy are advancing around the globe. The survival of our friends is in danger. And yet no war has been declared, no borders have been crossed by marching troops, no missiles have been fired.

If the press is awaiting a declaration of war before it imposes the self-discipline of combat conditions, then I can only say that no war ever posed a greater threat to our security. If you are awaiting a finding of "clear and present danger," then I can only say that the danger has never been more clear and its presence has never been more imminent.

It requires a change in outlook, a change in tactics, a change in missions—by the government, by the people, by every businessman or labor leader, and by every newspaper. For we are opposed around the world by a monolithic and ruthless conspiracy that relies primarily on covert means for expanding its sphere of influence—on infiltration instead of invasion, on subversion instead of elections, on intimidation instead of free choice, on guerrillas by night instead of armies by day. It is a system which has conscripted vast human and material resources into the building of a tightly knit, highly efficient machine that combines military, diplomatic, intelligence, economic, scientific and political operations.

Its preparations are concealed, not published. Its mistakes are buried, not headlined. Its dissenters are silenced, not praised. No expenditure is questioned, no rumor is printed, no secret is revealed. It conducts the Cold War, in short, with a war-time discipline no democracy would ever hope or wish to match.
—President John F. Kennedy, 1961[45]

In 1961, President Kennedy was mired in a growing Cold War between the nations that were in the process of embracing communism and those who weren't. It was a period filled with high anxiety and fear due to the heightened awareness of nuclear weapons and the existential threat it presented to the global population. In his speech to the press as quoted above, he rightfully identified the tactics and strategies for how communism (and socialism) spreads. Little would he know that his own beloved Democratic Party would come to wholly embrace and then champion the tenets of communism not even a full generation later. For there to be global government, as the Great Reset demands, there must be socialism. And where there is socialism, communism is always the final outcome.

To summarize even further, the world has almost always existed as empires and territories. The twentieth century has flirted briefly with the experiment of self-rule by individual nations, but that has only given us two World Wars and a hundred other lesser wars and conflicts. The general consensus now amongst the globe's elite is that the world needs to go back to the top-down, authoritarian form of empirical rule. Only this time, instead of there being competing empires, the world will be united under a single domain, with a small, elite group at the top making all the decisions.

In regard to the push for globalism, it hasn't been for a lack of trying during the twentieth century that's held it at bay. Neither has it been Islam or even communism; it's been the American Constitution. These documents (the Declaration of Independence and the Constitution) and our form of government (balance of powers) have been so successful in stifling this rush towards a global government that it has now become the globalists' primary target to destroy in order to finally achieve the Utopia they've come to believe must happen.

Our system was divinely inspired not because our founders were perfect (they weren't), but because they attributed governmental power to its true source: God. In so doing, God prophetically inspired them to create a system of governance designed to succeed to the degree that almost every nation around us and abroad has continually tried to emulate with little to no success. They get almost everything the same, except they continue to put themselves in the role of God. When any government attempts to replace God, it fails. This is why those same nations have constantly undergone changes in governments and constitutions while ours has remained constant.

Our Constitution also represented a form of divine restraint on global government. As the United States became the world's true superpower, its authority (in the form of our Constitutional documents) prevented too much government and kept us from ever subjugating ourselves to an international body politic. Even when one political party wanted to enter foreign entanglements, our political power was too diversified amongst the branches of government to ever willingly form a majority to subjugate ourselves.

The closest we came to losing this wasn't during the Civil War; rather, it was during the time between the Great Depression and the end of World War II. Can there be any doubt as to why God allowed the US to emerge victorious after both conflicts? It wasn't because He loved the Americans more than He loved everyone else. It was to prevent this New World Order from being formed too quickly. After World War I, the world rushed to create the League of Nations, an effort that lost its momentum when President Woodrow Wilson became sick and bedridden. After World War II, there was another strong push to create the United Nations, but still, our Constitution prevented us from ceding too much authority to them.

But the proponents of global government have been relentless. They have continually chipped away at our national sovereignty and freedom, always under the guise of collective security and cooperation. In reality, these organizations seem bent on treaties that make our foundational pillars resemble Swiss cheese, then solid marble. It will not be long before the overbearing weight of bloated governments finally buckles the pillars of Western civilization, causing it to come crashing down.

Looking back, we can see below the sampling of globalist efforts to unify political, military, and economic authority by way of crises, common technologies, finance, health, and other human domains in an effort to create new, major, political bodies:

- 1920- The League of Nations (Woodrow Wilson)
- 1921- Council on Foreign Relations (David Rockefeller since 1930)
- 1927- The Round Table (by Louis Marchesi)
- 1944- World Bank
- 1945- The United Nations (UN)
- 1945- International Monetary Fund (IMF)
- 1946- UN Children's Fund (UNICEF)
- 1948- World Health Organization (WHO)
- 1949- North Atlantic Treaty Organization (NATO)
- 1954- The Bilderberg Group
- 1968- The Club of Rome (Rockefeller)
- 1971- World Economic Forum
- 1973- The Trilateral Commission (Rockefeller)
- 1995- World Trade Organization (WTO)
- 1995- Union for the Mediterranean (UfM)
- 2004- Internet Governance Project

Although these are the best known, there are hundreds of American and European organizations dedicated to a single global system. There are more than 160 political and humanitarian groups funded by George Soros alone. The powerful esoteric groups listed below have also long been involved in consolidating power into the hands of an elite few:

1. The Vatican
2. The Illuminati
3. The Freemasons
4. Skull and Bones Society
5. National Socialists (Nazis) and sympathizers (Operation Paperclip)

Below are some quotes from some of the most powerful leaders in the world about how they see globalism.

In the next century, nations as we know it will be obsolete; all states will recognize a single, global authority. National sovereignty wasn't such a great idea after all. —US Deputy Secretary of State Strobe Talbot, July 20, 1992

The New World Order will have to be built from the bottom up rather than from the top down...run around national sovereignty, eroding it piece by piece will accomplish much more than the old-fashioned frontal assault. —Richard Gardner, US Council on Foreign Relations Journal *Foreign Affairs*, April 1974

We are on the verge of a global transformation. All we need is the right major crisis and the nations will accept the New World Order. —US billionaire David Rockefeller, to UN Business Conference, 1991

Today Americans would be outraged if U.N. troops entered Los Angeles to restore order; tomorrow they will be grateful. This is especially true if they were told there was an outside threat from beyond, whether real or promulgated, that threatened our very existence. It is then that all peoples of the world will plead with world leaders to deliver them from this evil. The one thing every man fears is the unknown. When presented with this scenario, individual rights will be willingly relinquished for the guarantee of their well-being granted to them by their world government. —US Secretary of State Henry Kissinger

To achieve world government, it is necessary to remove from the minds of men their individualism, loyalty to family traditions, national patriotism, and religious dogmas.—Brock Adams, director of UN Health Organization

There are numerous similar quotes from many others advocating for a single world government. The main difference today (as opposed to decades ago) is that the new technocracy (powerful technological corporations) such as Google, Huawei, Apple, Twitter, IBM, and so forth are piling aboard the globalist bandwagon as well.

They're doing that because of how interconnected the world's economy has become in the age of information. Hundreds of powerful technological corporations are involved in a countless number of efforts that can be used at some future point to corral humanity under a single banner: data processing, artificial intelligence, unmanned autonomous systems, 5G networks, low-earth-orbit satellites, the Internet of things, cloud computing, digital currency, block-chain technology, gene editing, 3D printing, holographic technology, nanotechnology, etc. In fact, the term "New World Order" itself has become antiquated. So as not to be labeled as outdated, the World Economic Forum's Klaus Schwab rebranded it with a new name—the "Fourth Industrial Revolution":

The fourth industrial revolution…is not only about smart and connected machines and systems. Its scope is much wider. Occurring simultaneously are waves of further breakthroughs in areas ranging from gene sequencing to nanotechnology, from renewables to quantum computing. It is the fusion of these technologies and their interaction across the physical, digital and biological domains that make the fourth industrial revolution fundamentally different from previous revolutions.[46] —Klaus Schwab, *The Fourth Industrial Revolution*

Paradox Gained

Even though the public opinion or awareness of global governance has waxed and waned over the past hundred years, *the plan* has never wavered from the globalists' minds. The continual push toward a single world government has wrought havoc everywhere it's been implemented, and thus, as stated at the outset, the effort has been successful. The victory is not in achieving global government, but in creating the geopolitical and societal destabilization necessary for the peoples of the earth to cry out for one. Their relentless chipping away at the US Constitution has put us dangerously close to the tipping point. As of 2022, it wouldn't take much for us to collapse nationally; a simple *nudge* would move us into any number of existential crises.

COVID-19—and the political, economic, and social disruptions it has caused—is fundamentally changing the traditional context for decision-making. The inconsistencies, inadequacies, and contradictions of multiple systems—from health and finance to energy and education—are more exposed than ever amidst a global context of concern for lives, livelihoods, and the planet. Leaders find themselves at a historic crossroads, managing short-term pressures against medium- to long-term uncertainties with one-size-fits-all solutions.

As we enter a unique window of opportunity to shape the recovery, this initiative will offer insights to help inform all those determining the future state of global relations, the direction of national economies, the priorities of societies, the nature of business models, and the management of a global commons. Drawing from the vision and vast expertise of the leaders engaged across the World

Economic Forum's communities, the Great Reset initiative has a set of dimensions to build a new social contract that honours the dignity of every human being.[47]

Nevertheless, we have two complementing agendas afoot. The first is *incrementalism*, or *gradualism*, which continually seeks to chip away at the foundations of a nation or empire. An example of this is the poisonous injection of postmodernism into our public education systems. These are slow-moving agendas that ultimately aim their sights at undermining the foundation.

The second is *opportunism*, which makes every crisis an opportunity for rapid change. There is no shortage of examples for radical opportunism, including climate change, global warming, pandemics, financial depressions, terrorism, social justice, etc.

Only a crisis—actual or perceived—produces real change. When that crisis occurs, the actions that are taken depend on the ideas that are lying around. That, I believe, is our basic function: to develop alternatives to existing policies, to keep them alive and available until the politically impossible becomes the politically inevitable. —Milton Friedman, *Capitalism and Freedom*[48]

Although many of these products and systems are designed to make life in the twenty-first century better, safer, and more efficient, they also have the potential for great and terrible abuse in the wrong hands. What these New-World-Order types seem to be bent on is not making our lives better, but cementing their power for generations to come. And, according to Scripture, if we can be so bold as to read between the lines, they will be.

He causes all, both small and great, rich and poor, free and slave, to receive a mark on their right hand or on their foreheads, and that no one may buy or sell except one who has the mark or the name of the beast, or the number of his name.

Here is wisdom. Let him who has understanding calculate the number of the beast, for it is the number of a man: His number is 666. (Revelation 13:16–18)

TEN

NWO: FACT OR FICTION?

Elitism has always been the dark side of illuminism; the revolutionary vanguard that seizes control because it *knows* what's good for the people, the philosopher-king who *knows* the truth, the technocrat who *knows* how to run societies and wars- all try to hoard the light at the top of the pyramid. Reason, which can be used to rescue man from churches and kings, can also be used to enslave him with dogmas of its own. Knowledge is power that can be abused.

GEORGE JOHNSON, *ARCHITECTS OF FEAR*[49]

ISN'T THE NEW WORLD ORDER just one giant conspiracy theory?

Let us compare two quotes. The first is from late US Congressman Larry P. McDonald:

> The drive of the Rockefellers and their allies is to create a one-world government combining supercapitalism and Communism under the same tent, all under their control. ... Do I mean conspiracy? Yes I do. I am convinced there is such a plot, international in scope, generations old in planning, and incredibly evil in intent.[50]

Next, let's look at a quote from David Rockefeller himself, in his autobiography, *Memoirs*, to see if this "conspiracy theory" holds any weight.

For more than a century ideological extremists at either end of the political spectrum have seized upon well-publicized incidents such as my encounter with Castro to attack the Rockefeller family for the inordinate influence they claim we wield over American political and economic institutions. Some even believe we are part of a secret cabal working against the best interests of the United States, characterizing my family and me as "internationalists" and of conspiring with others around the world to build a more integrated global political and economic structure—one world, if you will. If that's the charge, I stand guilty, and I am proud of it.[51]

"New World Order" is an often maligned and misused phrase that frequently centers on the idea of the creation of a single, all-powerful, global government, presumably controlled by a small group of elites. It is also a phrase that is many times mocked and lauded as a conspiracy-fringe idea that deserves the utmost derision.

But does it?

In truth, a "new world order" happens quite regularly. Any time the global power shifts from one nation or empire to another, there is in a sense, a "new world order." The phrase *Novus Ordo Seclorum* appears on our own currency. It simply means "the new order of the ages." However, the phrase in question here is more than that. It is the idea of a new, single, all-powerful global government—not just of a nation, but of the world. If this had originated from a bunch of loser-nobodies hanging out in their parents' basements, it should be mocked. Sadly, that is not the case.

However, the idea of New World Order, aside from being plastered to our national currency, has remained the buzz amongst the world's political, economic, and military elite for centuries. This is not some passing fad or work of science fiction, but a real thing—whether we choose to believe it or not.

In other words, the concept is a serious one and is originating from the highest echelons amongst the most powerful leaders in the world.

Considering that many of these men and women have all the wealth and resources and are seemingly on their way to making it happen, it must be taken seriously. However, the news of it—rather, the *lack* of news of it—has never diminished the intrepid march towards this goal.

> The loss of public interest, however, did not mean the end of world order aspirations. Quite the opposite; the "big idea" of world organization remained active within elite circles, largely operating beyond the knowledge or concern of the public. A corollary was this: As public memory fogged with the advance of time, the notion of world government—once openly identified and celebrated—faded into our cultural background, eventually slipping into the realm of "conspiracy theory."[52] —Carl Teichrib, *Game of Gods*

But, as history has borne out, taking the world from nationalism to globalism is not easy. It took the Great War to create the League of Nations. It took the Second World War to create the United Nations. The globalist types know that so long as the United States remains the leader of the free world, there will be no true New World Order—hence the bull's-eye on the Constitution.

This should explain how we have arrived at the lunacy of 2020 and beyond. It has been a century-long, concerted effort to: a) dumb down the population; b) get America's youth to hate both our past and our present; c) take control over the major institutions that control the flow of information; and d) completely take over our two major political parties. As stated at the outset, these schemes were never designed to *replace* our own competent system. They are designed to *destroy* it. For example:

> Liberal billionaire George Soros said Thursday that the U.S. economy could be headed for calamity as a result of President Donald Trump's efforts to juice American business and stock prices ahead of the 2020 election.
>
> "Trump's economic team has managed to overheat an already

buoyant economy," Soros warned his guests at an informal dinner at the World Economic Forum in Davos, Switzerland.

"The stock market, already celebrating Trump's military success, is breaking out to reach new heights," he said. "But an overheated economy can't be kept boiling for too long. If all this had happened closer to the elections, it would have assured his reelection."[53]

Notice how Soros stated this last sentence as if Trump's defeat had been a foregone conclusion? Mind you, this was also around the same time the US-funded Chinese coronavirus was making its maiden voyage to the United States. It's often hard to wrap our minds around the idea that our reality is not just happening in the natural order of things, but rather is being intentionally and artificially shaped to fit some globalist agenda. Like the assassinations of Abraham Lincoln, John F. Kennedy, and Martin Luther King, as well as the wars of Korea, Vietnam, Afghanistan, and Iraq, things are happening that are seemingly attempting to hijack our natural, national trajectory.

Events are being shaped by men and women under the influence of dark, spiritual forces that are actively seeking the demise of the United States and the imposition of Satan's original *world order*. (See the account of Nimrod and the Tower of Babel in Genesis 10–11.)

Now, some of you are saying, "Wait a minute; didn't you just write that God is the final arbiter of human history?"

Yes, we did.

Let's clarify this seemingly juxtaposed position. People may shape the present events, but they cannot control the outcome. God alone reserves that authority. Humankind is very much the tempest in the teapot—furious, but over-exaggerated. God has the ultimate say on what and when things happen. (Read Psalm 2 for more clarity on this.)

Nevertheless, we know that, according to Scripture, no nation like the United States is in existence during the last days. The final world superpower will come out of the boundaries of the old Roman Empire

(Daniel 2, 7–9). Ergo, something must happen to us between now and then that knocks us down a whole bunch of pegs. Sadly, our demise is as inevitable as the setting of the sun after a long day. We cannot prevent it, nor can we slow its approach.

However, if our downfall is certain, who cares which party wins the next election?

Well, we care, primarily because we don't know when the Lord will return.

If the Lord tarries another ten to twenty years, should we suffer unnecessarily under the totalitarian machinations of the Democratic-Socialist Party? A party that lauds abortion on demand, genderless children, and emasculated men; invites war and terrorist attacks; and promotes the general lawlessness of anarchy on every street?

Or should we "occupy until He comes," as our Lord instructs in Luke 19:13?

We are commanded to be the salt and light until He returns. Furthermore, as history has ascertained, it is much easier to share the Gospel when we are free than when we are under a totalitarian dictatorship. One could argue that truer converts are made during times of persecution, and that may be true; however, each of us who is certain of our salvation today was, at one point, converted. Is our conversion any less valid because we did it without duress? Can Christ still redeem the freedman (Galatians 3:28)?

Given Over

The sad reality is that, in the process of abandoning God, people are forced to abandon the truth. When they abandon the truth, they then abandon common sense and reality. By this point, God will give people over to their delusions because they never loved the truth. A perfect example of this is Pope Francis' 2015 encyclical letter, *Laudato Si*, which was nothing more than a quasi-theological puff piece promoting sustainable development (UN code for "depopulation," "wealth redistribution," "global healthcare," and "citizenry"); the imminent perils of man-made climate change; and the virtues of globalism over nationalism. Mind you, the "vicar of Christ" and the so-called leader of all Christians on the earth has seemingly placed Al Gore's false predictions above God's promise (see Genesis 8:22), which tells us that perhaps he's not as close to God as he seems to think. We only mention him because, in this article for his closing statement in the encyclical, he deifies Mary as the "Queen of Creation."

> Mary, the Mother who cared for Jesus, now cares with maternal affection and pain for this wounded world. Just as her pierced heart mourned the death of Jesus, so now she grieves for the sufferings of the crucified poor and for the creatures of this world laid waste by human power. Completely transfigured, she now lives with Jesus, and all creatures sing of her fairness. She is the Woman, "clothed in the sun, with the moon under her feet, and on her head a crown of twelve stars" (Rev 12:1). Carried up into heaven, she is the Mother and Queen of all creation. In her glorified body, together with the Risen Christ, part of creation has reached the fullness of its beauty. She treasures the entire life of Jesus in her heart (cf. Lk 2:19, 51), and now understands the meaning of all things. Hence, we can ask her to enable us to look at this world with eyes of wisdom.[54]

It's no mystery that the Roman Catholic Church has long venerated Mary above even Christ for centuries now. However, when we take the entirety of the pope's encyclical, it is attempting to insert crisis into its deeply flawed theology to promote unbridled globalism. His words show a complete departure from biblical discernment, biblical understanding, basic science, and even common sense.

Granted, Pope Francis is just one man; however, he theoretically speaks for nearly one billion people on the planet, which is a frightening thought—perhaps even more so now that the Reformation is supposedly over, according to the late Bishop Tony Palmer.

But because we here in the trans-Atlantic West have neglected our duties as Christians to "occupy" until Jesus returns, the fact that the inmates are out of the asylum and running the country is not surprising. What *is* surprising is that American Christendom is still surprised. However, we should expect that, after decades of progressive, socialist, humanist, and Marxist indoctrination in our educational systems, a generation will rise up that can no longer understand right from wrong, and no longer differentiate between up and down, black and white, or male and female. Their moral compass has rotted from the inside out and is spinning freely—with whichever way the wind is blowing.

God has allowed this process of being "given over" ever since we attempted to kick Him out of our homes, our schools, our businesses, and our government. Thus, God is permitting this fleeting moment for the wicked to appear victorious as a means of punishment. In other words, He is restraining one form of wrath (the fire-and-brimstone kind) in favor of another, the *wrath of abandonment*, which is worse. Woe to those who fall under this form of judgment.

For the wrath of God is revealed from heaven against all ungodliness and unrighteousness of men, who suppress the truth in unrighteousness, because what may be known of God is manifest in them, for God has shown *it* to them…. Therefore God also *gave them up to* uncleanness, in the lusts of their hearts, to dishonor their bodies among themselves…. For this reason God *gave them up* to vile passions. For even their women exchanged the natural use for what is against nature. Likewise also the men, leaving the natural use of the woman, burned in their lust for one another, men with men committing what is shameful, and receiving in themselves the penalty of their error which was due….

And even as they did not like to retain God in their knowledge, God *gave them over* to a debased mind, to do those things which are not fitting;…being filled with all unrighteousness, sexual immorality, wickedness, covetousness, maliciousness; full of envy, murder, strife, deceit, evil-mindedness; they are whisperers, backbiters, haters of God, violent, proud, boasters, inventors of evil things, disobedient to parents, undiscerning, untrustworthy, unloving, unforgiving, unmerciful; who, knowing the righteous judgment of God, that those who practice such things are deserving of death, not only do the same but also approve of those who practice them. (Romans 1:18–32, emphasis added)

Aren't we already here, though? Public acceptance of homosexuality is in its final stage of normalization. Now, not only have homosexuals come out of the closet, but they have moved in, taken over, and demanded our children as recompense. They are, even now, moving to legalize and push for the public acceptance of pedophilia, because that is the final stage in their agenda.

Today, almost every Fortune 500 company, federal institution, and public university, as well as many churches, are kowtowing to the LGBTQ mob. That's not because they care, mind you; they fear the economic backlash from the media and Hollywood if they don't.

The new "woke" generation ignorantly promotes Marxism by masquerading it as "equality." However, the new Brown Shirts are not walking around with swastikas, but with black fists and ANTIFA armbands. These mobs are the unofficial army of the liberal elite. Their purpose is to promote lawlessness so the people will demand more authoritarian law and order. The Hegelian dialectic being played out right before our eyes.

They think they are evolving into more enlightened human beings. However, their progressivist postmodernism is clouding their judgment with lies and half-truths. They're becoming a generation unable to know the truth as to how to be saved, and this has Satan's fingerprints all over it.

Satan's goal, as it has been since the days of Babel, is to unite the entire world under the leadership of one man, his Antichrist. This goal is what drove Alexander the Great, the Romans, the Muslims, the Mongols, Napoleon, and Hitler, and it will one day drive the world's final ruler. The difference between the Antichrist and all those who come before him will be that he finally will have the technology to control the entire world. He will have that capability because corporations are feverishly "whoring" themselves to create terrible systems of control that will one day fall into the wrong hands.

> A really efficient totalitarian state would be one in which the all-powerful executive of political bosses and their army of managers control a population of slaves who do not have to be coerced, because they love their servitude.[55] —Aldous Huxley, *Brave New World*

Clearly, there are forces at work beyond the political boundaries. Spiritual powers are moving. Demonic princes are attempting to maintain their poisonous stranglehold over their territories. The message of the Gospel is being spread across enemy territory with the advent of the Internet and satellite television. The battlefield is aflame, and we are on the verge of a titanic shift in prophetic, global geopolitics.

The politicians and powerbrokers with means are the ones using the mob to bring about the New World Order. They have embraced the ever-changing tenets of postmodern progressivism. They have embraced the delusional machinations of intersectionality and social justice. They have embraced the suicidal ideations of relativism. However, the George Soroses and David Rockefellers of the world are pawns, too, albeit to a much older, darker, power.

Let us not kid ourselves: Nationalism is dead and America is gone. There is no returning to the *old* normal of the pre-COVID-19 days. While we believe God has used imperfect people throughout history to effect change, change still came. Men like Nebuchadnezzar, Cyrus, Washington, Lincoln, Churchill, and Trump are merely designed to carry out some facet of God's plan; however, God's plan is still to let things continue to worsen until He institutes the final crisis that drives the world together into the final Beast government.

Waving the False Flag

One of the most powerful tools the globalists have used in recent decades is a form of psychological warfare called the "false flag." Here is the definition of "false flag":

1: a hostile or harmful action (such as an attack) that is designed
   to look like it was perpetrated by
2: a deliberate misrepresentation of motives or identity
3: a flag used to disguise the identity of something (such as a ship)[56]

Since the advent of the Cold War (1945), the US government intelligentsia has mushroomed from one agency to seventeen (as of 2022). These agencies specialize in information warfare, and it should be no small concern to the average citizen that, if the globalists want to drive our nation in a particular direction, and they have the means (power and wealth) to do so, they will use these agencies to accomplish those goals. Seems like common sense that they would, which brings up the issue of agendas and why tragedies will always be exploited by these groups to achieve those ends.

Whether we're talking about the major news events of our day highlighting some new and terrible calamity, or just watching our communities and cities succumb to the atrophying effects of sin, things are falling apart. The global elite intend to use this increasing lawlessness to further destabilize formerly civilized nations. There is no arguing that sad reality. On any given day, there are at least twenty different threats to undo Western civilization. But there is one aspect of this we would like to hone in on here—the erosion of public trust. It is this point we want to spend the rest of the chapter discussing. Here is Henry Olsen of the *Washington Post* addressing the very issue about which we write:

Confidence in public institutions is falling in part because of the
belief that the people within those institutions do not work for

the public's benefit. Worse, many of those who exercise terrible judgment, such as the Federal Reserve governors who presided over the 2008 financial collapse and today's entirely foreseeable inflation surge, keep their jobs.

Nearly a year after the devastating and chaotic withdrawal from Afghanistan, none of the senior military officials who presided over the catastrophe have been fired. The idea that there are two sets of rules—one for the powerful and another for the rest of the country—is gaining credence precisely because there are so many examples that it is true.

This wasn't always the case. Generals who lost important battles, such as the mauling of Allied forces at Kasserine Pass in World War II, were relieved of command because of their failures. Now, the "too big to fail" mantra that has been applied to large financial institutions seems to have morphed into "too important to face the consequences" for many high-ranking officials.[57]

The "confidence" noted in this article, meaning the public trust in institutions that are supposed to be looking out for our best interests, has been lost. Mr. Olsen wrote this in response to the cowardly/inept response of law enforcement officials in the school shootings in places like Parkland, Florida, and Uvalde, Texas, as well as in other mass-casualty events. But it's more than simply blaming inept law enforcement, isn't it? Consider the *increasingly* frequent cycle we, the general public, endure in an *increasingly* familiar process in response to these *increasingly* frequent and horrific events now happening.

- **Shock:** We are brought the news of some event that shocks our intellect and senses.
- **Desensitization:** The news coverage blankets everything else for a brief moment in time, causing us to become saturated with the crisis *du jour.*

- **Politicization:** Lawmakers come out of the woodwork promising knee-jerk, draconian legislation as if mass shootings/killings weren't already illegal enough.
- **Anger:** As government officials (local/city/state/federal) begin to close down discussion on the situation, the millions of unanswered questions the public still has remain unanswered. So, with the government-sanctioned obfuscation comes growing anger and mistrust amongst the public that recognizes something is amiss.
- **Moving on:** A new day brings new crises, new scandals, and new news. The mass casualty event is summarily minimized until it becomes a historical footnote mentioned only in passing until the next mass casualty event occurs.
- **Rinse/Wash/Repeat:** Thus, the cycle begins again.

Now, numerous questions have begun to arise (as they often do) as to how and why mass shooters do what they do. The government and media seemingly are never interested in issues like how an unemployed eighteen-year-old high school dropout could afford two high-end rifles (manufactured by Daniel Defense) worth at least two thousand dollars apiece, a seven-hundred-dollar optic, sixty clips, body armor, and sixteen hundred rounds of ammunition—all totaling around nine thousand dollars. Could this kid have saved enough money to purchase it all? Sure. It seems unlikely, but it is possible. However, the attention always seems to revolve around how we can restrict guns and undo the Second Amendment rather than why someone decides to shoot up anything. As far as questions go, we have some surrounding numerous past tragedies, including the following.

John F. Kennedy Assassination, 1963
- Who aided Lee Harvey Oswald in the assassination of JFK?
- If Oswald acted alone, then what do we make of his assassination by Dallas nightclub owner Jack Ruby?
- Why the decades-long cover-up?

The Vietnam War, 1964

- Who authorized the Gulf of Tonkin narrative, and why?

The Oklahoma City Bombing, 1995

- The 1995 Omnibus Counterterrorism Bill was first introduced in February of 1995, but did not get voted on due to its massive violations of Americans' civil liberties. The Oklahoma City bombing happened in April of 1995, which seemed (at least to us) the last-ditch effort to get the Omnibus bill back on the table. It wasn't. However, six short years later (September 11, 2001) this same bill was resurrected, rebranded as the Patriot Act, and was summarily voted on, approved, and made into law within thirty days of 9/11.

Terrorist Attacks on the US, September 11, 2001

- Why weren't all the surveillance cameras around the Pentagon (except one across the parking lot) working on this date?

Sandy Hook Elementary, December 2012

- What is up with all the bizarre CIA-Hollywood connections and weird absurdities surrounding the 2012 Sandy Hook Massacre?
  - Is it a coincidence that there was an active shooter exercise (FEMA L-366 Planning for the Needs of Children in Disasters) at the Carmel Elementary School in Bridgeport, Connecticut (fourteen miles away from Newton, Connecticut), on the same day as the Sandy Hook Elementary massacre?[58]
  - Is it also a coincidence that Robert Holmes (father of James Holmes, aka "Dark Knight" theater mass murderer in Aurora, Colorado) and Peter Lanza (father of Adam Lanza, the Sandy Hook mass murderer) were both set to testify in the Libor Scandal?[59,60] (See endnote 58 for more information on the LIBOR scandal.)

Las Vegas Country Music Festival Shooting, October 2017

- How did the 2017 Las Vegas shooter, Stephen Paddock, kill and wound 573 people from his thirty-second-story hotel window with little to no *known* weapons training?[61]
- Why wasn't the media screaming the dangers of "white power extremism" (as they always do) after learning Paddock was in fact, a white guy? The only thing anyone seemed to care about after the Vegas shooting were "bump stocks."[62]
- How was Paddock able to move all those weapons and ammo to his room unnoticed—and keep it unnoticed by housekeeping personnel?

Jeffrey Epstein, August 2019

- Why was Jeffrey Epstein, the infamous pedophile financier to the wealthy, isolated in a jail cell with a broken surveillance camera?
- Why have none of the clients of Epstein and his madame, Ghislaine Maxwell, ever been made public?

General Questions

- Why do so many mass murderers claim to hear voices prior to their dastardly deeds?
- Have the intelligence agencies resurrected an MKUltra-like CIA program to help sway both the government and the general population to disarm? MKUltra had been deemed a conspiracy theory for years until it was unequivocally proven to have been a real government program.[63]
- Why is there almost never any discussion on other contributing factors to the psyche of the criminals, such as behavior-modifying medication (pharmaceuticals), violent video games, music, and movies. As far as we know, thirty-seven mass murderers were taking behavior-modifying medications. Why isn't this ever discussed?[64]

- How come none of the people who knew the perpetrators (before the events) felt compelled to report them to law enforcement (due to the telltale warning signs of bizarre and dangerous behavior)?
- An even more disturbing question is this: What if they did report them to law enforcement, yet law enforcement did nothing about it? Who then should be held accountable?

Whether it was violent attacks on the Pilgrims by the indigenous pagans (i.e., American Indians) on the East Coast or the military campaigns against the colonies by the British armies under King George III, this nation has been under attack since its founding. There has always been someone attempting to prevent this nation from being established. In true fashion, once Satan's initial attempts to abort the US from becoming a nation failed, he shifted tactics. He reasoned that if he cannot destroy this nation from without (foreign powers), he would destroy it from within. Beginning with the encoding of Freemason symbolism into our founding documents, Satan would use both corruption and division (slavery and states' rights) to help tear apart the United States. Beginning with the 1820 Missouri Compromise, Satan worked diligently until he could push the nations to the point of Civil War.

After the Civil War failed to permanently divide the nation, Satan began a subtler form of subversion by importing European liberalism and Marxism into the US under the guise of academia (both religious and secular), banking, and big business. He used the Democratic Party to continue perpetuating systemic racism throughout the nation (i.e., Jim Crow Laws, Ku Klux Klan [KKK], eugenics, Margaret Sanger [founder of Planned Parenthood], federal segregation, Japanese internment camps, etc.) while corrupting every institution that made this nation great. Since the turn of the century, it has been one ideological struggle after another, with the left increasingly inching farther and farther left, finally making enough headway to become mainstays in Hollywood, academia, and government bureaucracies since the 1960s.

All of the craziness we've been witnessing since that pivotal decade begins to make more sense when we understand the powers that be are not just political or economic. They are primarily demonic and use politics and economics as dangerous tools to shape the direction of empires and nations. They are dark and malevolent spiritual forces that use their *campaign of whispers* to influence their possessed servants like human meat puppets. These demonic forces, who are lords and princes of vice and territories, are using proven tactics and strategies to drive an increasingly desperate citizenry to demand a more totalitarian government. In other words, we are living through a real-life version of the Hegelian dialectic, wherein those in control already have a prescribed solution in hand. Mass-casualty events are but symptoms of a deeper and more systemic rot in the underbelly of our nation.

If you consider people like President Joe Biden, Speaker of the House Nancy Pelosi, Senate Majority Leader Chuck Schumer, Representative Adam Schiff, Representative Liz Cheney, and the rest of their ilk, they really aren't that smart. In fact, they aren't intelligent at all. They for sure aren't smart enough to conjure up all the things that are being done now in the name of global governance (digital currencies, man-made climate change, COVID-19, etc.) They are, however, being influenced by smart people behind the scenes like billionaire businessmen George Soros, Larry Fink, and Bill Gates, as well as World Economic Forum Chairman Klaus Schwab. These are the ones who have, we believe it is likely, bent their ears to listen to these demonic overlords.

They're using tried-and-tested strategies to create an increasingly desperate situation (crisis) wherein the citizens of (pick a nation) finally come to think global government is the be-all and end-all solution. Since these problems are being artificially created to generate the facade of crisis, they should be just as easily resolved. Perhaps we need only ask who Prince (now King) Charles was referring to in his speech back in October 2021 at the 26th UN Climate Change Conference of the Parties (COP26) in Glasgow, Scotland.

We also know that countries, many of whom are burdened by growing levels of debt, simply cannot afford to go green. Here we need a vast military style campaign to marsh the strength of the global private sector, with trillions at *his* disposal far beyond global GDP, and with the greatest respect, beyond even the governments of the world's leaders. It offers the only real prospect of achieving fundamental economic transition.[65] (Emphasis added)

Artificial Crises Created by Leftists and Globalists

- $30 trillion in national debt with another $171 trillion in unfunded liabilities
- Open borders and unchecked illegal immigration
- Rampant lawlessness in our Democrat-run cities
- Creating a new generation of self-entitled narcissists
- Reconstructing our educational bedrock with postmodernism and cultural relativism
- The systemic revisionism of our nation's history and heritage
- Government promotion of poisonous political ideologies like Marxism, socialism, and fascism
- Tolerating politicians who openly commit treason by partnering with international bodies committed to the destruction of our nation

But we tolerate these things. The real question is why? Why do we allow this?

First, we're busy. Life has us so wrapped up in making money, building careers, and keeping up with Joneses that we are too busy to care. For those who have "arrived" at the good life, they are too comfortable, complacent, and lazy to care. For the poor, well, they are just too busy trying to survive to care. We aren't just pointing our fingers at you. We are pointing our fingers at ourselves as well. We all bought into the charade of the American Dream, and we've all (to one degree or another) been guilty of chasing it. But here we are. This is where God planted us, and we must do the best with the gifts God has given each of us with the time we each have remaining.

Second, our government has become way too big. It's an abomination, bloated to the gills with unnecessary bureaucratic agencies and departments that are not accountable to its citizenry. We have allowed a swamp (the permanent bureaucratic class) to go unchecked for decades. And any time a president has tried to take it on (Kennedy, Reagan, Trump), they got dealt with.

Third, we have allowed special-interest lobbies to control our political parties. Actor and comedian Robin Williams once said, "Politicians should wear sponsor jackets like NASCAR drivers, so we knew who owned them." We wholeheartedly agree.

Fourth, under the guise of winning the Cold War, we have allowed for the creation of the most powerful intelligence agencies the world had ever seen. As these agencies came to life, they fed like selfish piglets on the teats of the American government. As they transitioned off of milk onto solid sustenance, their appetites became even more voracious. But instead of meat and meal, they fed off of war, conflict, and crisis to continue justifying their own existence.

- This is why we went into Cuba (Bay of Pigs) and Vietnam.
- It's why we funded Saddam Hussein's war against Iran and the Taliban's war against the Soviet Union.
- It's why we continued to grow NATO even after the Soviet Union collapsed.
- It's why we waged a twenty-year War on Terror.
- It's why we goaded Ukraine into taunting Russia.
- It's why we need a Chinese threat.

Without conflict, these agencies face the budgetary chopping block, and they will not go quietly into the night.

Fifth, and last, we abandoned the idea of a balanced budget nearly eight decades ago. Perhaps it was those dastardly progressives like Franklin D. Roosevelt (delinking our currency from gold) or the crafters of the Bretton-Woods Agreement. Perhaps. For sure, by the time Lyndon B. Johnson implemented his costly *Great Society Initiative* while simultaneously waging an expensive land war in Asia, we were quickly heading toward economic dire straits. By the 1970s, an ingenious plan was created to link US currency with OPEC stability (i.e., military reassurances) that caused all nations on the planet to have to keep US dollars as their reserve currency. This fiscal maneuver bought us some wiggle room, but it wasn't a permanent solution.

During the Jimmy Carter administration, globalists like Zbigniew Brzezinski and Henry Kissinger (*vis a vis* the Council on Foreign Relations and Trilateral Commission), along with the Bilderbergers, the Rockefeller Foundation, and so forth, convinced our leadership to spend ourselves out of debt. They knew Keynesian economics doesn't work, but they needed our "almighty dollar" to collapse to bring about a global currency. ("Keynesian economics" is a macroeconomic theory of total spending in the economy and its effects on output, employment, and inflation. It was developed by British economist John Maynard Keynes during the 1930s in an attempt to understand the Great Depression.)[66]

Aside from the fact that the technology wasn't there, the globalists were trying to force God's timeline. Instead, God gave our nation a reprieve in the form of Ronald Reagan. Another four administrations (George H. W. Bush, Bill Clinton, George W. Bush, and Barack Obama) would follow by doing everything they could to reverse Reaganomics and usher in a New World Order. Once again, they were trying to force God's timeline, but instead, He gave us a reprieve in the form of Donald Trump. Now we are at the very end of ourselves. We are not just an empire in decline; we have declined past the point of no return and are now living off of borrowed time. We are out of road on which to kick the can down.

We are out of runway on which to safely land. We are out of tricks up our sleeve. We (as a nation) are hanging on by a thread with at least twenty existential threats to our national sovereignty.

We used to wonder how the educated and advanced German people of the 1920s and '30s could have followed a man like Adolf Hitler—with his funny-looking moustache—and his brown-shirted National Socialists into the Third Reich. Didn't they realize what a nutcase this guy was? But then we realized the German propagandists were masters at creating a façade. They had duped the German people in World War I up until Armistice Day, November 11, 1918, portraying the German Imperial Army as undefeated. So defeat was the *last thing* a shocked German nation ever expected. Even that moment of national weakness was exploited and allowed a man like Hitler to step in and quickly garner supporters who began to champion his vision of a thousand-year Third Reich.

We've seen that same look in the eyes of those who were told over and over by practically everyone that Hillary Clinton was an absolute shoo-in, and then watched all of that propaganda deconstruct before their very eyes on the night of November 9, 2016. That disillusionment turned to visceral and irrational hatred for Donald Trump and anyone who followed him, so our nation became more divided than ever before.

This certainly explains the level of vitriol the leftists and Democrats displayed over the course of Trump's presidency and the absolute blatant desperation to which the left would sabotage the 2020 elections (damn the consequences!). This was the same level of desperation the left turned to with a dementia-addled candidate like Joe Biden. Even then, they couldn't get enough votes to drag him across the finish line, so they had to stop the counting and flip the script in four states to ensure that Trump couldn't win, which tells us God allowed this for a reason.

What we are watching now is a generation quickly and intentionally being given over. We have an entire age bracket of folks who are blatantly rejecting obvious truths under the illusion of intersectionality, equity, and diversity. *Mark our words*, any nation that can't define what a woman is, what an unborn baby is, or how many genders there are is ripe for a grand delusion. This is the same kind of delusion the German people bought into a generation ago, and they are the same kind of people who would overwhelmingly embrace another man like Hitler.

Of course, Joe Biden isn't the next Führer. Biden doesn't know where he is half the time or how to even string together a coherent sentence. Joe is more like aging Kaiser Wilhelm II, who, after losing WWI, faded miserably into history only to watch his nation succumb to the allure of National Socialism (Nazism).

Neither will the next evil dictator (an antichrist) come in with a funny mustache and wearing khaki Cub Scout attire. No, the next one will be *the Antichrist* and will appear attractive, vibrant, and tolerant. He will use his advanced intellect and flowery language to win over the widest group of people possible. But don't let his debonair looks and mastery of public speaking fool you. Although he won't look like Herr Hitler, he will be that same devil in sheep's clothing.

He is going to preach tolerance while being the most intolerant man who ever existed. He will specialize in doublespeak, saying one thing but meaning another. He will appear to be a great peacemaker, but will be a man of extreme violence who is wicked to the core. He will come in at the right moment (right after a global crisis) and get the whole world to follow him by promising to bring peace and security (a new thousand-year kingdom).

But just as God did with Hitler, He will curtail that final Gentile kingdom down to seven years. He then will toss both the Antichrist and his henchman (the False Prophet) directly into the lake of fire a thousand years ahead of everyone else, because they will have been responsible for sending billions of souls straight to Hell.

The fact that we are seeing our nation plummeting as quickly as it is now, while troubling, is also reassuring for the students of Bible prophecy. As bad as things look (economically, politically, religiously, and culturally), the Bible tells us that this is what the last days will look like ("perilous times"; 2 Timothy 3). While we don't delight in seeing our world collapse, we don't despair either. We must get busy sharing the Gospel so that in the few precious moments we have remaining, we can bring as many with us to Heaven as possible.

> When these things begin to take place, stand up and lift up your heads, because your redemption is drawing near. (Luke 21:28)

ELEVEN

THE GREAT RESET

To achieve a better outcome, the world must act jointly and swiftly to revamp all aspects of our societies and economies, from education to social contracts and working conditions. Every country, from the United States to China, must participate, and every industry, from oil and gas to tech, must be transformed. In short, we need a "Great Reset" of capitalism.[67]

KLAUS SCHWAB, WORLD ECONOMIC FORUM

IN HONOR OF THE newly minted global holiday, Earth Week, we thought it pertinent to bring back the discussion of how things begin and end. Contrastingly, those who are foolishly trying to separate the Creator from His creation love to promote the idea of uniformitarianism. By definition, "uniformitarianism is the principle or assumption that the same natural laws and processes that operate in the universe now have always operated in the universe in the past and apply everywhere in the universe."[68] This idea has been a mainstay in humanist reasoning since Aristotle first proposed the universe had no beginning.

Due to the discovery of an expanding universe, science has since abandoned the idea of an eternal one. For the godless, the only logical solution to explain both the existence and complexity of our world, apart from there being a divine Creator, is to add time to the equation...lots of time. Thus, the universe would have begun at some point long before recorded history—perhaps tens of millions, or even billions, of years ago.

Adding an indeterminate amount of time to the equation would not only allow for a gradual transition from single-celled organisms to what we are today, but would do so without the ability to verify said claims. In other words, make it so long ago that it can't be disproven, then use state-controlled academia, media, and pop culture to beat the message into the consciousness of every citizen as if the "science is settled." As far as recorded human history goes, civilization simply began about ten thousand years ago, once the Cro-Magnons decided to upgrade from the cave to the farm.

> For this they willfully forget: that by the word of God the heavens were of old, and the earth standing out of water and in the water, by which the world that then existed perished, being flooded with water. (2 Peter 3:5–6)

While most atheists, human secularists, evolutionists, free thinkers, and skeptics mostly agree that our presence here is likely the result of a cosmic accident billions of years ago, they do seem particularly divided over how it all ends. They can't seem to get their extinction-level ducks in a row. Thus, the "experts," aka scientists, media pundits, professors, politicians, etc., have become the modern-day doomsday prophets warning us of virtually every kind of apocalypse under the sun—except for the biblical one. These are not promoted as theory, but as "settled science," despite the fact that their "settled science" seems to change about every ten years.

In the 1970s, environmental apocalypticism was predicated on an impending ice age. In the mid 1990s–2000s, the ice age forecasts gave way to warnings of looming global warming. In the 2010s, due to an unfortunate run of severely cold winters, ice buildup over the poles, and numerous failed doomsday dates (much to Al Gore's chagrin), global warming was no longer scaring anyone. The scare tactics had to be changed to something else. Something scarier. Something as vague as the all-encompassing "climate change." By this, they willfully ignore God's pronouncement after the Noahic Flood:

While the earth remains,
Seedtime and harvest,
Cold and heat,
Winter and summer,
And day and night
Shall not cease.
(Genesis 8:22)

But now, our global demise has become a smorgasbord of potential earth-ending calamities: everything from cosmic threats such as a severe solar storm to a rogue asteroid/planet striking the Earth, to terrestrial threats such as massive earthquakes, supervolcanoes, and global plagues. Regardless of the actual cause for the calamities, all of these earth-ending events are somehow directly related to driving a large SUV, cow flatulence, or setting our home air conditioners to 70 degrees. In other words, the "experts" have no idea what's coming, or when, but will exploit it to the uttermost nonetheless.

Enter nefarious character stage left.

What began in the 1970s as a bunch of disconnected, radical (fringe), environmentalist factions fighting to save the planet (Green Peace, Earth Liberation Front [ELF], Animal Liberation Front [ALF], etc.), began to coalesce into a united political front by the 1980s. Famine in Africa had become the new *cause célèbre*, culminating with one of the most cringe-worthy events/songs ever written, "We Are the World."

Cashing in on the sudden popularity of political-environmentalist sensationalism were the globalist-minded individuals who were quick to hijack the "save the planet" message. By the early 1990s, they had finally found *the way* to create a worldwide government. They needed a terrifying threat to humanity, one that only an all-powerful global government could solve. Thus, they began preparing the narrative of catastrophic environmental disasters. Global cooling, global warming, and climate change were going to be the crises the world got, regardless of whether they were crises or not. Take, for example, the following quotes:

The common enemy of humanity is man. In searching for a new enemy to unite us, we came up with the idea that pollution, the threat of global warming, water shortages, famine, and the like would fit the bill. All these dangers are caused by human intervention, and it is only through changed attitudes and behavior that they can be overcome. The real enemy then is humanity itself.[69]
—Alexander King and Bertrand Schneider, Club of Rome

Isn't the only hope for the planet that the industrialized civilizations collapse? Isn't it our responsibility to bring that about?[70]
—Maurice Strong, founder of the UN Environment Program and grandfather of Agenda 21

This agenda began in the bowels of the United Nations in the late 1980s under the name of "Agenda 21" and was signed into *soft law* by President George H. W. Bush at the 1992 Earth Summit in Rio de Janeiro. This meant that, although it was created outside of our own nation's legislative branch and was technically nonbinding, it was still strongly encouraged through voluntary local, state, and federal efforts; to date, some six hundred US cities have signed on as partners. President Clinton later re-signed the United States as signatories to this law, effectively advancing the precedence of global governance and perpetuating the necessity for a New World Order.

(Authors' note: Apologies for the length of the quote below, but the original UN document is four hundred pages long. This is as brief and accurate a summation as we could find.)

Translation of the UN's "2030 Agenda Blueprint for Globalist Government" (controlled by corporate interests)

Goal 1) End poverty in all its forms everywhere.
Translation: Put everyone on government welfare, food stamps, housing subsidies, and handouts that make them obe-

dient slaves to global government. Never allow people upward mobility to help themselves. Instead, teach mass victimization and obedience to a government that provides monthly "allowance" money for basic essentials like food and medicine. Label it "ending poverty."

Goal 2) End hunger, achieve food security and improved nutrition, and promote sustainable agriculture

Translation: Invade the entire planet with GMOs and Monsanto's patented seeds while increasing the use of deadly herbicides under the false claim of "increased output" of food crops. Engineer genetically modified plants to boost specific vitamin chemicals while having no idea of the long-term consequences of genetic pollution or cross-species genetic experiments carried out openly in a fragile ecosystem.

Goal 3) Ensure healthy lives and promote well-being for all at all ages

Translation: Mandate 100+ jabs for all children and adults at gunpoint, threatening parents with arrest and imprisonment if they refuse to cooperate. Push heavy medication use on children and teens while rolling out "screening" programs. Call mass medication "prevention" programs and claim they improve the health of citizens.

Goal 4) Ensure inclusive and equitable quality education and promote lifelong learning opportunities for all

Translation: Push a false history and a dumbed-down education under "Common Core" education standards that produce obedient workers rather than independent thinkers. Never let people learn real history, or else they might realize they don't want to repeat it.

Goal 5) Achieve gender equality and empower all women and girls

Translation: Criminalize Christianity, marginalize heterosexuality, demonize males and promote the LGBTQ agenda everywhere.

The real goal is never "equality" but rather the marginalization and shaming of anyone who expresses any male characteristics whatsoever. The ultimate goal is to feminize society, creating widespread acceptance of "gentle obedience" along with the self-weakening ideas of communal property and "sharing" everything. Because only male energy has the strength to rise up against oppression and fight for human rights, the suppression of male energy is key to keeping the population in a state of eternal acquiescence.

Goal 6) Ensure availability and sustainable management of water and sanitation for all

Translation: Allow powerful corporations to seize control of the world's water supplies and charge monopoly prices to "build new water delivery infrastructure" that "ensures availability."

Goal 7) Ensure access to affordable, reliable, sustainable, and modern energy for all

Translation: Penalize coal, gas, and oil while pushing doomed-to-fail "green" energy subsidies to brain-dead startups headed by friends of the White House who all go bankrupt in five years or less. The green startups make for impressive speeches and media coverage, but because these companies are led by corrupt idiots rather than capable entrepreneurs, they always go broke. (And the media hopes you don't remember all the fanfare surrounding their original launch.)

Goal 8) Promote sustained, inclusive, and sustainable economic growth, full and productive employment, and decent work for all

Translation: Regulate small businesses out of existence with government-mandated minimum wages that bankrupt entire sectors of the economy. Force employers to meet hiring quotas of LGBTQ workers while mandating wage tiers under a centrally planned work economy dictated by the government. Destroy free-market economics and deny permits and licenses to those companies that don't obey government dictates.

Goal 9) Build resilient infrastructure, promote inclusive and sustainable industrialization, and foster innovation

Translation: Put nations into extreme debt with the World Bank, spending debt money to hire corrupt American corporations to build large-scale infrastructure projects that trap developing nations in an endless spiral of debt. See the book *Confessions of an Economic Hit Man* by John Perkins to understand the details of how this scheme has been repeated countless times over the last several decades.

Goal 10) Reduce inequality within and among countries

Translation: Punish the rich, the entrepreneurs, and the innovators, confiscating nearly all gains by those who choose to work and excel. Redistribute the confiscated wealth to the masses of non-working human parasites that feed off a productive economy while contributing nothing to it…all while screaming about "equality!"

Goal 11) Make cities and human settlements inclusive, safe, resilient, and sustainable

Translation: Ban all gun ownership by private citizens, concentrating guns into the hands of obedient government enforcers who rule over an unarmed, enslaved class of impoverished workers. Criminalize living in most rural areas by instituting Hunger Games-style "protected areas" which the government will claim are owned by "the People" even though no people are allowed to live there. Force all humans into densely packed, tightly controlled cities where they are under 24/7 surveillance and subject to easy manipulation by government.

Goal 12) Ensure sustainable consumption and production patterns

Translation: Begin levying punitive taxes on the consumption of fossil fuels and electricity, forcing people to live under conditions of worsening standards of living that increasingly resemble Third World conditions. Use social influence campaigns in TV, movies and social media to shame people who use gasoline, water or electricity, establishing a social construct of ninnies and tattlers who rat out their neighbors in exchange for food credit rewards.

Goal 13) Take urgent action to combat climate change and its impacts

Translation: Set energy consumption quotas on each human being and start punishing or even criminalizing "lifestyle decisions" that exceed energy usage limits set by governments. Institute total surveillance of individuals in order to track and calculate their energy consumption. Penalize private vehicle ownership and force the masses onto public transit, where TSA grunts and facial recognition cameras can monitor and record the movement of every person in society, like a scene ripped right out of *Minority Report.*

Goal 14) Conserve and sustainably use the oceans, seas, and marine resources for sustainable development

Translation: Ban most ocean fishing, plunging the food supply into an extreme shortage and causing runaway food price inflation that puts even more people into economic desperation. Criminalize the operation of private fishing vessels and place all ocean fishing operations under the control of government central planning. Only allow favored corporations to conduct ocean fishing operations (and make this decision based entirely on which corporations give the most campaign contributions to corrupt lawmakers).

Goal 15) Protect, restore and promote sustainable use of terrestrial ecosystems, sustainably manage forests, combat desertification, and halt and reverse land degradation and halt biodiversity loss

Translation: Roll out Agenda 21 and force humans off the land and into controlled cities. Criminalize private land ownership, including ranches and agricultural tracts. Tightly control all agriculture through a corporate-corrupted government bureaucracy whose policies are determined almost entirely by Monsanto while being rubber-stamped by the USDA. Ban woodstoves, rainwater collection and home gardening in order to criminalize self-reliance and force total dependence on government.

Goal 16) Promote peaceful and inclusive societies for sustainable development, provide access to justice for all, and build effective, accountable and inclusive institutions at all levels

Translation: Grant legal immunity to illegal aliens and "protected" minority groups, which will be free to engage in any illegal activity — including openly calling for the mass murder of police officers — because they are the new protected class in society. "Inclusive institutions" means granting favorable tax structures and government grants to corporations that hire LGBTQ workers or whatever groups are currently in favor with the central planners in government. Use the IRS and other federal agencies to selectively punish unfavorable groups with punitive audits and regulatory harassment, all while ignoring the criminal activities of favored corporations that are friends of the political elite.

Goal 17) Strengthen the means of implementation and revitalize the global partnership for sustainable development

Translation: Enact global trade mandates that override national laws while granting unrestricted imperialism powers to companies like Monsanto, Dow Chemical, RJ Reynolds, Coca-Cola and Merck. Pass global trade pacts that bypass a nation's lawmakers and override intellectual property laws to make sure the world's most powerful corporations maintain total monopolies over drugs, seeds, chemicals and technology. Nullify national laws and demand total global obedience to trade agreements authored by powerful corporations and rubber-stamped by the UN.

Their goal: Total enslavement of the planet by 2030. But don't take our word for it.

As the UN document says: "We commit ourselves to working tirelessly for the full implementation of this Agenda by 2030.[71]

Funny Money

By a continuing process of inflation, government can confiscate, secretly and unobserved, an important part of the wealth of their citizens. —John Maynard Keynes

Politically, the German Third Reich lasted twelve years—from 1933–1945. The Third Reich's money, on the other hand, the *reichsmark*, held its value for about double that, from 1924–1948 (twenty-four years), after which it was changed to the *deutsche mark*. That lasted from 1948 to 2002, when the euro became the common currency in Germany and the rest of the European Union. The *reichsmark's* fate was sealed due to the changing geopolitical realities on the ground.

For reasons unknown (demonically driven paranoia, perhaps), and despite his advisors urging him against it, Hitler was driven to open up a second war front by invading the Soviet Union in the brutal Operation Barbarossa. In so doing, he doomed not just his nation, but the national currency as well. The *reichsmark's* collapse also triggered other financial currency collapses across Europe for those who had either been accosted by the *reichsmark* or were dependent upon it for their own stability. However, by 1944, the Third Reich was in a death spiral, and Nazi officials everywhere were getting nervous and looking for highly mobile valuables (gold, diamonds, etc.) to use after Germany's inevitable demise.

Although we have the luxury of historical hindsight, even a casual observer back then could see that Hitler's policies were both unconscionable (i.e., the Final Solution) as well as unsustainable (i.e., the Four Year Plan). But if we make the comparisons to the US today, what does that say for us? We know our policies are both unconscionable (the abortion holocaust, endless wars, etc.) as well as unsustainable ($169 trillion in national debt). Can our leaders today not see the writing on the wall as evidence of our imminent financial collapse?

Perhaps.

Perhaps they don't care.

Not to compare modern investors with Nazi officials, but both are/ were frantically looking to diversify their holdings. Back then, it was in precious metals and stones. Today, it's in stock-market options, bonds, and cryptocurrency. Like the Titanic, the "SS Dollar" has already hit the iceberg and is slowly sinking into the Atlantic. But investors are not the only indicators of our impending collapse. Simply look at the globalists who used to operate in the shadows but are now working boldly to expedite the dismantlement of our once-great nation. Put another way, at the height of US global dominance, they never would have done the things they're doing now. Now, they are no longer hiding their true intentions.

Enter the World Economic Forum's (WEF) Great Reset.

Give me control of a nation's money and I care not who makes the laws. —Mayer Amschel Rothschild (1744–1812)[72]

If money equals power, and power equals influence, then influence (ideas and ideology) makes the world go round. The 1940s Bretton-Woods Agreement was intent on keeping global influence firmly in American hands. From then until the 1970s, the international economy was largely led by the US economy and US dollar. The way it was set up, it was in the world's best interest to keep the US dollar strong, which would, in turn, help keep every other currency stable.

However, given the increasingly advanced technological developments we are seeing each passing day, the US dollar's global hegemony is increasingly becoming a twentieth-century holdover that is trying desperately to stay relevant past its expiration date...and the globalists know it. They are in the process of bankrupting us just as we did the Soviet Union in the 1980s, through strategically imbalanced climate and economic policies, weaponized illegal immigration, expansion of the welfare state, and an endless war footing.

Maybe this is why our government over the past several Congresses and administrations doesn't seem to care about writing multi-trillion-dollar legislative bills, controlling our borders, instituting universal basic income and healthcare, or providing $450,000 reparations to illegal aliens. They don't care about the national debt, because they know this whole system is collapsing anyway. From their perspective, we are already too far gone, so they might as well jockey for their positions in the New World Order by expediting its arrival. After all, if globalist-minded politicians and corporate oligarchs' primary goals are to stay in power, they will do whatever is in their best interests to ensure this happens—regardless of what it does to the rest of us. Hence, the Great Reset.

Since the onset of COVID-19 in March of 2020, the response to the scourge has consolidated the monopolistic corporations' grip on the economy on top, while advancing "actually existing socialism" below. In partnership with Big Tech, Big Pharma, the legacy media, national and international health agencies, and compliant populations, hitherto "democratic" Western states are increasingly being transformed into totalitarian regimes modeled after China, seemingly overnight. I need not provide a litany of the tyranny and abuses. You can read about them on alternative news sites—until you can no longer read about them even there.

> The Great Reset, then, is not merely a conspiracy theory; it is an open, avowed, and planned project, and it is well underway. But because capitalism with Chinese characteristics, or corporate-socialist statism, lacks free markets and depends on the absence of free will and individual liberty, it is, ironically, "unsustainable," and doomed to fail. The question is just how much suffering and distortion will be endured until it does. —Michael Rectenwald[73]

Globalists such as Klaus Schwab, Bill Gates, George Soros, British royalty, the United Nations (and its various appendages), Blackrock, State Street, Vanguard, Berkshire Hathaway, and countless others are of *one mind* regarding this coming global change. They truly believe that the only way to save the planet is to be the ones controlling it. They are feverishly planning this regime change under a number of different auspices, namely through the legislative initiatives set forth by the United Nations'

Agenda 21/Agenda 2030 programs while using climate change as the new threat *du jour*. These initiatives are then repackaged by other globalist groups such as the Web Economic Forum (WEF), Bilderberg Group, Council on Foreign Relations (CFR), the Rockefeller Foundation, etc., into more palatable and benign terms such as "the Fourth Industrial Revolution," "Building Back Better," "Environmental, Social, and Governance (ESG)", and the Great Reset, which are then propagandized by the *fifth-column*[74] mainstream media.

According to Scripture, the final world government (as described in Daniel 2, 7; Revelation 13–18) will be headed by the Antichrist, aided by the False Prophet, and will control the entire world for a period of, at most, seven years.

Many emperors and kings in the past have tried in vain to conquer the world. Alexander the Great, the Roman Caesars, Genghis Khan, Napoleon, Adolf Hitler, Islamists, etc., have all had a go at it. And while their endeavors met with varying degrees of success, none ever conquered the entire world. Furthermore, none could even completely control the territories they had already conquered. What will be different with this final government is that, through the totalitarian policies being put in place today, along with the rapid advancements in information technology and artificial intelligence, the final Beast system will be able to control everything with 100 percent efficiency. This is the convergence we see coming together today.

This convergence did not happen overnight; it came in stages. The First World War saw the dismantlement of the Ottoman Empire and the creation of the League of Nations. The Second World War saw the undoing of global colonialism, the raising of the Iron Curtain, and the creation of the United Nations and NATO.

Out of these two global events came a world government (the United Nations), the rebirth of the nation of Israel, the reunification of Europe, and a meteoric explosion of technological advancements across every sector. The convergence (listed below) marks the prophetic areas that are critical to Satan's agenda of achieving total global domination. The fact that we are seeing the formation of these things even now should alert us to the lateness of the hour. Two key areas will greatly expedite the world's transition from our world today to the final world government to come:

1. **Quantum computing**: For those not very familiar with quantum technology, a single quantum computer could easily power everything on the list below and then some. Quantum computers are thousands of times faster and more powerful than even our highest-level computers today. With that said, there are at present around twenty major companies in the US alone that are rapidly developing quantum technologies.[75]

2. **Artificial intelligence (i.e., machine/deep learning)**: Along with quantum technologies, many nations and organizations are racing toward developing the first superior artificial intelligence system. As digitally connected as the world is becoming, the development of quantum technologies will be critical to the Antichrist's ability to control, organize, and process an overwhelming amount of information. Artificial intelligence will be critical in using that information to assert control over large areas of governance.[76]

These are the two new arms races for the twenty-first century. The fact that these two technologies are linked hand in glove should testify to the terrifying power this final government will one day wield. If you want to know how one man could control all the buying and selling in the world at the same time, this is how it begins. Listed below are the disparate parts and pieces being developed (often independent of each other) that will come together at the right crisis.

- **Global Government**: The rider on the white horse (the first beast) represents the coming of a global imperial system that will be divided into ten regions. Out of these ten, another will arise, subdue three, and then assume control of the entire system.
- **Global Religion**: The second beast is described as having horns

like a lamb, but speaking like a dragon. He will work hand in glove with the white horse to promote this new Beast kingdom, serving as its spiritual propaganda arm.

- **Global Military:** The red horse of war will remove peace from the earth and cause the world's militaries to realign into coalitions and regions instead of individual nations.

- **Global Economy:** The rider on the black horse with the balances will signal that an economic collapse and reset are coming. Something will have to give in order to get the world moved from our present model to the system of the Beast.

- **Global Finance:** The black horse with the balances indicates that redesigning the economy will not be enough. There needs to be a complete overhaul by replacing the twentieth-century-based fiat currencies with the twenty-first-century digital one, namely, the mark of the Beast. This digital system will have three basic functions: identification, a universal basic income, and access.[77]

All of the above already exist in our world today and are gaining momentum by way of crisis-based governance. Realizing mankind will never unite without some kind of external threat, the globalists have long been championing the fear-mongering as early as the 1950s with the atomic arms race, the Cold War, global cooling, global warming, the war on terror, the indefinable *climate change,* and now, pandemics (both real and artificial). These so-called crises were designed to keep sovereign nations in a perpetual state of fear, in the hopes that they would be more prone to giving up more and more of their national sovereignty. And while most of the world went along with this, the globalists could not get the US to fully come along.

While most of these globalist groups all want the same thing, they remain fragmented and separated by varying interests internal to their respective organizations. It is our belief that the key to all the above coming together into a single, cohesive organization, is the collapse of the United States.

For the record, the collapse of the US will not come until the Rapture of the Church. The reason we believe this is that, as recorded in Matthew 24:36–41 and Luke 17:26–36, Jesus spoke of the time just before the end as carrying on with a sense of normalcy. He stated that His return would catch the world off-guard; the people will be buying and selling, eating and drinking, marrying and giving in marriage…and then sudden destruction will come upon them, and they will not escape. This certainly couldn't be said of the time just prior to the Second Coming, because for the seven years leading up to that great event, the world will have undergone twenty-one of the most severe divine judgments ever recorded in human history.

At present, we already have a global government. However, the UN is powerless without the full backing of the United States. We also have a global economy—which, again, is hamstrung by US laws that protect its financial interests over other nations. As for global military and global religion, these two will not become a reality until after the Rapture.

Just as we saw the wholesale abandonment of billions of dollars' worth of military equipment in Afghanistan, after the Rapture, the US military arsenal will become a free-for-all for the remaining world powers. With the US in varying states of disarray and lawlessness, we expect that the European Union, China, and Russia will cross the pond and take control of our nuclear assets, weapons systems, submarines, aircraft carriers, and aircraft, etc., rather quickly. This will be how they rapidly arm themselves and become the well-armed powerbrokers in the last days. NATO will be redesignated as the new EU defense force. Russia (newly armed and emboldened) will decide to join with Turkey and Iran and take out Israel. With the US no longer a threat, China will consolidate its control over the entirety of Asia.

Westernization, coupled with globalization, has created an afflu-
ent and leisured elite that now gravitates to universities, the media,
bureaucracies, and world organizations, all places where wealth is
not created, but analyzed, critiqued, and lavishly spent.[78] —Victor
Davis Hanson

Moreover, because we are in the digital age and our economies are already largely tied together through cyber networks, an economic *coup d'état* is easier today than it ever has been. So much has already been prepared and readied for a one-currency system based upon the US dollar today that all it will take is a little nudge to get the nations lined up. If the US dollar crashes, it will drag every other currency down with it. Out of the ashes, a financial phoenix will arise, probably in the form of a quantum-based cryptocurrency that biometrically ties the person (the user) to the system.[79]

This is very much the same as how, for example, the 2001 Patriot Act came to be. The act (or the core of it) was written both before (as the 1995 Omnibus Counterterrorism Act) and after the Oklahoma City bombing (the 1996 Antiterrorism and Effective Death Penalty Act). Once 9/11 happened, there was enough political consensus and raw emotion to simply add in the intelligence-sharing-and-collecting measures to make it broad in scope. This has since been renewed in four-year intervals, often with additions to the original provision. What could not be done by the government (constitutional constraints aside) was simply handed to private businesses such as cell phone companies, social media, or Internet companies to hold on behalf of the government for later collection.

All that to say this: When this final government comes into being, it may not make a grand, sweeping entrance onto the global stage, as many are led to believe. This world government is already in place, and has been coming in stages for quite some time. The Rapture, in terms of geopolitical effects, gives mankind that final *nudge* to abandon nationalism forever. The creeping Orwellian antiterrorism measures we have seen expanded over the last few decades could not have passed were it not for the devastating terrorist attacks in Oklahoma and on 9/11. Again, crisis proves the perfect catalyst for rapid change.

So, where are we today in terms of seeing this final government coming into being?

- The world's economies must be fragile and easily unbalanced due to emerging technologies and massive debt. *Check.*

- The world's economies must be interwoven to the point that should one fall (i.e., the United States), the rest would also collapse. *Check.*
- There needs to exist some structure/system (the Internet) through which all the countries *could* be controlled. *Check.*
- There needs to be some sort of crisis that both frightens and unites the world leadership into ceding their autonomy into a collective economic/political system. *Pending.*

However, creating an all-powerful and overarching global government would still be a daunting, nigh impossible task if it wasn't for our technological advancements. The world would need an Internet system and computers powerful enough to blanket the entire earth. Although we do not see it today, the process for free global Internet is already in motion. The justification (for providing free Internet access to those around the world who either don't have it or can't afford it) seems altruistic enough. But, like everything else, what begins as something *for* mankind will quickly become something that is used *against* mankind.[80]

Furthermore, with quantum computing and cloud technology coming into the fray more and more each day, this final government system will not only have the global reach, but the power to process massive amounts of information effortlessly and limitlessly. This will be used not only for tying all of the world's economies together, but also for global surveillance, biometrics, military and political propaganda campaigns, artificial intelligence, and information warfare—simultaneously. The race is on amongst tech companies (IBM, Google, D-Wave, Rigetti, etc.) to see who will gain *quantum supremacy* first—not just amongst private industries, but nations:

The European Commission is preparing the ground for the launch in 2018 of a €1 billion flagship initiative on quantum technologies, which can put Europe at the forefront of the second quantum revolution, bringing transformative advances to science, industry and society. The flagship initiative is expected to turn Europe's excellent research results in areas like quantum secure communication, quantum sensing and quantum simulation and computing into concrete technological opportunities that can be taken up by industry.[81]

In terms of national unity, the EU leads the world in its efforts to achieve quantum supremacy, and it even has a *quantum manifesto*.[82] However, it is not just the one billion euros they are dropping on this quantum bet, but also the eighty billion euros they have invested in technological growth and research in their project Horizon 2020. They are determined to lead, and we believe that what the Apostle John saw in the imagery described in Revelation 13 was the manifestation of a revived Roman Empire coming on the heels of a major crisis such as the Rapture, aided by this quantum technology breakthrough. When this advancement happens, it will absolutely revolutionize how people live on earth. In fact, it will be so groundbreaking in terms of its power and scope, the world will say: "Who is like the beast? Who is able to make war with him?" (Revelation 13:4).

What John also saw was global government being displayed as having seven heads and ten crowns. It will be arrayed with subordinate commands that function at the regional levels. Below them will be the nation-states, all of which are subordinate to the Beast. However, at a certain point, all of that government's power and authority will be concentrated into the hands of just one man, *the Antichrist*, largely aided by another man, the *False Prophet*.

So how do we get from where we are today to where the Bible says we will be in such a short period of time?

In stages at first, then after a giant shove.

The final thrust into this system will come on the heels of the crisis of the Rapture.

If "necessity is the mother of all inventions," then "necessity rooted in *the mother of all crises*" is what invents this final governmental system.

However, change like that is exceedingly painful (i.e., replacing dying empires), and nations at the top will not go quietly into the night. This means two things are certain on our horizon: the Rapture of the Church and total war.

The Rapture of the Church (the "blessed hope") will decimate the United States and, to lesser degrees, the rest of the world. When Christ removes His Church from the earth, it will force a realignment to the current world order. Since we can know without any hesitation that the Bible teaches a pre-Tribulation Rapture, that change to the world order will happen immediately after that event. This also means that *total war* is on the horizon, because nations less affected will jockey to fill the vacuum left by the world's undisputed superpower. The EU will win that race to fill the vacuum by way of its heavy investments in technology today. That fits exactly with what prophetic Scripture has already laid out.

TWELVE

THE NEW ABNORMAL

Most Americans are unaware of a decline in individual liberty, and the reason is obvious: the decline rarely takes the form of sudden personal deprivation but, instead, takes the form of unnoticed erosion and, thus, we come to regard whatever state we are in as a normal condition.

LEONARD E. READ, "HOW TO ADVANCE LIBERTY"[83]

IF YOU'RE WONDERING why the world is as crazy as it seems today, it is because we can see all seventeen of these agendas mentioned in the previous chapter being enforced around the world. It would seem, given what we now know, that the recent 2020 "plandemic" wasn't about a real crisis at all, but a course correction. The globalists were desperate to counteract the "Trump effect" of American exceptionalism and put the world back on track toward global governance by 2030. This should also tell you that they will do all within their power to intentionally nullify the midterm Republican victories by attempting to crash the American dollar either right before or right after the election, forcing all Americans onto a central bank digital currency (CBDC). Adding to the global Agenda 2030 lunacy will be the coming food shortages that we can see coming a mile away:

- The culling of tens of millions of chickens in China and the US
- The culling of thousands of heads of cattle in the US

- Forty percent of the world's wheat, corn, soy, and fertilizer being cut off due to the Ukraine-Russia conflict
- Cataclysmic lockdown of one of the world's major port cities (Shanghai, China)
- Skyrocketing fuel prices and inflation
- The sudden rash of fires and explosions in more than twenty food processing and fertilizer plants in the US

What is unknown by many, though, is the real end-state for this "sustainable development" plan (i.e., Agenda 21/2030). It's not just to create a global government or to impose environmental lunacy everywhere; it is to get the global population back down under five hundred million people. Despite all the flowery and bureaucratic doublespeak, the true key to sustainable development (in their minds) is the global depopulation of the planet by some 95 percent (aka the Great Reset). Of course, this is not really a secret, since it has been (literally) written in stone since 1980.

According to the formerly standing Georgia Guidestones in Elbert County, Georgia, the globalists' first goal is to "maintain humanity at or below 500,000 in perpetual balance with nature." If the aim is to reduce the world's population by 95 percent in order to achieve "sustainable development," who are the remaining 5 percent?

As it appears, the fringe nineteenth-century theories of a master race (i.e., Social Darwinism and Eugenics) never actually died out with the German Third Reich. You can't go from eight billion people down to five hundred million (a net loss of 7.5 billion people) without committing mass genocide. And nobody is willingly going to throw themselves into the fire just so the ultra-elite can have their utopia.

So who dies?

Conversely, if you are among the ones at the top and in the position to determine who is going to live to inherit this new global utopia, you're not going to hand it over to third-world commoners or MAGA ("Make America Great Again")-type conservatives. No, you are going to carefully select the "who's who" of the most genetically enhanced and politically connected people in the world to help propagate the *new* New World Order.[84]

They believe they will be able to extend their life spans back to centuries. There has been a concerted effort to advance "anti-aging" technologies through numerous fronts like the Methuselah Foundation and the Gilgamesh Project. These might sound like fringe science on the surface, but billions of dollars, euros, yen, and other currencies are being pumped into this to do anything to extend human life beyond one hundred years again. Ultimately, this all boils down to the original lie of being able to become "like God" so many have bought into.

> Then the serpent said to the woman, "You will not surely die. For God knows that in the day you eat of it your eyes will be opened, and *you will be like God*, knowing good and evil." (Genesis 3:5–6, emphasis added)

Needless to say, Satan has been feeding this tripe to the global elite for millennia. Like an infectious disease, these theories (and the ones of immortality that predate them) simply spread from kingdom to kingdom, nation to nation, poisoning the minds of each generation of world leaders down through the ages. It feeds on people's pride and their willingness to reject God's free offer of eternal life for salvation for their own glory. Little do they realize that the world is about to undergo a massive depopulation campaign. It won't be by the global elite or any UN mandate, but by God Himself.

> When He opened the fourth seal, I heard the voice of the fourth living creature saying, "Come and see." So I looked, and behold, a pale horse. And the name of him who sat on it was Death, and Hades followed with him. And power was given to them *over a fourth of the earth*, to kill with sword, with hunger, with death, and by the beasts of the earth. (Revelation 6:7–8, emphasis added)

By current population standards, a fourth of eight billion people is two billion. This will reduce the world population to around six billion survivors at the end of the seal judgments. During the trumpet judgments, a third of that six billion are killed. That means another 1.8 billion are killed, leaving the global population to just 4.2 billion.

$$8,000,000,000 - 2,000,000,000 = \mathbf{6,000,000,000}$$
(at the end of the seal judgments)

$$6,000,000,000 - 1,800,000,000 = \mathbf{4,200,000,000}$$
(at the end of the trumpet judgments)

This doesn't even take into account all the Christians and children removed by Rapture before the seal judgments. Assuming that 10 ten percent of the global population is raptured (10% of 8B = 80M):

$4,200,000,000 - 80,000,000 = \mathbf{4,120,000,000}$ (remainder by the end of the trumpet judgments)

The bowl judgments and the Armageddon campaign will reduce the global population even further, so much so, that if Jesus doesn't intervene at the Second Coming, no flesh will survive.

> For then there will be great tribulation, such as has not been since
> the beginning of the world until this time, no, nor ever shall be.
> And unless those days were shortened, no flesh would be saved;
> but for *the elect's sake* [believing Israel] those days will be short-
> ened. (Matthew 24:21–22, emphasis added)

Aside from the numerous prophecies concerning the geopolitical alignment of nations, the apostatizing from within Christendom (Laodicea), the general deterioration of mankind, increasing natural calamities, and a supernatural hatred towards Israel…there are also the signs that the love of many will grow cold (or calloused) in these last days.

Western civilization is becoming "Gospel-resistant" and hardening its hearts against the Gospel of Jesus Christ because of centuries of leftist, socialist, Marxist, human-secularist brainwashing that has tricked them into believing they don't need God. This poisonous ideology has infected nearly every facet of our society today. We went from being a nation that actively called on God for His provision to one that:

- earnestly acknowledged Him for our blessings;
- generally thanked Him in passing;
- thanked themselves or no one at all; and
- raised their fists against Him.

In fact, there is no sector of government, military, media, academia, entertainment, or even a growing number of pulpits today that hasn't been tainted by this antichrist spirit. Globally speaking, there is such a minute remnant of true believers left alive that to believe Christ is actually coming back puts us squarely in the same company as the "flat-earthers." In fact, one UK study shows more Brits believe in extraterrestrial aliens than in Jesus Christ. If Charles Spurgeon were still lying dead in his grave, he'd be rolling over in it![85]

God will not be mocked by our attempts at self-deification. He separated humankind for a reason back at the Tower of Babel (Genesis 11:6–7). While He is longsuffering in that all should come to repentance, His patience is not without its limits. God set a schedule, and He will keep it.

When the world least expects it, that trumpet is going to *sound*, and that shouted command from the archangel is going to be heard, and then we who are alive and remain will be caught up in the air to meet those who had previously passed and receive our glorified bodies so we can live with our Lord forevermore.

What remains after His Bride the Church is removed?

God's fury.

It will begin when Jesus opens the seal judgments, which trigger the trumpet judgments, which finally unleash the horrific bowl judgments.

God will literally bring Hell to earth for the sole purpose of a) destroying all the nations of the world; and b) disciplining Israel into repentance (Jeremiah 30:7–11). And, despite centuries of meticulous scheming by Satan and the carefully contrived machinations of evil people, at least they will get one thing correct: Global warming and depopulation are coming.

Resetting the Reset

For the Lord Himself will descend from heaven with a shout, with the voice of an archangel, and with the trumpet of God. And the dead in Christ will rise first. Then we who are alive and remain shall be caught up together with them in the clouds to meet the Lord in the air. And thus we shall always be with the Lord… For when they say, "Peace and safety!" then sudden destruction comes upon them, as labor pains upon a pregnant woman. And they shall not escape. (1 Thessalonians 4:16–17, 5:3, NKJV)

D-Day

The Rapture event breaks into human history in two specific ways: immediately and disturbingly. The event itself is immediate, in that it doesn't take days, weeks, and months to happen, but it happens instantly. It occurs so quickly, in fact, the human brain does not have time to process it all. The suddenness catches a sleeping world off-guard.

It is disturbing in much the same way it was unnerving for those travelling with the Pharisee Saul on the road to Damascus (Acts 9:7) or to those with Daniel when he was down near the river (Daniel 10:7). There is a noise and sound of something having just transpired, and it is *known* (people know something just happened), yet *unknown* (they don't know *what* happened). It is also profoundly disturbing in the sense that, after the reality of it sets in, people know life will never be the same.

Among the first, most immediate effects of the Rapture are traffic accidents. Some planes crash, but the primary mode of travel in the United States is by car, and in an instant, thousands of cars crash at the same time. The very next thing people notice is that a number of their family members, friends, and coworkers are nowhere to be found, and there are no longer any children and babies. Between just those two results of the widespread disappearance of so many people—car crashes and missing persons—whatever is left of the law enforcement system is overwhelmed to the point that the entire 911 system crashes. There is also a noticeably marked increase in "target of opportunity" thefts and robberies because of shops that are now unattended, cars that are left open, purses and wallets that have been dropped by their owners, and open houses that have been abandoned, etc. While most people are trying to figure out what just happened, criminals take advantage of the chaos.

Local news reports go out that an unknown event has just transpired and thousands of people have just gone missing. Of course, the numbers cited in those reports continue to trend upwards to millions as more details become available. Nevertheless, throughout the day, the ramifications of the sudden disappearance become more apparent as the counts continue to skyrocket. Both cities and states declare lockdowns and/or curfews as the "crisis" overwhelms all existing (or remaining) emergency services and law-enforcement agencies. Churches are magnets for those left behind, as frightened and confused folks seek solace or information, knowing that what just happened must have something to do with that "Rapture thing" their "crazy" friends and families have been going on about.

Day 1

The mainstream media begins to report widespread disappearances across the nation and the world as government leaders scratch their heads trying to determine the cause of the event. The immediate concerns are the outbreak of numerous fires, looting, and massive transportation blockages as abandoned vehicles clog the roads. At some point within the first day or two, a reporter asks curiously, "Could this be the Rapture?" Once that idea is given traction, the remaining population starts to see the general breakdown of society, as chaos and looting become extensive. Public officials plead for calm as people begin a run on the banks and stores for cash, food, and necessities.

Days 2–7

Before the end of the first week, the president announces that martial law is in effect. Congress and the courts are recessed. Having already relocated to a secure site such as Camp David, members of the executive branch attempt to conduct damage control. The states enact a ban on travel outside the home as cities begin to systematically shut down. What the US law enforcement and military lacks in manpower, they try to compensate for in advanced artificial intelligence systems and surveillance technologies.

Cities like Atlanta, New York, Houston, Chicago, and Los Angeles lose whole sections to the criminal elements. The gangs who are prepared now take advantage of the chaos and solidify their own territorial holdings. Outside the larger cities, biker gangs (motorcycle clubs) attempt to dominate the open roads and smaller towns. Jails, prisons, and federal penitentiaries are the first targets for these groups as they try to retrieve incarcerated compatriots to boost the numbers of their rank and file.

Average citizens caught up in the mix of the chaos flee the cities looking for places of refuge. This is where the "impromptu" resettlement camps come into play, as authorities look to secure the people in areas they can control. This is the first step in separating the general populace from the criminals. Military and law enforcement groups, largely borrowing the tactics and techniques acquired in places like Fallujah and Sadr City (Iraq), begin quarantining vast swaths of areas that they can't control. Biometrics are 100 percent enforced, and those with critical job skills are identified for later use in their fields, or specialties.

DAY 7—WEEK 8

By the end of the seventh or eighth week, all basic goods such as fuel, food, hygiene, and medical products have been stripped from stores and hoarded. The US dollar is no longer sufficient for payment, as nations around the world have abandoned it wholesale, and people resort to bartering or taking things by force. The dollar's collapse has a destabilizing effect on the global economy, but the nations that relied heavily on the US dollar are hit the hardest.

Global Reaction

As nations around the world start to get a handle on their own internal crises, the European Union takes the lead in calling for a global summit. Currently, the EU and the US constitute the two largest economies in the world, followed closely by China. They have to rise because it defaults to them. The EU calls for the world to be broken up into regional authorities since the old order of political power has collapsed. All regional governments and a temporary digital currency answer to the United Nations. The UN has already abandoned its New York City address for a more secure and central location. Most likely, it seeks to take up residence in a place minimally impacted by the Rapture, which is either Europe or the Middle East.

As city, state, and regional governments begin to get "a handle" on the ensuing crisis, they also attempt to gain control of the narrative of what happened. Simultaneous to all of this from day one through the following weeks is an explosion of UFO/UAP activity in the atmosphere. These become the *de facto* causes for what has happened, and any discussion of the Rapture is quickly shut down/censored as "conspiracy theory" as fact checkers quickly dismiss any mention of it. Still, the average person who has been exposed to this knowledge before it happened will know better. This clamp-down on the messaging begins the underground Tribulation saints' movement.

Daniel 7 states the final version of the Roman Empire comes to dominate the whole world. This requires time. How much time, we are uncertain, as it largely depends on how quickly things move after the

Rapture itself. Most likely, there is a gap of time from a year to several years. It means the EU gets an advantage on everyone else in order to solidify that kind of control. But for the EU to gain the edge on the other regional blocs, it has to acquire military expertise and technology, which is most likely transferred to the EU through what used to be NATO. Similar to the criminal elements inside the US, rogue regimes also seek to take advantage of the chaos, especially in light of America's inability to flex its muscles anywhere else in the world.

Financial Armageddon

The US currently has roughly 330 million citizens. Now imagine that 10 percent of that population (thirty million people) is comprised of true, born-again Christians, and they suddenly disappear…

If that many people are no longer participating in activities such as buying or selling, paying bills and being paid, providing various industrial and technical skills, etc., how quickly does the American experiment come to a halt?

If thirty million people are no longer making house payments or going to work, there aren't enough taxes that can save our nation from defaulting to foreign creditors, let alone our own citizens. It isn't just about buying or selling; the Rapture shutters the entire educational system from daycare to universities, with hundreds of thousands of teachers left without jobs. Furthermore, do the people left behind feel compelled to keep paying their bills if something like the Rapture happens?

When we include teens, children, babies, and the mentally disabled… that number of thirty million citizens is significantly higher. The true tally for the United States alone is around 157 million. But even if only 10 percent go up in the Rapture, the impact is catastrophic.

At the very least, at least six months need to transpire between the Rapture (and the collapse of the US) to the rise of a revived Roman Empire through the European Union. This doesn't take into account natural or supernatural disasters that also occur during this time, prolonging these groups from getting their acts together. These left-behind govern-ments come up with a plan in short order to seemingly have some kind of ground to stand on to offer any kind of covenant with Israel. It seems that these events take place during the time between the Rapture and the start of the Tribulation. How long it takes is subject to debate, but two to three years seems reasonable. Here is a list of what we expect to happen during that "gap":

1. A Psalm 83 event occurs that removes the immediate threat to Israel.
2. After Israel succeeds in neutralizing this immediate threat, it establishes a certain degree of safety and security.
3. The Ezekiel 38–39 event (the battle of Gog-Magog) seeks revenge and attacks Israel for its natural resources, wealth, and religious real estate.
4. After God destroys this military coalition, the Jewish Temple is rebuilt. (This takes around a year if the effort is allowed to pro-ceed unimpeded.) Israel currently doesn't have the political will to do this just yet.
5. The world aligns into at least ten regional areas. This might involve more (or less) at the outset, but before it's all said and done, it is ten regions or ten super-nations—all under the same political authority.
6. A global digital currency is established as the main currency of the world.
7. One world religion rises up after the Rapture. This seems to be the result of the failed Psalm 83 and Ezekiel 38–39 wars neutral-izing militant Islam, opening the door for a hybrid Christian/Islam/Hindu/Buddhist/Pagan ecumenical religion. This new reli-gion is accompanied by "lying signs and wonders."

Many possible scenarios can play out as to how specifically the nations align and how they come under the influence of the Antichrist. Since

Satan is in the habit of imitating God, he could bring back another group of ancient people in their own version of a nationalist rebirth, most likely after the wars of Psalm 83 and Ezekiel 38–39. The two most plausible choices are the Kurds or the Assyrians. Both have managed to maintain their ethnic autonomy and currently reside in nations such as Syria, Iraq, Turkey, Iran, and Azerbaijan.

If the Antichrist were to control the majority of the world's oil, he could make "his mark," the reserve currency, in much the same way OPEC enforces all its transactions to be in US dollars (petrodollars). This would force everyone to use it, since we have yet to find a suitable alternative to petroleum-based energy.

Lastly, all the things that need to happen during the Tribulation require more than the seven years allotted for the Seventieth Week of Daniel (Tribulation) itself. While we believe there is a time gap between the Rapture and the Tribulation, we are not dogmatic about exactly how long that period is.

THIRTEEN

WARS AND RUMORS OF WAR

So they asked Him, saying, "Teacher, but when will these things be? And what sign will there be when these things are about to take place?" And He said: "Take heed that you not be deceived. For many will come in My name, saying, 'I am He,' and, 'The time has drawn near.' Therefore do not go after them. But when you hear of wars and commotions, do not be terrified; for these things must come to pass first, but the end will not come immediately. Then He said to them, "Nation will rise against nation, and kingdom against kingdom."

LUKE 21:7–10

IN RESPONDING to the questions posed to Him, Jesus gave a series of signs that would herald the end of the age and His return in power. Interestingly, most things on the list are not signs in and of themselves, but rather, they indicate *how* the signs would come. That is the sign; it's not so much the *what*, but the *how*. They would come like birth pangs upon a pregnant woman, increasing in frequency and intensity and converging upon a single generation.

Of the items listed, and with respect to warfare, the twentieth century has been the bloodiest and most violent century on record. While skeptics will attribute this ghastly reality to the rapid population explosion, the development of weapons of mass destruction, or the introduction of new kinds of warfare (e.g., air, space, subterranean, cyber, etc.), the mind-numbing body count simply belies the reality of something far more ominous: We are that generation.

We know some out there will say, "Hey, wait a minute. There have always been wars! How is our century any different?"

It is true: Wars and rumors thereof have been a mainstay in the human condition since time immemorial. However, as stated above, the twentieth (and now the twenty-first) century stands alone as the bloodiest and most terrifying on record for a reason. Modern technology has afforded frightening new levels of executing violence upon each other. Furthermore, while humankind has always existed in a sinful state and is prone to violence on an individual level, it takes something more to rally whole nations to brutally murder each other. It takes large-scale motivation to galvanize the wrath of a nation into taking up arms against another. This motivation almost always comes in the form of some kind of state-sanctioned propaganda.

> **Propaganda:** the spreading of ideas, information, or rumor for the purpose of helping or injuring an institution, a cause, or a person; ideas, facts, or allegations spread deliberately to further one's cause or to damage an opposing cause.[86]

Although propaganda has been around forever, it wasn't until the twentieth century that it got a supercharge with the advent of mass-communications platforms. What began as an extension of the First Amendment (free speech) and a check on government expansion in the eighteenth and nineteenth centuries was soon co-opted by the government in the twentieth (and twenty-first) to do its messaging.

With the advent of broadcast radio, it soon became easier than ever for governments of one nation to villainize another. Movies were employed for large-scale propaganda (for example, Germany's *Triumph of the Will* and the American *The Great Dictator*); later, television (largely out of Hollywood) got into the action serving as a fifth column for the

US government. It has become an increasingly powerful and effective tool to wield against an intentionally dumbed-down population in influencing a generation.

Nevertheless, while early twentieth-century propaganda can be considered overtly crude, propagandists continued to relentlessly refine their influence operations to the point that, today, most people don't even realize they're being targeted. Regardless of the subtleties, if one simply looks at any message and asks the old Latin question, *Cui bono*? ("who benefits?"), one could easily decipher who is pushing the message and to what end.

But how does government propaganda fit into Jesus' warning about wars and rumors of war? Propaganda is akin to the very oxygen that can fan the flames of war. It feeds a steady diet of lies and half-truths, which nurtures the necessary amounts of irrational hatred toward others in order to dehumanize the other party. This provocation ultimately reaches a point that war (even civil war) becomes the only recourse.

After sacrificing two generations of young men by 1945, the twentieth-century powers that be seemingly lost their appetite for large-scale warfare. "Peace at any cost" became the new mantra. However, with two ideologically opposed and nuclear-armed global powers dominating geopolitics (the US and the USSR), the policy of mutually assured destruction (MAD) required war by other means to become the new standard of warfare in order for each side to keep each other in check. What followed has evolved into one of the greatest psychological-intelligence operations in history.

Rumors of War

Thus, before the dust even settled in Hiroshima and Nagasaki, the new "Cold War" was beginning to heat up. With Mao Tse-tung's defeat of Chiang Kai-shek in 1949, a new post-war era arose. This multi-decade conflict indirectly pitted two superpowers (plus China) against each other, most often fighting in what is known as proxy wars. We saw this to a lesser degree in places like the Taiwan Strait Crisis (1954–55), the Suez Canal (1956–57), the Lebanese Crisis (1958), and the Tibetan Uprising (1959), and in a greater degree in the wars in Korea, Vietnam, and Afghanistan (the 1980s). This Cold War came to increasingly depend upon technology, shadowy intelligence agencies, and Tier-One military operators with seemingly bottomless black budgets to increasingly shape the twentieth century. These clandestine agencies (both civilian and military) began to specialize in what is known as "gray zone" operations, or "asymmetric" warfare. These are military conflicts that are essentially wars without wars, that stay just below the threshold of declared war, and primarily operate in what Carl von Clausewitz once deemed the fog of war.

> War is the realm of uncertainty; three-quarters of the factors on which action in war is based are wrapped in a fog of greater or lesser uncertainty. A sensitive and discriminating judgment is called for; a skilled intelligence to scent out the truth.—Carl von Clausewitz, *On War*[87]

They took what was one of warfare's greatest detriments (confusion) and exploited it. This was done intentionally so that any interested outside parties would have very little understanding of what was actually happening on the ground, or who was fighting whom. This intentional confusion was created to add in both plausible deniability as well as quick exit strategies should they be required. Two recent examples of this are the Syrian Civil War and the 2008–2020 Ukrainian-Russian conflict. This kind of warfare was perfected during the forty-plus years of the Cold War era and was also the same time the US created most of its more than seventeen intelligence agencies, as well as that of the Soviet KGB, Israeli Mossad, and the German *Bundesnachrichtendienst* (BND).

Intelligence agencies made it their mission to collect information on everyone as well as to destabilize and overthrow hostile governments while installing friendly regimes (i.e., friendly to Western interests). This meant that most (if not all) of the twentieth-century *coups d'états* and revolutions were either directly or indirectly funded and managed by Western and Eastern intelligence agencies and their governments. With two powerful and diametrically opposed ideologies competing against each other, the new currency for the second half of the twentieth century was information.

Project Echelon, the largest and most clandestine information-gathering operation in the world, is located at RAF Menwith Hill, North Yorkshire, United Kingdom. The genesis for Echelon began back in World War II as the Allies (United States and United Kingdom) began to collaborate on how to break both the secret code language of the Nazis (Enigma) and the Japanese (Purple). So secretive was this project that most would never have known it existed had the US not revealed these capabilities in our justification to the UN for invading Iraq. While Menwith Hill is still a Royal Airforce Base, ownership of the mission was transferred to the American National Security Agency (NSA) back in the 1970s to cover the growing satellite communications that were beginning to develop.

In summary, Project Echelon is a global network of spy stations that collects millions of communication messages, bank records, Internet records, satellite transmissions, metadata, etc. for analysis and action. All of this data, though, requires massive computer networks (created by Lockheed Martin no less) for storage. While this mass surveillance project began in the UK (initially to bypass our Constitution), we know it works in conjunction with other information-gathering hubs around the world (Pine Gap, AUS; Titanpointe, NYC, etc.). This is being used to collect and sweep all electronic information from "high-profile targets" around the world.[88]

Little did most Americans realize that those same intelligence agencies would become so powerful that, once they had said power, they would never let it go. They justified the Patriot Act after 9/11 by declaring a "War on Terror," only later redefining what "terror" meant to include anyone who disagreed with their globalist agenda. These unelected bureaucrats (whether American or otherwise) would collect information not just against their foreign enemies, but their domestic ones as well. Furthermore, they would apply those same tried-and-true tactics of regime change not just abroad, but at home as well. We got a full four years of this after Donald Trump announced his candidacy for president in 2015.

Again, the justification for Cold War activities was (according to leaders then) to avoid war, especially nuclear war. Nevertheless, this kind of foreign meddling by "sneaky" intelligence agencies and their special forces usually ended up dragging in their regular army counterparts anyway to clean up their "special military operations."

Again, most of these Cold War operations were designed to contain communism (or, for Soviets, to promote it) and influence foreign affairs without using declared war. Thankfully, the one thing both sides could agree on was that neither wanted World War III. Everyone knew that was a zero-sum game. However, in the Cold War, everything—including currency manipulation, blackmail schemes, bribery, anti-government propaganda, regime change, and targeted political assassinations—was still fair game.

Adding to the creation of all these intelligence agencies and the prolific use of propaganda by media and governments was also the greatest expansion of technological advances the world had ever seen, encompassing:

- Satellite technology and the space race
- The Internet and computers
- Advances in non-nuclear WMD
- Energy and EMP weapons
- Robotization and AI
- Smart technology
- Nanotechnology
- Quantum computing

The greatest challenge that has really come about from these "rumors of wars" is not in the above-mentioned realities (although they bring their own complications into the mix) but in the relentless attack on truth and information that has added so much uncertainty and confusion in the last moments of the last days. The explosion of communication meant it was almost impossible to keep the hard-fought and potentially explosive secrets in, simply due to the number of ways people could now share them.

Nation and Kingdoms

Part of Jesus' description of the last days would be the rise of conflicts between nations and kingdoms. From an English rendering of this passage, it seems redundant to state both. However, as many of you already know, when we look at this in the original Koine Greek, it makes more sense.

The Greek word for "nation" is *ethnos*. It simply means "people"—or, if used about a national group of people, it means "nation."[89] Our English word "ethnic" is derived from this Greek word. Since "*ethnos* is set against *ethnos*" in this context, it must mean a "nation," like Canada or Mexico. On the other hand, the Greek word for "kingdom" is *basileia*, which simply means "the territory ruled over by a king." James Morison elaborates, saying it means, "literally, upon nation. One nation shall rise in its anger to come down upon another." But what is the relationship between nation and kingdom?

At the very least, "nation" and "kingdom" are synonyms for national entities. However, it appears to me from the context that there is a progression from nation (*ethnos*) to a confederation of nations that form a kingdom (*basileia*). Morison says the notion of kingdom could include "greater communities, or empire, embracing within one political sphere various distinct nationalities." If this is the case, then the passage is saying that nations will be fighting against nations and groups of nations will also be fighting against each other.

If this escalation between nations and kingdoms is true, then it certainly causes one to pause and wonder whether these two great global conflicts in the first half of the twentieth century were not a marked departure from all previous wars. If WWI and WWII fit the category of the "mother of all" multi-nation wars, then certainly the seventy-plus years of the Cold War suffices as the "mother of all" rumors of wars.

Technological advancements, media, government mass propaganda, and information warfare have created an almost impenetrable fog of war that has become part of the new normal the world has endured for the past seventy years. An old Russian joke says, "The future is certain; it is only the past that is unpredictable." Thanks to historical revisionism, faulty calendars, and newly discovered translations, it's not just the Russians who are wondering about the past any longer.

Nothing is what it seems. History is not what it was. The future is not what we think. There is so much confusion these days about where we are and where we are heading that it seems this is exactly where Satan wants us to be: confused and beleaguered to the point of apathy. He has been busy sowing distress and perplexity amongst the nations solely so he can bring them to the point of desperation wherein everyone will willingly trade their liberty for security. Therefore, for the born-again believer, living in these final years requires an incredible amount of discernment that can only come about through the Holy Spirit.

However, given the transformation of communication over the millennia and the rapid development of technology that can spread this misinformation, Jesus prophetically identified the greatest challenge to those living in the final generation. It would not be wars, pandemics, and earthquakes (although their birth-pang-like increase would be troubling); it would be *deception*. This is why Jesus sternly warned at least four times (Matthew's account of the Olivet Discourse) that they (that generation) needed to take great care so as not to be deceived. In other words, He told them, "Keep your head on a swivel and know that these things must increase…but the end is not yet." Well, if the wars began in earnest in 1914 (with the onset of WWI), then certainly the Cold War was the ultimate manifestation of "rumors of war." Now, if we are coming to the end of this particular "pregnancy," what do those birth pangs produce?

A child.

For the earnest expectation of the creation eagerly waits for the revealing of the sons of God. For the creation was subjected to futility, not willingly, but because of Him who subjected it in hope; because the creation itself also will be delivered from the bondage of corruption into the glorious liberty of the children of God. For we know that the whole creation groans and labors with birth pangs together until now. Not only that, but we also who have the firstfruits of the Spirit, even we ourselves groan within ourselves, eagerly waiting for the adoption, the redemption of our body. (Romans 8:19–23, emphasis added)

WEAPONS OF MASS DISTRACTION

The coming of the lawless one is according to the working of Satan,
with all power, signs, and lying wonders, and with all unrighteous
deception among those who perish, because they did not receive the
love of the truth, that they might be saved. And for this reason God
will send them strong delusion, that they should believe the lie.

2 THESSALONIANS 2:9–11, EMPHASIS ADDED

SOMETHING WE'VE OVERLOOKED for years is found at the beginning
of this passage written by Paul in his second letter to the Thessalonians.
Notice it doesn't say "at" the arrival or "after" the arrival of the lawless one,
but at his "coming" (Greek: *parousia*)—as in prior to his arriving fully, in
conjunction with his future arrival. With his (the Antichrist's) coming,
or in the process of his coming/manifesting, the "lawless one" will do so
according to the supernatural outworking or power (Greek: *energeia*) of
Satan.

We like to think of this supernatural process of manifesting as that of
a plough wind or outflow boundary that precedes a major storm front.
It kicks up the wind something fierce and drops the temperature so we
know that a storm is on its way. This is what we're seeing today with
regards to the Luciferian zeitgeist sweeping the planet. Common sense
and reasoning are tossed out the window for those who did not receive
the love of the truth. They are being given over to—and will come to
embrace—the great delusion when it arrives. As we've often said, a global-
level crisis requires a global-level distraction.

And Satan intends to put on one heck of a light show in the moments after the Rapture of the Church. But before we get to that, let's do a quick overview of the differing, yet overlapping constructs that presently exist, and upon which this great delusion will be placed.

Geopolitical

The Times of the Gentiles

The times we are in now were called by Jesus the "times of the Gentiles" (Luke 21:24). This speaks to the ongoing Gentile domination that would basically control the earth during the interim between Christ's First and Second Comings. However, it also includes the following major Gentile powers that preceded the days of Christ, according to Daniel chapters 2, 7–8 and Revelation 17:10. These are Egypt, Assyria (included in Revelation 17:10's "eight"), Babylon (gold/lion), Persia (silver/bear), Greece (bronze/leopard), Rome (iron/ferocious beast), and a future revived Roman Empire (iron mixed with clay).

Rome was the dominant world power in Jesus' day, and in truth, it has never fully lost its power and influence. Western Rome collapsed politically, culturally, militarily, and economically around AD 476, but Eastern Rome (*vis a vis* the Byzantine Empire) continued on until the fifteenth century. Western Rome was revived under the guise of the Holy Roman Empire in AD 800 (the Frankish King Charlemagne) and has since morphed into varying colonial empires until it culminated with the founding of the United States of America, which is a product of the English, Dutch, French, Italian, and Spanish. It's interesting how invested Satan is in keeping this particular empire intact.

Birth Pangs

Addressing the question of the last days, Jesus referred to the horrendous lead-up to the final moments of human history as being similar to that of "birth pangs" (Matthew 24:8). Paul used a similar metaphor in 1 Thessalonians 5:3. Since the signs Jesus mentioned pointing us towards the end are fairly common mainstays throughout the human drama (earthquakes, wars, rumors of wars, pestilences, deception, etc.) what He was referring to was not that they will happen, but *how* they will happen. He said they would increase in both frequency and intensity, like birth pangs, until reaching a crescendo point at the very end of time. One could conclusively argue that the twentieth century certainly achieved that status as being the most violent and transformative century in history.

Spiritual

The Fullness of the Gentiles

Paul spoke of national Israel's spiritual blindness being in place until the "fullness of the Gentiles" has come in (Romans 11:25). While Jesus' comment regarding the Gentiles concerned geopolitical domination, Paul here was describing the populations Jesus would use to build His Church (i.e., the Gentile populations) as the Gospel continued to spread around the world. Like a beautiful mosaic, the Church is being built into a single, yet corporate body of believers from all tribes and tongues during this particular age. The fullness will continue until it is complete and reaches a point known only to God.

Perilous Times

Here there is a paradoxical relationship of sorts, in which, on the one hand, Jesus referred to these times as the "days of Noah" and "days of Lot," speaking to the seeming normalcy bias that will be prevalent upon the earth. On the other hand, Paul called these same days "perilous times" (2 Timothy 3), meaning wickedness will continue to escalate globally until it reaches unprecedented and unbearable levels. So the evil and wickedness that will continue to fester will be so commonplace as to be accepted as normal, or "just the way things are." But even then, the depravity will rise so noticeably toward the end that it will become unbearable to the righteous (similar to how Lot's soul was "vexed" daily in 2 Peter 2:7).

The other writers of the New Testament expressed similar sentiments about the rising tide of evil in the last days (James 5:1–6; 2 Peter 3:3–7; 1 John 2:15–19; Jude 1:14–19). The truth is, we are at the tail-end of this two-thousand-year stretch of time since Christ first walked the earth. It should not surprise us that we are seeing the escalation in both wickedness and entropy as we draw near to the conclusion of the convergence of Bible prophecy.

Technology

Having briefly discussed both the geopolitical and spiritual conditions of the world upon reaching the last days, let us move on to events now that are moving us even faster into the final moments. Think about all of the recent twenty-first-century concepts that have been introduced into our modern lexicon of common knowledge through pop culture, academia, science, and even government sanctions. These are redefining reality for many people and are expanding, in our honest opinion, the venues Satan will use to introduce delusion and confusion. For example:

- The Internet of things (IoT)
- Blockchain
- The metaverse
- The multiverse
- Cryptocurrency
- AI cloud services
- 5G bandwidth
- Graphene
- Singularity
- Quantum computing
- Artificial general intelligence
- UAPs (unidentified aerial phenomena)

- Critical race theory
- Multi-domain operations
- The gray zone

Now, most of these things are not necessarily evil in and of themselves. But they are tools that will be used to enslave humanity. We would venture to say that, prior to the year 2000, none of these items on this list were commonly known or understood outside a small, select group of military, scientific, or academic professionals. Even then, it was almost always in the theoretical sense, never as an actual or physical reality. For instance, we've known about quantum physics since Albert Einstein walked the earth, but it was only a theory that seemed plausible. It wasn't until 1998 that there was an actual physical quantum computer, even if it was a rudimentary version of what we have today.[90]

The term "Internet of things" (IoT) was first coined/defined in 1999, but it wasn't really implemented until 2002–03. Again, its beginning was embryonic. Blockchain technology (as a reality) was unheard of until 2008. If we'd gone up to someone prior to the advent and development of smart devices and asked about cloud services, very few (if any) would understand what that meant. Graphene was discovered to be a byproduct of graphite in 2004. Not only was it found to be harder than steel and thinner than paper, but it conducted both electricity and radio frequencies extremely well. Many researches have suggested that the reason graphine (in the form of nanoparticles) was purposefully added into several variants of the recent mRNA vaccines was so that it could later be triggered by governments (and other entities) by using 18 GHz pulse blasts should the need ever be required.[91]

Below is an abstract from an article titled: "Potential of Graphene-based Materials to Combat COVID-19: Properties, Perspectives, and Prospects," found on the National Library of Medicine website:

Severe acute respiratory syndrome coronavirus 2 (SARS-CoV-2), a new virus in the coronavirus family that causes coronavirus disease (COVID-19), emerges as a big threat to the human race. To date, there is no medicine and vaccine available for COVID-19 treatment. While the development of medicines and vaccines are essentially and urgently required, *what is also extremely important is the repurposing of smart materials to design effective systems for combating COVID-19. Graphene and graphene-related materials (GRMs) exhibit extraordinary physicochemical, electrical, optical, antiviral, antimicrobial, and other fascinating properties that warrant them as potential candidates for designing and development of high-performance components and devices required for COVID-19 pandemic and other futuristic calamities.* In this article, we discuss the potential of graphene and GRMs for healthcare applications and how they may contribute to fighting against COVID-19. (Emphasis added)[92]

The article was dated just prior to the delivery of COVID-19 mRNA therapies by Moderna and Pfizer. The intent of mentioning it here is simply to say that science and medical research have long been looking at adding graphene to injectables as a means of exploiting its properties with regard to putting technology into the human body.

As crazy as that sounds, artificial intelligence was popularly known long before the year 2000, but only as a category of science fiction—never in reality. Certainly, things like "singularity" were theoretical concepts prior to the turn of the century, but its reality seemed about as distant as putting humans on Mars. Now it is within reach.

The same idea goes with things like the gray zone. Obviously, people knew what irregular, guerrilla, and hybrid warfare meant prior to the turn of the century, but the gray zone definition (the space between peace and war) took on a whole new meaning when multi-domain operations came to be. They expanded conflict beyond simply land, sea, and air to include space, cyberspace, information technology, and the subterranean realms (multi-domain operations). Now mankind must also contend with the very real cyber world of the metaverse (adds complexity), as well as the fictional yet delusional concept of the multiverse (adds confusion).

Lying Signs and Wonders

Speaking of confusion, UAPs (formerly known as UFOs) became the *official* government definition that describes the unknown entities gallivanting unchallenged across our atmosphere while breaking the laws of physics. Clearly, the presence of UFOs had been common knowledge during the mid to late twentieth century but was a thing the government either profusely denied existing, or at least denied admitting publicly until 2017. Now that the governments of the world have officially acknowledged their existence, you can bet this information will be used in the future to muddy the waters surrounding the Rapture of the Church.

Something curious has happened recently that has a lot of Bible prophecy watchers both perplexed and excited. The US government has finally come out of the UFO-denial closet and admitted something the general public already knew and had been saying for decades:

UFOs are real.

Up until about three years ago, the US government had been vigorously hiding information (via classification systems) about the existence of UFOs or UAPs, as they are now known, from the general public for at least seventy years. The government routinely found itself in a major catch-22. On one hand, officials either refused to comment on it publicly—or if/when it did, they chose outright denial. On the other hand, they were simultaneously maintaining all information about the subject at the highest levels of security classification, (formerly known as the code name UMBRA), which really meant they do have relative information about the subject to keep from the public.

UMBRA: In the annals of intelligence, no word is more associated with secret government intelligence reports, especially those produced for policymakers based on raw intelligence. This undisclosed information included UFO reports in the 1950s; the most brittle reporting on Soviet leadership intentions; and intercepted phone calls between Chinese and Pakistani nuclear officials. Way back when—at least since the middle of the 1950s—the intelligence community used the UMBRA code word to inform the reader of a certain report that the *original source* for the intelligence was of the most sensitive category. At the National Security Agency (NSA) back then, there were three levels of source sensitivity. UMBRA was the five-letter code word used for Category III sources. If a document was stamped "TOP SECRET UMBRA" at the top and the bottom, you'd know the agency had gone to great lengths to obtain the embedded information.[93]

Let's be honest: If UFOs weren't a real thing, they wouldn't have anything to classify as UMBRA, right? We mean, does the US government have classified information on Santa Claus, the Easter Bunny, and the Decepticons? We're guessing they don't, largely because these are all imaginary entities. However, by that same standard, why would the government keep information about UFOs/UAPs at the highest classification level if they weren't real?

Nevertheless, the fact that everyone knows the government keeps this "secret" has become one of the longest-running jokes in pop-culture history. In fact, it has spawned an entire conspiracy-theory genre (G-Men, Men in Black, etc.) popularized by television shows like *The X-Files* and *Fringe*, as well as movies like *Independence Day*, *Men in Black 1–3*, and *Stargate*. These shows have themes centered on the government's full knowledge (and full denial) of dimensional portals, extraterrestrials, interstellar travel, and other deep-fringe topics.

All the same, it's not as if the public needs the federal government to admit something spooky is happening in our atmosphere for them to believe. There is simply too much evidence of it already (via video, photos, eyewitnesses, etc.) floating through the ethersphere. With the rapid advent of technology, this evidence has evolved somewhat spectacularly. It isn't just the grainy 8mm footage caught by some loner with shaky hands on a dark country road anymore. It's closed-circuit television (CCTV) footage from the International Space Station. Its declassified Apollo mission footage showing aircraft (or something) flying out of the Moon. Its military and Federal Aviation Administration (FAA) radar and forward-looking infrared (FLIR) camera footage from elite military aircraft. It is eyewitness testimony from reluctant, but freaked-out, airline pilots.

However, the US government's recent admissions of funding top-secret initiatives to study these supernatural events is finally removing the stigma and doubt many have had regarding the issue. One might liken it to the floodgates being opened.

In 2021, Senator Marco Rubio (R-FL), chairman of the Senate Intelligence Committee, quietly included an interesting clause into the 2020–2021 Senate Intelligence Authorization Act, which was signed into law by President Trump. The clause directed the Department of National Intelligence (DNI), in partnership with the Department of Defense and other agencies, to prepare a declassified brief to the Senate Intelligence Committee no later than June 25, 2021, with their assessments on the subject of unidentified anomalous aircraft. The premise for the added language centers on our national security and whether or not the numerous reports of unidentified anomalous aircraft flying unchallenged over the US and its territories pose a threat to these areas. Speaking to this:

John Ratcliffe, who served as director of national intelligence under former President Donald Trump, was asked on Fox News by host Maria Bartiromo what he knows about unidentified flying objects that have captured people's imaginations for generations.

"There are a lot more sightings than have been made public," Ratcliffe said. "Some of those have been declassified. And when we talk about sightings, we are talking about objects that have been seen by Navy or Air Force pilots, or have been picked up by satellite imagery that frankly engage in actions that are difficult to explain. Movements that are hard to replicate that we don't have the technology for. Or traveling at speeds that exceed the sound barrier without a sonic boom."

After saying that there have been sightings all around the world, Ratcliffe insisted that reports of "unidentified aerial phenomena" already in the public eye are only part of the bigger picture.

"When we talk about sightings, the other thing I will tell you is, it's not just a pilot or just a satellite, or some intelligence collection," Ratcliffe said. "Usually we have multiple sensors that are picking up these things, and…some of these are unexplained phenomenon, and there is actually quite a few more than have been made public."[94]

The Truth Is OUT There

Since at least the late 1970s, increasing public pressure has been building for the government to either release the information it has on the subject, or at least publicly acknowledge its existence. There have even been a few court cases wherein people and organizations have sued the government *vis a vis* the Freedom of Information Act (FOIA) to get them to disclose the truth.[95]

The truth is that there are a great many things operating over our nation's airspace that the collective "we" don't understand. Although many sightings can be explained or debunked, others defy explanation. This pressure—and in some cases, sheer curiosity—has also funded NASA ventures like SETI (Search for Extraterrestrial Intelligence).

In 2007, then Senate leader, Harry Reid (D-NV), had appropriated funds ($22 million) and approval to begin the Advanced Aerospace Threat Identification Program (AATIP) to further look into the same things Senator Rubio is attempting to get investigated nearly twelve years later. The program officially ended in 2012 when the funding priorities shifted to other areas, but unofficially, it continued until 2017. Lue Elizondo, a former intelligence officer and the director of AATIP from 2007–17, has since come out of the shadows and has spoken rather candidly about the existence of all this, and has arguably moved the needle on the discussion from "kook-fringe" into the mainstream. Thus far, he has been interviewed by *60 Minutes*, CNN, Fox, and dozens of other news and media agencies.

Elizondo would, admittedly, rather not discuss who these things are or what their intentions might be; rather, he simply addresses the capabilities these "aircraft" demonstrate that seemingly defy our laws of physics. He's seen multi-sensor reports that show these "aircraft" traveling at speeds up to 15,000 mph and make 90-degree turns at these same great speeds without deceleration. This far exceeds any known technology anyone has on planet earth as of 2022. By our laws of physics, this is an impossibility, given the limitations we face with mass, inertia, g-forces (gravitational forces—positive, negative, and linear), structural limits, etc.

Setting aside the aircraft for a moment, the pilots of these crafts (if they are biological entities) would still be affected by g-forces. According to the tolerance levels as described in NASA's *Bioastronautics Data Book*, (SP-3006, 1964), "G Tolerance in 4 vectors," the average human (without a special suit and training) can usually only withstand 6Gs (positive gravitational forces; i.e., the feeling of pressure in a turn) before losing consciousness. A US F-16 jet can withstand up to a little over 10 Gs before structural damage begins to occur. Many of these UFO crafts have been observed doing 300–400 Gs, well beyond the limits of any technology we humans possess. Given such advanced capabilities these other-earthly flying objects have exhibited, if movies like *Independence Day*, *Avengers*, *Transformers*, and *War of the Worlds* are true (many people without a biblical worldview believe they are), then these statistics are truly frightening. Such a great difference in technology appears that it would be like sending our modernized 101st Airborne Division back in time with all of their modern equipment to fight in the Civil or Revolutionary War. It wouldn't even be fair.

However, Elizondo went on to clarify the seeming contradiction in what eyewitnesses are seeing versus what we know as the truth about our present physical reality. Speaking to the seemingly law-defying feats these *trans-medium aircraft* (meaning they function at the same level of efficiency whether in air, space, or water) operate at:

> They're not breaking the laws of physics, there just seems to be an understanding of quantum physics in a way that we have not yet been successfully…able to apply, specifically as it relates to Einstein's "space and time." We are all used to Newtonian Physics that came about at the end of the Renaissance. Sir Isaac Newton, presented

the physics we are all comfortable with, gravity, an apple falling from the tree, Force = Mass x Acceleration, etc., etc. Then came along last century, a guy with crazy hair named Einstein, who proposes that there is actually a different model for the universe. In fact that while Newtonian Physics is true, there is an overlaying physics called Relativity where space-time is actually connected, not separate, and that space-time is flexible, you can compress it, and you can stretch it. In fact, mass does it, mass perturbs space-time. Then, of course, forty years ago, Quantum Physics really begins to come out and rock science on its heels.... It turns out that Quantum Physics has some very elegant solutions for the things we are seeing for this phenomenon.[96] —Luis Elizondo, the Basement Office Interview

If this is true, and these otherworldly visitors understand quantum physics like we understand Newtonian physics, then we are the Aztecs and they are the Spanish Conquistadors. Perhaps our government understood how woefully underprepared we were to fight this (if it ever came to that) and decided to shield the public from this terrible truth.

That, of course, is a fair argument to make on behalf of the government. However, its refusal to acknowledge these bizarre phenomena has only added fuel to the conspiracy-theory fire. Thus far, the government's ability to shield itself against lawful requests via the Freedom of Information Act (FOIA)—by layering its information with strata of classification labels—seems to finally have run its course. Has full disclosure finally seen its day? Or will the government double down on returning to the 1950s-level Project Blue Book by throwing the baby out with the bathwater on every sighting, regardless of how credible?

The revelation of June 25, 2021's Senate hearing was less than overwhelming. Nevertheless, what was astonishing was the US government's final public admission (after more than seventy years of secrecy) that there are things traversing our atmosphere and heavens that we have little to no understanding of.

And there will be signs in the sun, in the moon, and in the stars; and on the earth distress of nations, with perplexity, the sea and the waves roaring; men's hearts failing them from fear and the expectation of those things which are coming on the earth, for the powers of the heavens will be shaken. (Luke 21:25–26, emphasis added)

For believers who take their Bibles seriously, there is little doubt as to what these so-called extraterrestrial beings really are: demons or fallen angels (depending on how you interpret their nature). They employ what is known as "transmedium travel," meaning these vehicles possess the ability to travel through multiple environments with seeming ease (space, high-earth orbit, low-earth orbit, the varying atmospheres, and even water).

The truth is, these crafts are interdimensional in nature, which is why they either don't have to obey our laws of physics or understand it so much better than we do. In his book, *Fallen: Sons of God and the Nephilim*, Tim Chaffey addressed how the demonic activity has changed through the centuries, and how that deception seems to morph with how fast humanity advances. If we were to go back to Europe in the Dark Ages, large populations claimed to have seen sylvan, elves, and fairies. Fast-tracking to our modern era, these same sightings are now sophisticated and unexplainable *aircraft*. These supernatural sightings always seem to coalesce with the technology available at the time.[97]

For example, if a fifteenth-century peasant had seen a silvery, disk-shaped UFO with blinking lights whizzing through the sky, it would have made zero sense to him, because there was nothing he could compare it to (aside from birds). Therefore, the supernatural has to be relatable to the times in which people live in order for the deception to be relevant (hence, the fairies and werewolves, etc.) Similarly, this is why, instead of seeing massive reports of fairies and werewolves in the twenty-first century, we see UFOs and other strange phenomena. They are ever-present, but just outside the grasp of 100 percent, rock-solid verification. Furthermore, given the immensity of our universe, why do these almost always hover around the earth or our moon? Surely, if there were life outside of earth in other places, they would be more exciting than our complicated little blue rock.

For those who have had close contact of the fifth kind (personal contact) with these beings, almost all of the unidentified entities somehow have a "New Age" message to bring to the hapless earthlings. These aliens seem very keen on dissuading everyone they contact to avoid Jesus (and Christians) at all costs. My question is always if Jesus wasn't who He said He was (God in the flesh), then why should they care? Why should they care about some Jewish Messiah wannabe who lived and died nearly two thousand years ago? Why don't they warn people about Buddha, Mohammed, or Joseph Smith?

Because these men are dead and have gone onto their final, eternal destination.

Also, the enemies never attack the fakes. They pose no threat to them.

Now, what, as believers, are we to do with all this information?

Jesus stated that one of the markers of the last days would be that the world would see signs in the sun, moon, and stars. Do these signs include demonic deception in the heavens? It sure seems so. Now, if we correlate this idea with the ongoing desensitization we are being exposed to from godless Hollywood (since the 1940s), and knowing both seem to serve the same master, Satan, it seems much more likely.

Since the rebirth of the nation of Israel in 1948, Satan realizes he is living on borrowed time. More to the point, he realizes the Rapture of the Church could happen at any moment, and thus has taken off the kid gloves to wage an all-out deception campaign to introduce as much confusion and doubt about the Rapture as possible.

You might be asking: What does the Rapture have to do with UFOs and aliens?

Well, in a majority of close encounters in which humans have either been visited or abducted by these strange "grays," all come back with the same or similar messages from these "heavenly" visitors.

Dr. Leo Sprinkle, PhD, Professor Emeritus of counseling at Wyoming University, summarizes the experiences by saying: "UFO contactees have been chosen...no UFO contact is accidental...and that the manifestations are designed to influence the worldview of contactees."[98]

What follows is a summary of these claims about UFO experiences and related conditions:

- UFO contactees have been chosen; no UFO contact is accidental.
- Contactees are ordinary people who exhibit a caring or a loving concern for all humankind.
- UFO experiences include paraphysical, parapsychological, and spiritual manifestations that are designed to influence the "world view" of contactees.
- Contactees are programmed for a variety of "future" activities, including awareness of their own contacts and desire to share their messages and knowledge with other contactees.
- The lives of contactees move in the direction of greater self-awareness, greater concern for the welfare of planet earth, and a greater sense of cosmic citizenship with other beings in the universe.
- The personal metamorphosis of UFO contactees is the forerunner of a social transformation in human consciousness, which now is leading to changes in the economic, educational, military, political, and religious institutions of nations of the Earth: the "New Age" of true science and spirituality.[99]

Even if we dismiss their testimonies of physically being taken into a spaceship and probed, what stands out is the consistent theme these "deceiving spirits" impart to those they harass. In the list below, I have added in parentheses the likely reason they are saying these things.

1. Adam and Eve were not the only ones; there is life on many planets. *(You are not unique; Jesus is not unique.)*

2. They (the aliens) put Adam and Eve here and/or sped up the evolutionary process by planting Adam and Eve in the Garden. *(This is their attempt to disconnect the creation from the Creator.)*

3. They are here to either preserve the world from destruction or shepherd the survivors of the coming apocalypse *(nuclear/environmental, not biblical)*.

4. Many people will be taken to seed life on other planets *(possible Rapture explanation)*.

5. Humanity was about to take another huge evolutionary step forward. *(The mark of the Beast could be sold as enabling this.)*

As Christians, we know Satan is a defeated enemy. We also know how this all ends. For us, the beginning of the end is our glorious "catching up" at the true top-secret event, the Rapture of the Church. Since the Holy Spirit, working through the Church, serves as the Restrainer of evil in this current dispensation, we can assume that, after our departure, this restraint against deceiving spirits will be lifted and there will be some sort of full-scale "invasion" by these beings. Now, we're not going to be dogmatic about exactly how that plays out, but the Rapture itself will be a supernatural event that will shake the world's understanding of reality to its core. What we should take note of is that we are starting to see this deception campaign ramp up like never before. If we are seeing what is necessary for after the Rapture, then just how close must we be to the event itself?

Those left behind will want—no, *need*—to make sense of what just happened, and in this moment of great crisis and calamity, a man will come forth who seemingly has the answers. Simultaneous to this will be some large-scale disclosure during this time between the Rapture and the beginning of the Seventieth Week of Daniel. All those events that transpire exceed the scope of our discussion here, but suffice it to say these beings will somehow make contact and give their full endorsement and supernatural backing to this coming Man of Sin. *Lying signs and wonders* indeed!

What do all of the aforementioned twenty-first-century technologies and realities have in common? Well, as prophecy expert and pastor Dr.

Andy Woods has often said, "These things always point toward the fulfillment of Bible prophecy; never away from it." Just as the geopolitical
unwinding and cultural wickedness points mankind toward the end of
the age, so too has the rise of these advanced digital, economic, scientific,
and military concepts and technologies, as well as extraterrestrial visits,
thrust us into the conditions necessary for the final week of years to manifest—the dreaded Seventieth Week of Daniel.

When that final Gentile kingdom (the Beast) comes to power, it
will bring the first person since Nimrod who is able to physically control the entire human population all at the same time. Many powerful
empires have come and gone, but none have been able to do that. In
Nimrod's day, his absolute control was due to the limited population
(descendants of Shem, Ham, and Japheth) and the confined geographic
location (plains of Shinar) where the entire human population lived that
enabled him to do it. In our day, it will be the aforementioned technologies that will entrap humanity under an authoritarian system so brutal
and wicked that there will be no escape (save death) for those who seek
freedom (Revelation 13:7). Indeed, people around the world will marvel
at the power of this final kingdom and ask, "Who is able to make war
with him?" As with this particular scenario, we are going to focus on
the brief period between the Rapture of the Church and the start of the
Seventieth Week of Daniel. We don't know how long that gap of time is,
but knowing what will need to transpire may help us better understand
a general time frame.

- The battle of Gog and Magog
- The coalescing of the ten-nation/region empire
- Rebuilding the Third Temple
- (Re)Building the city of Babylon

These are things that must happen and yet don't seem to fit wholly
within the confines of the Seventieth Week proper. We know (or at least,
strongly presume) that the Rapture event itself will throw the world into

chaos. We know (or presume) that the ten kings, the False Prophet, and the Antichrist (whoever that may be) will use that time to consolidate their power. While chaos in and of itself is a powerful enough catalyst to consolidate power, it's not enough to assuage the growing panic that will consume the nations of the world, particularly those with Christians in them. For example, there is presumably more residual knowledge of what the Rapture is in, say, Australia, versus Nepal. The reason is fairly simple. One nation has more Christians talking/discussing/arguing about the Rapture versus a nation with hardly any Christians at all.

For nations that have a decent-sized population of born-again Christians, a satanic excuse for what just happened (Rapture) will be provided. Whether that event is attributed to extraterrestrials, Gaia cleansing the earth, or a zombie apocalypse (or a combination of the three), those reasons cannot exist in a vacuum. It requires both the preparatory groundwork (where we are now) as well as a sufficient enough illusionary façade or charade to deceive the left-behind masses. It won't be necessary to overwhelmingly convince everyone, but it needs to be enough to introduce sufficient reasonable doubt or confusion into the situation that nobody really knows what to believe. Whatever deception it ends up being, as long as it's not the Rapture, Satan will use it. This confusion/deception will become particularly exacerbated if this can also coincide with a Singularity-like event. Imagine the following scenario:

The Rapture of the Church happens on a particular day. In the hours following the event, city and state law and emergency officials quickly become inundated and then overwhelmed with calls and responses to fires, vehicle crashes, and looting. The states appeal for federal aid, but the federal government is thrown equally into the chaos, as numerous politicians, judges, and federal officials are missing.

The executive branch approves a hasty Department of Defense request to initiate martial law, which is quickly adopted by each of the fifty states. In the interim, the United States government shuts down and moves its executive branch operations to Camp David. Simultaneously, nations around the world begin to initiate varying forms of martial law, lockdowns, and complete news blackouts.

Within a week of the event, most major cities are burning and have been looted to the point of insolvency. The government (or what remains) initiates its Zombie Apocalypse Kill Switch (ZAKS) program in predetermined locations (with 5G access) to neutralize/minimalize the lawlessness in those major urban areas. They hand over much of the day-to-day functioning to the new quantum AI program that keeps the major nuclear and other highly sensitive facilities running unmanned. The remaining government also institutes safe havens at hundreds of newly built FEMA camps strategically located outside of major urban areas. Military bases, already suffering significant loss of personnel, are converted to housing for any survivors who can make it there.

The Internet is not entirely shut down, but is throttled and censored to such a degree that using it is impractical. Meanwhile, network communications (radio, broadband, and even some satellites) are either not working or are being so heavily censored by the backup AI bots that communication is at a standstill. Information is the new currency, and no one seems to know what's really happening.

A broadcast designed to calm the masses begins to make hourly reports that a new, regional government is forming and nations around the world are signing on. Information is still forthcoming, but it appears that people are moving toward the coasts and resettling into sanctuary communities.

In the meantime, the skies overhead have turned kinetic, with a marked increase in frenzied activities of UAPs and other anomalous events causing people to become panicked and increasingly frightened. The rural areas are given over to the gangs and criminals, who set up mobile "Mad Max" fiefdoms with cruel efficiency. However, as locations begin to run scarce on food and fuel, the gangs move in, spreading like locusts. Those who have chosen to remain in the country are increasingly faced with the rapid entropic effect of nature's reclaiming of towns and the increase in and brazenness of wild animals.

Cities and states less impacted by the Rapture (the Pacific Northwest and North Atlantic) remain more intact longer than those in the nation's Bible Belt. Still, everywhere is affected equally by the loss of children and babies, causing immediate and profound angst and misery amongst the left-behind communities. Residents of Utah and other areas heavily populated with Mormons seem the most perplexed, yet best prepared for the ensuing lawlessness as they declare their independence from what was previously the United States of America.

As the United States rapidly disintegrates along ethnic and racial lines, tribalism sets in, and once-vibrant communities quickly see an escalation in violence and threats of violence. Likewise, this disintegration becomes evident at the national level, as Europe, Africa, and Asia quickly succumb to tribalism as their respective governments collapse economically. The United Nations calls a number of emergency meetings and decides that the most-intact nation for each of the ten regions is given charge to begin reorganizing into a regional authority.

Satan realizes several things up front.

First, he has no idea when the Rapture will happen, so he must maintain a heightened state of readiness at all times. This is a tremendous argument in favor of the Pre-Tribulation Rapture, since, if it were to occur within the confines of the Seventieth Week itself, it could be figured out rather easily. All Satan would have to do is wait for the midpoint, or the seal, trumpet, and bowl judgments, and then it would happen. But since it occurs prior to any part of the Seventieth Week, and the crisis the Rapture produces triggers the rest of the events, Satan doesn't know. No one knows,, except God Himself. That is why John wrote in his epistle:

> Little children, it is the last hour; and as you have heard that the Antichrist is coming, even now many antichrists have come, by which we know that it is the last hour. (1 John 2:18)

John distinguished between the Antichrist who is coming and the many antichrists who have already come, because, again, Satan doesn't know. He has to continually put forth candidates that turn out not to be the Antichrist because it's not yet time. But the moment the lightning-fast Rapture occurs, Satan *will have* to have his man in a position to assume authority quickly. That is why, even now, he is wasting no time in prepping the world to be ready for his final kingdom. He is enabling humankind to speed up technology. He is opening Pandora's Box of the occult, supernatural, and metaphysical so that we are desensitized to its presence once it manifests. He is darkening people's minds to embrace and normalize wickedness so that its arrival will seem normal and commonplace instead of shocking.

Second, Satan must frontload (or preload) as much as he can of this final kingdom into our current construct today so that he can save time on the back side (post-Rapture). The problem he is continually running into is the Restrainer (the Holy Spirit-infused Body of Christ upon the earth), who is serving as salt and light in an increasingly dark world. As soon as Satan has some major gain in one part of the world, revival breaks out in another. Satan rushes in to crush or corrupt that movement, and another divine event happens that disrupts his plans. In other words, Satan has been stuck in the "whack-a-mole" business for the past two thousand years, which has been effectively disrupting and slowing down his plans of global domination.

> Then the devil, taking Him up on a high mountain, showed Him all the kingdoms of the world in a moment of time. And the devil said to Him, "*All this authority I will give You, and their glory; for this has been delivered to me, and I give it to whomever I wish. Therefore, if You will worship before me, all will be Yours.*" (Luke 4:5–7, emphasis added)

Although Satan spoke truthfully (albeit selectively) in his conversation while tempting Jesus in the wilderness, his ability to control the flow of kingdoms is still at the discretion of God's timing and purpose (Daniel 4:17; Acts 17:26). God determines their times and boundaries, and has decreed through divine judgment (the Flood, Babel, Babylon, etc.) the who, what, when, where, and why humanity progresses or stalls in its inevitable march towards the end. To this point, Satan has overplayed his hand over and over with regard to rushing ahead of God's timing.

But the fact that it is all seemingly coming together now, in our day, reinforces this idea put forth by Paul of being eyewitnesses to the Antichrist's *parousia* (coming) and the level of preparation required for this final kingdom to become a reality. This is why it is not just the threats of violence and the wickedness that are skyrocketing now, but the distractions of pop culture and modernity as well. In the US Army, almost every command is made up of different sections that handle everything from personnel and logistics to operations and information. The operations cell is usually broken down into two components—current ops and future ops. Current ops regard everything that will take place within the next forty-eight hours. Future ops are concerned with everything beyond that. The world right now (to include you and us) is being so inundated with current ops (work, family, bills, careers, news, politics, etc.) that we can't really see the forest for the trees any longer. We're moving from crisis to crisis without really being able to connect the dots.

As watchmen, though, we are peeking beyond the daily grind to the big picture of what is transpiring. We are seeing the Luciferian mosaic coming together, and are doing our best to warn our lost family and friends about what is coming. The sad truth is, while most will admit that something is not right in the world, most aren't ready to hear what is coming upon the earth. People have become addicted to this reality and to this world that is quickly passing away.

Do you not remember that when I was still with you I told you these things? And now you know what is restraining, that he may be revealed in his own time. For the mystery of lawlessness is already at work; *only He who now restrains will do so until He is taken out of the way. And then* the lawless one will be revealed, whom the Lord will consume with the breath of His mouth and destroy with the brightness of His coming. (2 Thessalonians 2:5–8, emphasis added)

If God isn't actively handing over the domains and nations of this world to Satan in the present, then He is, at least tacitly, allowing the Antichrist's kingdom to come to fruition insomuch as the Restrainer allows it. Nevertheless, as ominous and encroaching as this Antichrist kingdom appears on our horizon, it cannot come into its full manifestation so long as the Church physically remains on the earth. While that is encouraging news, it is also news that hearkens us to ramp up our evangelism efforts to share the Gospel and the prophetic truths with a lost and dying world.

Yes, salvation is the chief aim here, but if they will not listen or heed to the Holy Spirit's persistent drawing to Christ, then they should at least know what's coming—in the same vein as Christ telling His disciples of future events so that when those things happened, they would believe (John 13:19; 14:29; and 16:4). We don't think it's any mistake or coincidence that, at precisely the same time the Antichrist's kingdom is on the verge of physical manifestation, the message of salvation through Christ will have found its greatest avenue for reaching all the earth in the form of the Internet. Preachers now are able to minister not just to those in their congregations, but to people around the world. Bible teachers are finding enormous online audiences of people in all nations who are starving (locally) as spiritual famine comes upon the land. This book and chapter will be shared by many, and will reach many more people around the world far beyond what even we know.

We tell you all this not to woo you with our intelligence, knowledge, or writing skills, but to urge you to get busy sharing the Good News of salvation and Christ's soon return. Get busy in your own circles of influence, whether that be at work or home. Be bold(er) and do not worry about what others say. If the current world system had its way, the Gospel, the Bible, and Bible prophecy would be banned entirely from every channel and every pulpit. Don't wait for permission, because the world will never give it—or, if it does, that consent will come with strings attached. Be bold for the sake of Christ, because we are quickly running out of daylight.

And we urge you, brethren, to recognize those who labor among you, and are over you in the Lord and admonish you, and to esteem them very highly in love for their work's sake. Be at peace among yourselves. Now we exhort you, brethren, warn those who are unruly, comfort the fainthearted, uphold the weak, be patient with all. See that no one renders evil for evil to anyone, but always pursue what is good both for yourselves and for all. Rejoice always, pray without ceasing, in everything give thanks; for this is the will of God in Christ Jesus for you. Do not quench the Spirit. Do not despise prophecies. Test all things; hold fast what is good. Abstain from every form of evil. Now may the God of peace Himself sanctify you completely; and may your whole spirit, soul, and body be preserved blameless at the coming of our Lord Jesus Christ. He who calls you is faithful, who also will do it. (1 Thessalonians 5:12–24)

FIFTEEN

THE BEAST OUT OF THE SEA

Then I stood on the sand of the sea. And I saw *a beast rising up out of the sea*, having seven heads and ten horns, and on his horns ten crowns, and on his heads a blasphemous name.

REVELATION 13:1, EMPHASIS ADDED

THE END STATE from the global elite's perspective is a one-world government, a system that functions as a techno-humanist oligarchy. They envision the world being rid of any nationalist leanings and wholly given over to the idea of a single imperial government running the international affairs regionally. And they have worked diligently for many decades now to get it to this point. They've had the long game. The short sprints. They've used manipulative schemes to frighten the masses into surrendering their rights by politicizing crisis after crisis. They've encouraged the spirit of Antichrist that, itself, lends air to lawlessness and social/cultural wickedness. They've finally orchestrated enough of the influential governments to create powerful Orwellian technologies to gain the upper hand for command and controlling the populations. Then, the mother of all crises happens: Hundreds of millions of people just suddenly disappear. They finally have the requisite global crisis they need to cement this plan they've been staging for decades to bring to fruition. Now they are here.

This is the Beast (imperial government) rising out of the sea (of humanity).

197

Undoubtedly, Revelation 13:1 is one of the most prophetically loaded passages in all of the Bible. Reading through it one-dimensionally (as either entirely symbolic or completely literal), we miss the unique quality of the book of Revelation. Don't get us wrong; we are in the D. L. Cooper "Golden Rule of Interpretation" hermeneutical crowd—taking the literal, grammatical, historical view:

> When the plain sense of scripture makes common sense, seek no other sense; therefore, take every word at its primary, ordinary, usual, literal meaning *unless* the facts of the immediate context, studied in the light of related passages and axiomatic and fundamental truths indicate clearly otherwise.[100] —Dr. D. L. Cooper

However, even faithful adherence to this view renders our understanding of Revelation with some shortcomings and inconsistencies that are hard to wrap our heads around. Walk through this with us and, by the end, you will have (we hope) a much clearer understanding of all the horns, heads, and crowns that describe the last government coming upon the earth.

So let's begin by saying this: You can read the book of Revelation as being entirely symbolic. A lot of the more liberal or reformed denominations do this. However, if you do this, you will be grossly amiss in a number of places. This is the problem amillennialism, preterism, and postmillennialism run into, in that their symbolism is neither consistent nor is it honest in dealing with the things that are meant to be taken literally. You might get some overarching points correct (such as "God wins in the end"), but you get all or most of the details wrong. Thus, the *entirely symbolic* view is a broken hermeneutic.

Neither should you read the book as being entirely literal ("wooden literalism"). If you do this (as do some denominations and groups), then you will struggle mightily with the symbolism that is harder to codify into tangible (or relatable) explanations. There is also the problem of interpretational consistency, which leads to varying degrees of error across the general understanding of Bible prophecy. For example, if you believe the ten horns (Revelation 13) are ten literal kingdoms, then what do you do with the "Lamb" (Revelation 5:9) having seven horns? Are these kingdoms as well, or are they meant to represent something else? Let us quote the late, great Jack Kelley on this particular issue:

> Seven is the number of supernatural completion and our head is the location of our mind. Seven heads mean that the dragon (Satan) has complete supernatural wisdom. Ten stands for totality and horns are a symbol of authority. Having 10 horns means he has total authority on Earth (1 John 5:19). These attributes allow him to indwell the anti-Christ and lead the unbelieving world to think that they can defeat God in battle and take control of His Kingdom here. The seven crowns tell us that through the anti-Christ Satan will have complete rule over Planet Earth for a time. Rev. 17:17 says God will cause the Kings of the Earth to agree to this because it suits His purpose.[101]

So, given that understanding, the only consistent interpretation is to view the seven horns and eyes that are in/on the Lamb (Revelation 5:9–10) as being His complete authority and omniscience ("sees all"). This would also apply to the ten horns. If we are going to maintain any level of consistency in our symbolism interpretation, then that is the only view we can hold to. But what about the Revived Roman Empire, the ten kings, and the seven mountains, etc.?

Well, when the book of Revelation tells us that a number or symbol is more than just totality or perfection of some attribute, THEN we can apply the more corporeal understanding of what the symbolism is meant to be. First, let us list what we see in Revelation. But let's look at it in the order they should present themselves, and keep in mind that this is *all* in relation to when Revelation was written, how these kingdoms impact or relate to the nation of Israel, and lastly, how they tie in with the imagery from the book of Daniel.

NATION/ ENTITY	DANIEL 2	DANIEL 7-8	REVELATION 13	REV 17
1. Egypt	-	-	-	Fallen
2. Assyria	-	-	-	Fallen
3. Babylon	Head of gold	Lion w/ Wings	"mouth of a lion"	Fallen
4. Persia	Shoulders of silver	Bear w/ 3 ribs in mouth	"feet of a bear"	Fallen
5. Greece	Abdomen of brass	Leopard w/ four wings	"like a leopard"	Fallen
6. Rome	Legs of iron	Dreadful & terrible 4ᵗʰ beast w/ ten horns	Hybrid beast w/ all three attributes	One is (when written)
7. Revived Rome	Feet and toes of iron and clay	A *little horn* (the 11ᵗʰ) who plucks up three	The First Beast rising out of the sea	One is yet to come
The Harlot	-	-	The Second Beast rising in tandem with the First Beast	"Mystery Babylon"

A. Seven Kings (Revelation 17:10): These are the seven global powers that have either controlled or conquered Israel; "five are fallen, one is, one is yet to come."

B. The First Beast: This is a global (multinational) political system. It is this corporate government (oligarchy) that is intrinsically Antichrist in nature. This final political system arises out of the sea of nations. Revelation 17:15 states the "waters" (the sea) are "the peoples, multitudes, nations, and tongues" that make up this final political organization that will have total (seven heads, ten horns, ten crowns) control over the earth. At present, the only organization that *best* encompasses all of these attributes is the United Nations (UN). Yet, at present, the UN doesn't possess this kind of authority, primarily because the US prevents it from doing so.

However, at some point, this political system is personified by this man Antichrist. He becomes the face of it and takes total control over it. He leads the UN (or some rebranded version), and this renamed system represents a "rebirth" of the ancient imperial Roman Empire, much in the same way Israel was reborn as a nation in 1948. The UN takes on this new moniker to strip that uniqueness away from Israel by claiming the UN was reborn first (the UN was founded in 1945, three years prior to Israel's 1948 rebirth). This view also confirms the following prophecy the angel Gabriel gave Daniel:

And after the sixty-two weeks Messiah shall be cut off, but not for Himself; And *the people of the prince who is to come* Shall destroy the city and the sanctuary. (Daniel 9:26, emphasis added)

Historically, we know it was the Romans under the leadership of Titus Vespasian who destroyed the city of Jerusalem and the Temple in AD 70. This rebranding of the UN to some version of a revived Rome carries with it the historical baggage that "we took you away from being a people, and we brought you back" connotation. They may not come out and say it, but this rebranding definitely implies it.

C. Ten Horns: These are the ten kings (who serve in one or several of the following roles: kings, consuls, dictators, decimvir or magistrates, military tribunes, emperors or czars). Out of this first beast (the political system) come ten human rulers who exercise control over it (Daniel 2:41–42; Revelation 12:3). The number ten in biblical numerology signifies completeness or totality, especially regarding human governments. However, *in this case*, we know they are human rulers because Revelation later confirms they are (Revelation 17:12). They either represent individual nations or geopolitical regions, and they are "of one mind." This "one-mindedness" is a form of supernatural control, as it is unnatural for any group to get along, let alone agree on anything completely.

Out of the ten, one arises (the eleventh) to supplant three kings to secure total control over the other seven (for a total of ten). This one who rises up (the "little horn") is the Antichrist. He starts out as the Man of Sin but becomes the "son of perdition" when Satan physically possesses him at the midpoint of the seven-year covenant (2 Thessalonians 2:3).

D. Ten Crowns: These are the ten seats of power/authority/right to rule. The crowns represent the positions of power the kings possess over the ten-kingdom structures of the beast. Remember that in Luke 4:5–6, Satan declared to Jesus (during the wilderness temptation) that he had control of these kingdoms and could give them to whomever he wished.

In this final government, Satan gives control to ten kings, and the crowns represent that appointed authority.

E. Second Beast: The second beast is representative of the false religious system that rises up in tandem with the first beast (the political system). At some point, the False Prophet (religious leader), who actually precedes the Antichrist in order of arrival (in similar fashion to how John the Baptist prepared the way for Christ), becomes the face of this system. He personifies this movement just as Adolf Hitler personified Nazism.

The False Prophet will prepare the way for Antichrist and does this through the implementation of his apostate/Antichrist religious system (the harlot) that rises up in tandem with the Beast's political system. This harlot religion (all religions meshed into one) is not something the world of today would accept. There are far too many differences between Islam and Buddhism, or Hinduism and Roman Catholicism, for them to agree in totality. However, once the Restrainer's influence in the world is removed, these religious systems will unite.

It may be that he, even now, is not a well-known religious leader. He doesn't need to be. He creates a whole new system at least for the first three years. He first appears as a meek and humble man ("horns like a lamb"), but inwardly, he is vicious and wicked; that's why the Bible likens his voice to that of a dragon (Revelation 13:11). In other words, the ideas he puts forth are blasphemous and evil, yet he says them as a well-spoken, soft-mannered person. Furthermore, he, despite his "lamb-like" manner, has real supernatural power.

At a certain point (presumably the midpoint of the Seventieth Week) he directs all earth dwellers, on threat of death, to worship the first Beast (who is now personified by the Antichrist), uses supernatural signs and wonders to deceive the world, and implements the worship of the Beast, the image of the Beast, and the *mark of the Beast* (Revelation 13:11–18).

F. Seven Heads: These are the seven mountains where the harlot and the Beast sit. Again, seven represents perfection and thus indicates that this place may signify (to the people on earth) the most perfect place for global power to sit. Revelation 17:9 seems to indicate that this is a particular geographic location. Given the clues we have in Scripture, this "seems" to lead to Rome, a rebuilt Babylon, or Jerusalem (see also Revelation 11:8). If it is a city built upon seven hills, then there are numerous options.

G. The Harlot: This is the false religious system that arises to global dominance AFTER the Rapture of the Church. She is led by the False Prophet, and rises in tandem with the Beast political system. This system, given the attribute she's given (whore/harlot), appears to combine all religious systems together as being equally valid. It is the mechanism by which the great martyrdom against followers of Christ arises during the Tribulation (Revelation 17:6). At some future point inside the Seventieth Week, the Beast (the political system) comes to hate the harlot, and ultimately turns on her and destroys her (Revelation 17:16–18). Before this point, the False Prophet will have already abandoned her.

H. The Dragon: Satan. At the midpoint of the seven-year Tribulation, Satan and his forces are finally kicked out of Heaven and lose total access to the divine realm, meaning they are now confined to the earth. Satan possesses Antichrist and indwells him (similar to how he physically possessed Judas Iscariot). Revelation 12 confirms two things believers longed to know: 1) Satan is the one who possessed the serpent to deceive Eve (Genesis 3); and 2) when Lucifer (Satan) rebelled, he took one-third of the angels with him. This heavenly expulsion could not have happened back in the time of Genesis 3, because Satan still had access to Heaven nearly two thousand years later, during the days of Job (Job 1–2). Thus, this event must be future still.

So Revelation 13 confirms the formation of the unholy trinity with the three main players identified as Satan: the father; Antichrist: the son; and the False Prophet: the unholy spirit. The ten kings are then in some way counterparts to the disciples.

The symbolism revolving around the final world government in the books of Daniel and Revelation is intriguing. On one hand, we should take the seven heads and ten horns and crowns as literal numbers (i.e., seven kingdoms, ten kings, etc.). On the other hand, we should also be open to taking the symbolic as being something more than just the literal understanding. For example, we don't associate Jesus with actually having seven horns and seven eyes, do we?

> ...stood a Lamb as though it had been slain, having seven horns and seven eyes, which are the seven Spirits of God sent out into all the earth. (Revelation 5:6)

In this instance, no. We look at what the numbers seven, the horns, and the eyes are representative of. This form of interpretation is no different than applying a common-sense approach to other portions of Scripture. For example, consider the following:

> I am the door. If anyone enters by Me, he will be saved, and will go in and out and find pasture. (John 10:9)

We don't think Jesus is a "literal" door with hinges and a handle. Rather, we grasp what He is really saying, which is, "I am the only way through to salvation. No one can gain salvation apart from me." But we could go through dozens of Jesus' parables and see the deeper picture He is painting by the use of symbolism (bread, water, light, good shepherd, etc.).

Some Questions and Answers

Question: While true, born-again Christians will not know the identity of the Antichrist, it is presumed that we also won't know the identities of the False Prophet, and perhaps even of the ten kings. But is that assumption true?

Answer: We don't think so. The Bible states we will not definitively know the identity of the Antichrist. It makes no mention of whether or not we will know the identities of any of the other major players.

Question: Can we see anyone on the global stage right now who meets the criteria for the False Prophet or the ten kings? And how can we know?

Answer: Yes. Because they are of "one mind."

Question: What is the "one mind?"

Answer: They have wholly bought into this "spirit of Antichrist" that is consuming the world. While they support most of these things, it is fair to say they definitely are not opposed to any of them.

What is the "one mind" they all share?

- Indefinable man-caused climate change
- Open borders and global government
- Pro-death (abortion, euthanasia)
- Social-justice gospel
- Pro-authoritarianism
- Pro-human secularism
- Postmodernist
- Transhumanist
- Pro-hedonist
- Pro-LGBTQ
- Pro-Luciferian
- Pro-pantheist
- Pro-Marxism
- Pro-atheism
- Pro-paganism

Question: Do any current world leaders come to mind?

Answer: The truth is, almost all world leaders come to mind, because most have to buy into this anti-God/anti-Christ/anti-Bible worldview to even hold power.

Question: How will the Beast come about, and what will it look like?

Answer: This could be a really long answer, but to summarize what Scripture says about this topic, we need to go back to Daniel chapter 2. In this chapter, Daniel interpreted a dream for King Nebuchadnezzar. The dream was of a multi-metallic statue of a man with a head of gold (which we find out represents Babylon), shoulders of silver (Persia), an abdomen and waist of brass (Greece), legs of iron (Rome), and feet of iron mixed with miry clay (Rome 2.0). These are the kingdoms God said would rule the world until the end.

Daniel later received a different kind of dream that essentially said the same thing, but in a different way. Instead of it being an impressive and awe-inspiring statue, the kingdoms were represented by four chimeric (mixed creatures) beasts. The first beast represented, we find out, was—you guessed it—Babylon. The second beast indicated Persia; the third, Greece; and the fourth beast, Rome. There is no fifth beast, so the *Roman Empire is still ruling the Gentile nations*, according to that prophecy.

Eight of Seven

Here is where it gets interesting. In Daniel's vision, the fourth beast the prophet saw (which represents the Roman Empire) is said to "break" the "whole" world into "pieces":

> Thus he said, The fourth beast shall be the fourth kingdom upon earth, which shall be diverse from all kingdoms, and shall devour the whole earth, and shall tread it down, and break it in pieces. (Daniel 7:23)

Why is that? It is because the Roman Empire never ceased to exist. It expanded east and then progressed globally, spreading westward through Europe and then colonializing the world. Those colonial strongholds were then given back over to the individual states in the mid-twentieth century. So, as a matter of fact, Rome did "break" the "whole earth," just like the passage says.

That fourth kingdom is still carrying out the agenda the angelic messenger explained. It is treading down the earth and shattering it into nation-states. Even so, the little horn that becomes the Son of Perdition cannot appear in the Roman Empire until the Restrainer (the Holy Spirit) is taken out of the way (2 Thessalonians 2:3).

As noted previously, ever since the nations were divided at Babel, all globalization efforts have failed. In fact, any attempt to establish a one-world order will fail until God allows it to come to pass. The Restrainer will not permit it to happen until after the time of the Gentiles is fulfilled. That is because the only global Gentile government in Bible prophecy that will have dominion over the entire earth is the counterfeit kingdom of God identified as Babylon and the Beast. Even then, that only occurs for seven years at the end of the age, just prior to the Lord's coming to set up His own Kingdom. The satanic counterfeit cannot come as long as it is being restrained.

The first three kingdoms were identified with, in chronological order, the reigns of Nebuchadnezzar, Cyrus, and Alexander the Great. Although the fourth kingdom was the Romans', their kingdom has never completely ended, but morphed from west to east, then to the Holy Roman Empire, and then subsequent European powers until the offspring of the Romans (the United States). As for the feet of iron mixed with miry clay (the ten-toed regional Roman Empire), we do not have a clue about who the leader of this fourth beast could be linked to. We (pre-Rapture) will not be able to determine who that final Gentile king will be, because it takes the Rapture of the Church to set things (the great crisis) in motion… and no one knows the day or hour of that event (Matthew 24:36).

The book of Revelation tells us that five of the seven kings lived around the Mediterranean prior to the Apostle John. The sixth (Emperor Domitian) was ruling when John wrote Revelation. We believe the seventh king comes after the Church is raptured.

Revelation also tells us the eighth king will be one of the previous seven. Although we cannot say for certain, he most likely would be the seventh king, who, it seems, becomes incarnated by a supernatural being out of the abyss and then is identified as the eighth. He is the Beast/Antichrist figure that goes into perdition (Revelation17:11).

Confused yet?

Let's take it from macro to micro. So, a final king comes from the fourth beast/feet of iron and clay (which will be a revived Roman

Empire). This final king will become the Beast/Antichrist when he gains the majority of control over the rest of the beast system. He is called the Beast, as well as the Beast being a political (imperial) system. The reason he can be both is that he comes to personify the beast kingdom just as Hitler came to personify the Third Reich. Nevertheless, the seventh king, along with the False Prophet, will be the one to bring back together the broken pieces that was the former Roman Empire, and unite it under his leadership, which will go on to conquer the rest of the world (Revelation 6:1–2; 13:1–18).

We believe this king will become possessed after he is seemingly assassinated at the midpoint of the Seventieth Week. He will go from being the "man of sin," to the "son of perdition" during this transformation. For clarification, the only other person called the "son of perdition" in Scripture was Judas Iscariot, who was physically possessed by Satan (John 17:12, 2 Thessalonians 2:3).

After the assassination of the seventh king, his lifeless body, becomes possessed by a spirit that rises from the abyss (Apollyon) and incarnates the body and it somehow becomes a transhuman supernatural being. At that time, he becomes the eighth king. Scripture identifies him as a Beast rather than a descendant of Adam.

> He causes all, both small and great, rich and poor, free and slave, to receive a mark on their right hand or on their foreheads, and that no one may buy or sell except one who has the mark or the name of the beast, or the number of his name. (Revelation 13:16–17)

When people take the mark of the Beast, some sort of genetic editing creates changes to the nature of the bearer. That is why those who take the mark cannot be saved. Jesus died to save the souls of human men. If they change what it means to be human, then they will pay the eternal price for the sins of changing their created nature. Again, Christ came to redeemed the fallen Adamic race, not those who are post-Adamic.

Although we do not see the ten kings or the little horn in the world yet, we can see the stage setting for this final world government aligning itself according to Scripture. This tells us that this is at some point in the near future.[102]

The Seventieth Week of Daniel

And he [the prince who shall come] shall confirm the covenant with many for one week: and in the midst of the week he shall cause the sacrifice and oblation to cease, and for the overspreading of abominations he shall make it desolate, even until the consummation, and that determined shall be poured out upon the desolate. (Daniel 9:27)

The reason we list Revelation 13 ahead of this chapter for the explanation of the Seventieth Week is that we can already see the Beast kingdom rising in its "mystery" form. It has been rising since 1945 when World War II came to its decisive end. Seventy-seven years have passed, and everything geopolitically, technologically, religiously, and economically has been trending toward the creation of this final world government. All it needed was the right crisis. The Rapture of the Church will give the world that crisis, and in the months to years following, the world will be thrown into a state of chaos. Out of that chaos will rise the leadership of this newly revived Roman Empire. They won't identify as simply a government full of bureaucrats, because they know that will not hold everything together. They will rebrand into a regionalized imperial empire hearkening back to the glory days of Europe in the hopes of unifying a largely divided continent.

The Rapture of the Church doesn't begin the Seventieth Week of Daniel. Neither does the ensuing chaos, or even the official rise of the Beast kingdom. The Seventieth Week begins when the leader (the little horn/Antichrist) confirms a covenant with the nation of Israel. That is when the divine countdown and judgments begin.

And I saw in the right hand of Him who sat on the throne a scroll written inside and on the back, sealed with seven seals. Then I saw a strong angel proclaiming with a loud voice, "Who is worthy to open the scroll and to loose its seals?" And no one in heaven or on the earth or under the earth was able to open the scroll, or to look at it.

So I wept much, because no one was found worthy to open and read the scroll, or to look at it. But one of the elders said to me, "Do not weep. Behold, the Lion of the tribe of Judah, the Root of David, has prevailed to open the scroll and to loose its seven seals."

And I looked, and behold, in the midst of the throne and of the four living creatures, and in the midst of the elders, stood a Lamb as though it had been slain, having seven horns and seven eyes, which are the seven Spirits of God sent out into all the earth. Then He came and took the scroll out of the right hand of Him who sat on the throne.... Now I saw when the Lamb opened one of the seals; and I heard one of the four living creatures saying with a voice like thunder, "Come and see." (Revelation 5:1–7, 6:1)

The Seal Judgments: Jesus initiates the judgments by opening the first seal. In fact, He is the only One in all the universe who can open the seals, which, subsequently, triggers the rest of the twenty-one judgments. It should be understood that, as the seals are opened here at the beginning, they remain "in effect" throughout the entire Seventieth Week. Here is brief overview of the complete list.

Seal 1: White horse (political and religious conquest)

Seal 2: Red horse (military conquest)

Seal 3: Black horse (global famine and scarcity)

Seal 4: Pale horse (pestilence and plagues; one-fourth of the earth's population perishes)

Seal 5: The cry of the martyrs (the new global religious system takes aim at Tribulation saints)

Seal 6: Cosmic disturbances, great earthquake; the wrath of the Lamb is recognized

Seal 7: Silence in Heaven for about a half-hour (Heaven is never silent)

The Trumpet Judgments: These begin from the opening of the seventh seal. They represent an escalation of God's wrath upon the earth. The increase comes in thirds, as God begins channelizing and confining the world's populations back to one geographic location, namely that of the Old World (Europe, Asia, the Middle East, and Africa).

Trumpet 1: One-third of the earth's vegetation is struck (this seems to indicate a geographic location such as the Americas).

Trumpet 2: One-third of the seas are struck (this seems to indicate a particular body of water, such as the Atlantic Ocean).

Trumpet 3: One-third of fresh waters are struck (Wormwood; see trumpet 1).

Trumpet 4: One-third of the heavens are struck (obscuration from the earth blots out light for a third of the earth [Americas?]).

Trumpet 5 (woe #1): Demonic locusts arise from the bottomless pit.

Trumpet 6 (woe #2): Angels from the Euphrates are released and kill one-third of mankind. Seven thunders are proclaimed; they're not written down.

Trumpet 7 (woe #3): Kingdoms are proclaimed; Satan is confined to earth (Revelation 12:12).

The Bowl Judgments: These represent the full measure of God's wrath being poured out upon the earth. If these were to last even a minute longer, no flesh would survive, as the final moments resemble Hell more than Earth.

Bowl 1: Loathsome sores break out on those who bear the mark of the Beast.

Bowl 2: The rest of the seas turn to blood.

Bowl 3: The rest of the fresh waters turn to blood.

Bowl 4: Earth's inhabitants are scorched from the sun.

Bowl 5: Darkness and pain fall upon the earth.

Bowl 6: The Euphrates dries up and makes way for the arrival of the kings of the East.

Bowl 7: The earth is utterly shaken; one hundred-pound hailstones fall; fire mixed with blood rains down.

The seal judgments then, mark the beginning of the Seventieth Week of Daniel (the Tribulation), and are the opening salvo against a Christ-rejecting world. These are opened by none other than Jesus Christ Himself. Since the subsequent trumpet and bowl judgments are tied to the seal judgments, it is Christ who triggers ALL of the wrath during the Tribulation, period. Thus, we should deduce conclusively that Jesus is the one initiating the wrath of God upon the earth (Revelation 5:1–5).

At the end of the seven years, the Beast's armies, along with the kings of the East, gather in the Megiddo Valley (Israel) to try to destroy what remains of the Jewish people. The skies are rolled back and Christ returns in power and glory, followed by the armies of Heaven. Christ then destroys the armies gathered at Megiddo. The Beast and the False Prophet are cast alive into the lake of fire.

SIXTEEN

REGIME CHANGE

A potent testimony for the new earth and heavens being instituted
at the second coming is the association of the redemption of creation with the redemption of the believers in Romans 8:18-23. In
verse 21 we read, "creation itself will be delivered from the bondage of the current subjection to futility will be redressed (v. 20).
Its tendency to decay and degradation will be remedied (v. 21).
Its groans and travails will come to an end (v. 22). It receives its
deliverance at the same time as the saints.

LEE BRAINARD, *THE NEW HEAVENS AND EARTH*[103]

WHILE THE BOWL JUDGMENTS are being poured out from Heaven into
the earthly reality, we are watching these judgments transition from the
eternal dimension to the time-constrained, physical one. We believe the
"fullness of sin" is being stored in these bowls, which, when poured out,
will be the exact measure of wrath upon a Christ-rejecting world (Romans
12: 19; Revelation 15:1). Thus, as with all the judgments, their execution
(opening the seals, blowing the trumpets, issuing the thunders, and now
pouring out the bowls) may happen successively in Heaven, but they may
be time-proportionate on the earth.

After the midpoint of the Tribulation, the Dragon (Satan), the Antichrist (the Beast), and the False Prophet begin issuing decrees to summon
all military forces to Israel. These issuances come forth from the three and
appear to be commands. However, these commands are actually frog-
like demons, which go forth to deceive the leaders of the world to come

and fight one last glorious battle. They are being deceived into believing they can actually wage war against Heaven and win. It is beyond insanity, which is why they must be deceived into leading their armies against such overwhelming odds.

As the trumpet and bowl judgments are carried out, the military forces are being stranded in various parts of the earth. The naval forces of the Beast kingdom have largely been stranded at sea, as a third of the oceans have been turned to literal blood (second trumpet). Soon after, the second bowl judgment turn all the oceans to blood. The blood oceans, along with the scorching heat, unleash massive amounts of microorganisms (blood-borne pathogens) from all the sea creatures dying off, producing untold and even unknown bacteriological and viral outbreaks. The pounding of the waves and natural evaporation processes that take place within the hydrological cycle are quickly aerosolizing these microorganisms into the atmosphere.

Travel has become as treacherous in the air as in the oceans, with a third of the light having been struck to darkness (fourth trumpet). In addition, with the demonic army unleashed in the fifth trumpet judgment, pilots are grounded after suffering from terrible stings and demonic possessions, thus crippling the Beast's aerial forces. The scorching heat (fourth bowl) also quickly overheats almost any vehicle and weapon system, causing troops to be forced to move by foot or by horse. This later intensifies with one hundred-pound hailstones striking the earth from the skies (seventh bowl), destroying aircraft on the ground, in their hangars, or in the air. Anything that is not bunkered underground is presumably destroyed. Even those, however, are constrained by destroyed runways.

All of New Babylon is plunged into supernatural darkness, forcing the armies of the Beast to slowly move by land to the west. The oppressive heat, having already scorched the polar ice caps, raises the sea levels significantly, submerging the flood plains with the overflow of these oceans of blood. The smell from it is both putrid and suffocating. This, in effect, has a reverse-migration effect, causing those near the coastlines to move farther inland. Those who remain or cannot leave the hot, bloody bodies of water gag and suffocate due to the putridity. There is not only be a horrible smell, though; the air quickly fills up with dangerous microorganisms.

The forces of the Beast have to wait for the miserable heat wave to lessen and then come up with a plan to move out of New Babylon in total darkness. Still, through all this, mankind does not repent. Instead, the remaining population blames God for the afflictions and attempts to wage war against Him.

Now word has spread that the kings of the East are coming to join the fray. Although they've been summoned, the Beast worries that they will seek to dethrone him, so overwhelming are their numbers. He knows they won't be satisfied in just taking Jerusalem. They are coming to stay for good, and will be problematic for his rule moving forward. Mysteriously, the mighty Euphrates has dried up, which further adds to his concern, seeing as they now have nothing to slow them down as the barbarian horde descends upon the tiny nation of Israel. The Beast knows this massive assemblage of forces will not fit in or around Jerusalem; the terrain doesn't support it. They need to assemble in the Valley of Megiddo, from Bozrah to Jehosophat (Isaiah 63:1–6)—the world's most perfect battlefield.

The following is a general timeline for the events surrounding the War of Armageddon and the Second Coming of Christ.

1. **The satanic trinity gathers the armies of the world to Har Megiddo.**
   Then the sixth angel poured out his bowl on the great river Euphrates, and its water was dried up, *so that the way of the kings from the east might be prepared.* And I saw three unclean spirits like frogs coming out of the mouth of the dragon, out of the mouth of the beast, and out of the mouth of the false prophet. For they are spirits of demons, performing signs, which go out to the kings of the earth and of the whole world, *to gather them to the battle of that great day of God Almighty.* (Revelation 16:12–14, emphasis added)

In the books of Daniel and Revelation, the ten kings are represented as ten horns, with the Antichrist rising up as the eleventh and subduing three. After gaining the majority control, he demands obedience from the rest of the seven. While it is not evident during the first half of the seven-year Tribulation, at the midpoint (three and a half years into it), the Antichrist turns on Israel. He, the False Prophet, and Satan himself call forth the armies of the world to gather for war in Israel.

> The ten horns which you saw are ten kings who have received no kingdom as yet, but they receive authority for one hour as kings with the beast. These are of one mind, and they will give their power and authority to the beast. These will make war with the Lamb, and the Lamb will overcome them, for He is Lord of lords and King of kings; and those who are with Him are called, chosen, and faithful. (Revelation 17:12–13)

2. Religious Babylon is destroyed.

Near the midpoint of the Tribulation, the False Prophet, the Antichrist, and the rest of the ten kings overthrow the world's ecumenical, politically correct, militant religion (the harlot). They used her at first to rid the world of all the competing religious systems left in the wake of the Rapture. Now, the Antichrist wants all the worship to himself. He does not like to share his glory with another.

> So he carried me away in the Spirit into the wilderness. And I saw a woman sitting on a scarlet beast which was full of names of blasphemy, having seven heads and ten horns. The woman was arrayed in purple and scarlet, and adorned with gold and precious stones and pearls, having in her hand a golden cup full of abominations and the filthiness of her fornication. And on her forehead a name was written:
>
> MYSTERY, BABYLON THE GREAT, THE MOTHER OF HARLOTS AND OF THE ABOMINATIONS OF THE EARTH.

Then he said to me, "The waters which you saw, where the harlot sits, are peoples, multitudes, nations, and tongues. And the ten horns which you saw on the beast, these will hate the harlot, make her desolate and naked, eat her flesh and burn her with fire. For God has put it into their hearts to fulfill His purpose, to be of one mind, and to give their kingdom to the beast, until the words of God are fulfilled. And the woman whom you saw is that great city which reigns over the kings of the earth." (Revelation 17:3–5, 15–18)

3. Commercial Babylon is destroyed.

While the military forces are beginning to prepare to move toward Israel, the Antichrist and his forces start to plan their attack on Jerusalem. Presumably, this is around the midpoint of the Tribulation, right after the Antichrist kills the Two Witnesses, and commits the "abomination that causes desolation" (Matthew 24:15; 2 Thessalonians 2:4; Revelation 13:6). At this phase, the Antichrist might be splitting his time between his headquarters in Babylon and Jerusalem, which are around 660 miles apart (if using Baghdad, Iraq, as a point of reference). At a certain point after the mid-point (likely near the end of the bowl judgments), the Beast's headquarters in Babylon are utterly and supernaturally destroyed.

The kings of the earth who committed fornication and lived luxuriously with her will weep and lament for her, when they see the smoke of her burning, standing at a distance for fear of her torment, saying, "Alas, alas, that great city Babylon, that mighty city! For in one hour your judgment has come." (Revelation 18:9–10)

4. Half of Jerusalem is captured.

It is interesting to note that, from 1948–1967, half of Israel was already under Gentile domination (British/Jordanians). Since the victorious Six Day War, there has been an intense, fifty-plus-year struggle to wrest that city out of the hands of Israel. At some time after the midpoint, the Antichrist finally takes back a portion of Jerusalem, presumably the portion with the Temple Mount and the newly built Third Temple.

> Behold, the day of the Lord is coming, and your spoil will be divided in your midst.
> For I will gather all the nations to battle against Jerusalem; the city shall be taken, the houses rifled, and the women ravished.
> Half of the city shall go into captivity, but the remnant of the people shall not be cut off from the city. (Zechariah 14:1–2; see also Zechariah 12:1–9 and 14:1–2; Micah 4:11–5:1)

5. Antichrist moves against Petra and the remnant there.

Having taken Jerusalem, the Antichrist is furious that many have escaped. His hatred for the Jews eclipses even that of Reich Marshal Hermann Göring and Führer Adolf Hitler at the height of the power of the Third Reich. He rallies his forces to chase after the Jews in the same fashion that Pharaoh had his army pursue the Hebrews in the Exodus. Antichrist's flood of forces meets a fate similar to the that of the Egyptians after God parted the Red Sea; however, instead of being devoured by the ocean, Antichrist's forces are swallowed up by the earth like Korah (Numbers 26:10).

> Now when the dragon saw that he had been cast to the earth, he persecuted the woman who gave birth to the male Child. But the woman was given two wings of a great eagle, that she might fly into the wilderness to her place, where she is nourished for a time and times and half a time, from the presence of the serpent. So the serpent spewed water out of his mouth like a flood after the woman, that he might cause her to be carried away by the flood. But the earth helped the woman, and the earth opened its mouth and swallowed up the flood which the dragon had spewed out of his mouth. And the dragon was enraged with the woman, and he went to make war with the rest of her offspring, who keep the commandments of God and have the testimony

of Jesus Christ. (Revelation 12:14–17; see also Zechariah 13:8; Daniel 9:27; Isaiah 33:13–16; Jeremiah 49:13, 14; Micah 2:12; Matthew 24:15–31; Revelation 12:6, 14)

6. The Regeneration of Israel
In Matthew 23:37–39, Jesus stated:

O Jerusalem, Jerusalem, the one who kills the prophets and stones those who are sent to her! How often I wanted to gather your children together, as a hen gathers her chicks under her wings, but you were not willing! See! Your house is left to you desolate; for I say to you, you shall see Me no more till you say, "Blessed is He who comes in the name of the Lord!"

So it has been for nearly two millennia that Israel (at large) has nationally rejected Jesus as the one, true Messiah. Here, after the murdering of the Two Witnesses (and their subsequent Rapture), the desecration of their new Temple, the sacking of Jerusalem by the Antichrist, and their fleeing to Petra, the Jewish remnant, in desperation, finally has the veil lifted (2 Corinthians 3:15–16; see also Isaiah 53:1–9; Leviticus 26:40–42; Deuteronomy 4:29–31; 36:6–8; Jeremiah 3:11–18; Hosea 5:15; Joel 2:28–32; Isaiah 53:1–9; Isaiah 64; Zechariah 12:10; Matthew 23:37–39; Romans 1:25–27).

7. The Second Coming of Christ
After the remaining portion of Israel turns to Jesus Christ as their Messiah, this triggers a devastating and culminating response from Heaven. Jesus Himself steps forward and moves out of eternity toward earth. The first time He came to earth, He was an infant. The second time He comes to earth, He returns as its rightful King. From Revelation 19:11–6:

Now I saw heaven opened, and behold, a white horse. And He who sat on him was called Faithful and True, and in righteousness He judges and makes war. His eyes were like a flame of fire, and on His head were many crowns. He had a name written that no one knew except Himself. He was clothed with a robe dipped in blood, and His name is called The Word of God. And the armies in heaven, clothed in fine linen, white and clean, followed Him on white horses. Now out of His mouth goes a sharp sword, that with it He should strike the nations. And He Himself will rule them with a rod of iron. He Himself treads the winepress of the fierceness and wrath of Almighty God. And He has on His robe and on His thigh a name written: KING OF KINGS AND LORD OF LORDS.

8. The Final Campaign

Beginning at Bozrah, Jordan (Isaiah 34:6; 63:1–6), the skies tear open; Christ and His armies begin working their way up the two-hundred-mile stretch up the Jordan River Valley to the Kidron Valley (Jehosophat).

Then I saw an angel standing in the sun; and he cried with a loud voice, saying to all the birds that fly in the midst of heaven, "Come and gather together for the supper of the great God, that you may eat the flesh of kings, the flesh of captains, the flesh of mighty men, the flesh of horses and of those who sit on them, and the flesh of all people, free and slave, both small and great."

And I saw the beast, the kings of the earth, and their armies, gathered together to make war against Him who sat on the horse and against His army. Then the beast was captured, and with him the false prophet who worked signs in his presence, by which he deceived those who received the mark of the beast and those who worshiped his image. These two were cast alive into the lake of fire burning with brimstone. And the rest were killed with the sword which proceeded from the mouth of Him who sat on the horse. And all the birds were filled with their flesh. (Revelation 20:17–21; see also 2 Thessalonians 2:8; Joel 3:12, 13; Zechariah 14:12–15).

9. Jesus descends to the Mount of Olives

Immediately after the tribulation of those days the sun will be darkened, and the moon will not give its light; the stars will fall from heaven, and the powers of the heavens will be shaken. Then the sign of the Son of Man will appear in heaven, and then all the tribes of the earth will mourn, and they will see the Son of Man coming on the clouds of heaven with power and great glory. And He will send His angels with a great sound of a trumpet, and they will gather together His elect from the four winds, from one end of heaven to the other. (Matthew 24:29–31)

After Jesus crushes the armies of the Antichrist, He casts the two reprobates (the Antichrist and the False Prophet) alive into the lake of fire. These are the first and only inhabitants of this most dreadful place for the first thousand years. After their armies are destroyed, Jesus descends out of the sky and sets foot on the Mount of Olives (where He gave His famous Olivet Discourse), splitting the mount in half. This may in fact coincide with the seventh bowl judgment (Revelation 16:17–18).

Then the Lord will go forth and fight against those nations, as He fights in the day of battle. And in that day His feet will stand on the Mount of Olives, which faces Jerusalem on the east.

And the Mount of Olives shall be split in two, from east to west, making a very large valley;

Half of the mountain shall move toward the north and half of it toward the south.

Then you shall flee through My mountain valley, for the mountain valley shall reach to Azal.

Yes, you shall flee as you fled from the earthquake in the days of Uzziah king of Judah.

Thus the Lord my God will come, and all the saints with You. (Zechariah 14:3–5; see also Zechariah 14:3–5; Joel 3:14–16; Matthew 24:29; Revelation 16:17–21).

SEVENTEEN

THE REBIRTH OF LIBERTY

AMERICAN HISTORIAN AND PASTOR John S C Abbott, in his 1855 *History of Napoleon Bonaparte*, related a conversation between the French emperor and his close friend, General Henri Bertrand. The exchange centered on Christ's divinity and began with General Bertrand's words to Napoleon:

"I can not conceive, Sire, how a great man like you can believe that the Supreme Being ever exhibited himself to men under a human form, with a body, a face, mouth, and eyes. Let Jesus be whatever you please—the highest intelligence, the purest heart, the most profound legislator, and, in all respects, the most singular being who has ever existed. I grant it. Still he was simply a man, who taught his disciples, and deluded credulous people, as did Orpheus, Confucius, Brahma. Jesus caused himself to be adored, because his predecessors, Isis and Osiris, Jupiter and Juno, had proudly made themselves objects of worship. The ascendency of Jesus over his time, was like the ascendency of the gods and the heroes of fable. If Jesus has impassioned and attached to his chariot the multitude—if he has revolutionized the world—I see in that only the power of genius, and the action of a commanding spirit, which vanquishes the world, as so many conquerors have done—Alexander, Caesar, you, Sire, and Mohammed with a sword."

Napoleon offered a powerful response to the general's remarks:

"I know men, and I tell you that Jesus Christ is not a man. Superficial minds see a resemblance between Christ and the founders of empires and the gods of other religions. That resemblance does not exist. There is between Christianity and whatever other religion the distance of infinity.

"We can say to the authors of every other religion, 'You are neither gods nor the agents of the Deity. You are but missionaries of falsehood, moulded from the same clay with the rest of mortals. You are made with all the passions and vices inseparable from them. Your temples and your priests proclaim your origin. Such will be the judgment, the cry of conscience, of whoever examines the gods and the temples of paganism.

"Paganism was never accepted, as truth, by the wise men of Greece; neither by Socrates, Pythagoras, Plato, Anaxagoras, or Pericles. On the other side, the loftiest intellects, since the advent of Christianity, have had faith, a living faith, a practical faith, in the mysteries and the doctrines of the gospel ; not only Bossuet and Fenelon, who were preachers, but Descartes and Newton, Leibnitz and Pascal, Corneille and Racine, Charlemagne and Louis XIV...

"Christ, having but a few weak disciples, was condemned to death. He died the object of the wrath of the Jewish priests, and of the contempt of the nation, and abandoned and denied by his own disciples.

"'They are about to take me, and to crucify me,' said he. 'I shall be abandoned of all the world. My chief disciple will deny me at the commencement of my punishment. I shall be left to the wicked. But then, divine justice being satisfied, original sin being expiated by my sufferings, the bond of man to God will be renewed, and my death will be the life of my disciples. Then they will be more strong without me than with me; for they will see me rise again. I shall ascend to the skies; and I shall send to them, from heaven, a Spirit who will instruct them. The spirit of the cross will enable them to understand my gospel. In time, they will believe it; they will preach it; and they will convert the world.'

"And this strange promise, so aptly called by Paul the 'fool-ishness of the cross,' this prediction of one miserably crucified, is literally accomplished. And the mode of the accomplishment is perhaps more prodigious than the promise.

"It is not a day, nor a battle which has decided it. Is it the lifetime of a man? No! It is a war, a long combat of three hun-dred years, commenced by the apostles and continued by their successors and by succeeding generations of Christians. In this conflict all the kings and all the forces of the earth were arrayed on one side. Upon the other I see no army, but a mysterious energy; individuals scattered here and there, in all parts of the globe, hav-ing no other rallying sign than a common faith in the mysteries of the cross...

"You speak of Caesar, of Alexander; of their conquests, and of the enthusiasm which they enkindled in the hearts of their soldiers. But can you conceive of a dead man making conquests, with an army faithful and entirely devoted to his memory. My armies have forgotten me, even while living, as the Carthaginian army forgot Hannibal. Such is our power! A single battle lost crushes us, and adversity scatters our friends.

"Can you conceive of Cæsar as the eternal emperor of the Roman senate, and from the depths of his mausoleum governing the empire, watching over the destinies of Rome? Such is the history of the invasion and conquest of the world by Christianity. Such is the power of the God of the Christians; and such is the perpetual miracle of the progress of the faith and of the govern-ment of His church. Nations pass away, thrones crumble, but the church remains. What is then the power which has protected this church, thus assailed by the furious billows of rage and the hostility of ages? Whose is the arm which, for eighteen hundred years, has protected the church from so many storms which have threatened to engulf it?

"Alexander, Cæsar, Charlemagne, and myself founded empires. But upon what did we rest the creations of our genius? Upon force. Jesus Christ alone founded his empire upon love; and at this hour millions of men would die for him."[104]

Having first conquered the whole of creation by His great love, Christ, the victorious King of kings and Lord of lords, returns to reclaim the kingdom that was forfeited by Adam, now through great violence. He means to wage war, dethrone the usurper and his forces, and cast them into the winepress of His wrath.

The fabric of the skies tears open as He comes riding into the panorama of the earth, with the armies of Heaven behind Him. Out of His mouth, the word of God comes forth, cutting His foes into pieces and levelling mountains. His eyes are ablaze, His robe is dipped in blood; for the enemies of God, this is a frightful sight to behold.

Behold, He is coming with clouds, and every eye will see Him, even they who pierced Him. And all the tribes of the earth will mourn because of Him. Even so, Amen. (Revelation 1:7)

He does not come just on conquest, but on liberation. He is setting free not just humankind, but all of creation that was subjected to bondage because of Adam's transgressions. The earth, the sky, the waters, and all of the plants and creatures—all have suffered millennia under the bondage of sin's crushing embrace. Now, they will be free.

But humanity—in particular, fallen humanity—is still defiant, still foolishly attempting to wage war on the Creator. People have come to believe the way things are in this fallen world is the way things should be. They have become institutionalized within the broken system they think is reality. They cannot even conceive of what it means to be truly free.

And now, branded with the mark of death, they fight to their inevitable deaths and eternal reward of damnation and misery.

No, Christ is no mere man. He is the God-Man, the Alpha and Omega, and He is come to set His creation free.

One of the most common mental conditions for soldiers and prisoners coming out of long periods of enlistment or incarceration is the process known as institutionalism. Institutionalism (or being institutionalized) is a form of mental and social conditioning that produces expected routine behaviors that become ingrained in the individual—and they often remain far beyond the time those behaviors are needed. As an example, soldiers who retire or complete a long period of service may continue waking up before dawn even long after they're out of the military because they've conditioned their minds and bodies to do so. Similarly, ex-cons may continue to knock on doors before entering rooms even within their own houses, as that was the expected behavior during their incarceration.

With regards to the subject of this book, the institutionalism comes in the form of the projected "reality" that has existed on earth since shortly after Creation. In other words, all humans (with the exception of Adam and Eve) have only ever known a fallen and corrupted world, largely ruled by other people. That is the satanically imposed normalcy bias inculcated upon thousands of generations, because that's the only way it's ever been. The politically driven Great Reset was meant to be the culmination of that authoritarian control, but all it did was set the stage for what would come during the Tribulation.

The real change has come with the return of Christ to the earth at His Second Coming. The change is no longer coming; it is here. And it's not just a shift in the political or economic system; it's a pivotal transformation of the governance of the earth, the galaxy, and the entirety of the universe. There, by necessity, will be a fundamental rearrangement in the laws of nature, the laws of physics, and the natural order of the earth (and its ecosystems and atmosphere). This change is called the coming Theocratic Rule of Jesus Christ (Daniel 7:13–14; Luke 1:30–33). This is when the Creator Himself, Jesus Christ, will appear, peel back the sky, and descend upon earth as a conquering warrior defeating all the armies who have gathered against Him at the Armageddon campaign (Daniel 2:44–45, Zechariah 14:3–4, Revelation 19:11–19, 21).

From there, He will toss the two primary antagonists of the previous seven years (the Antichrist and the False Prophet), alive, into the lake of fire, which will burn forever and ever (Revelation 19:20). He then has an angel bind Satan in chains and toss him into the abyss for one thousand years. Jesus then steps foot on the Mount of Olives, splitting the mountain in two (east to west) and terraforming Jerusalem and Israel. He not only brings the Dead Sea back to life, but He also restores the entire nation of Israel to its full strength and bounty (Ezekiel 47:8–12; Zechariah 14:8; Isaiah 2; 11:4–9; 65:24–25).

Judgment of the Nations

Unbelievably, there will be peoples from all walks of life still alive at Christ's Second Coming. Here, Jesus divides the remaining populations in two: the sheep on His right, and the goats on His left. These nations will be judged based on how they treated the nation of Israel up until the end (Matthew 25:31–46). The nations that sided with those who sought Israel's destruction will be cast into outer darkness. Those who aided the survival of Israel will be allowed entrance (physically) into the Millennial Kingdom. The mortal humans who do survive the Tribulation will be allowed entrance into this new theocratic Millennial Kingdom, and they will go on to repopulate the earth.

It's hard to imagine a world like this, namely because we've never known any different. We've become institutionalized to the system of life on this fallen planet. We've come to believe the false genesis of our supposed accidental beginnings and our evolutionary ascendancy. We've grown accustomed to the history (both false and true) of the ancient ages of humankind. We've gotten comfortable with the never-ending cycle of the rising and falling of empires and kingdoms. We've adapted to accepting sin, wickedness, violence, and "acts of God" as being normal. We've even embraced the unavoidability of certain things like "death and taxes" as being normal. Yet, all of these thoughts and conditions are merely symptoms of a reality that has always been passing away.

The difference between then and now will be so stark that it will be unrecognizable to those who physically enter the Kingdom. This is the same Kingdom that was promised to Israel when Christ came the first time, yet, they rejected it. They didn't reject the preeminence this Kingdom would have afforded them, though; they rejected the Messenger who brought the standards for entrance into this Kingdom. It is for this very reason they crucified Him at Calvary. Since then, the Kingdom was in mystery form, operating through the Church (now glorified), and it did so throughout the Church Age (Pentecost—Rapture). Yes, the world will undergo a radical transformation, bringing it back to the way the world was originally intended.

Environmental Changes

For the creation was subjected to futility, not willingly, but because of Him who subjected it in hope; because the creation itself also will be delivered from the bondage of corruption into the glorious liberty of the children of God. For we know that the whole creation groans and labors with birth pangs together until now. (Romans 8:20–22)

During the Millennial Reign, Christ reigns upon the earth for, of course, one thousand years. His first order of business is restoration, beginning with Jerusalem and continuing with all of Israel. This means He lifts the sin curse upon the earth at the Second Coming, not at the end of the Millennium. This cleansing begins at Jerusalem, then ripples throughout the earth. While fire may have purged the heavens and the earth (2 Peter 3:10), it did not annihilate them. So, the planet is renovated to remove the blight, blood, and damage accrued not just during the previous seven years, but since the time when Cain slew Abel. Nature is restored to yield its full strength; the animal kingdom becomes peaceful and docile. From the wildest lion to the most cantankerous snake, all now dwell peacefully with everyone and everything.

After this baptism by fire, the kingdom restores the natural order to the earth and the atmosphere—down to even the molecular level. Harmful viruses, bacteria, and pests that have plagued mankind since the dawn of time are destroyed. Thorns, thistles, and other unpleasant protective measures employed by nature are no longer needed for plant life to be sustained. The oceans, once full of blood, are now clear and healthy, repopulated with their former sea life. The sea (the Mediterranean) ceases to exist, but the rest of the oceans flourish.

Territories formerly uninhabitable become lush and vibrant, full of life. The deepest depths are lifted up, and the highest heights are leveled. The largest mountain on the planet is Mt. Zion. Of all the changes in the Kingdom, the environmental one is the most startlingly different.

> The wolf and the lamb shall feed together, The lion shall eat straw like the ox, And dust shall be the serpent's food. They shall not hurt nor destroy in all My holy mountain," says the Lord. (Isaiah 65:25)

Political Changes

Jesus has two thrones in the Millennial Kingdom. One is in Jerusalem (the throne of David) and the other is in the New Jerusalem that encircles the globe like a satellite in low-earth orbit. From here, the Church comes and goes to the earth, ruling and co-reigning with Christ. However, the world now has one capital: Jerusalem. Inhabitants of all nations stream here to pay homage to the King of kings and Lord of lords. The nations no longer war against each other, nor are there even weapons; there is no need. The Lord rules through His saints, and the world itself begins to heal from the scarring humankind has put upon it for six thousand years. The theocratic rule is so perfect that it fundamentally destroys the need for crime, wickedness, violence, corruption, or vice—any of the mechanisms or trappings required for those actions to exist.

> Many people shall come and say, "Come, and let us go up to the mountain of the Lord, To the house of the God of Jacob; He will teach us His ways, And we shall walk in His paths."
> For out of Zion shall go forth the law, And the word of the Lord from Jerusalem. He shall judge between the nations, And rebuke many people;
> They shall beat their swords into plowshares, And their spears into pruning hooks;
> Nation shall not lift up sword against nation, Neither shall they learn war anymore. (Isaiah 2:3–4)

Religious Changes

There is only one religion: the worship of Jesus Christ Himself. On earth, as we said, Christ simultaneously rules from the New Jerusalem and from David's throne in the earthly Jerusalem (Luke 1:32; Psalm 2; Isaiah 2:1–4, 11; 65:17–25). We (like Him, in a similar manner) are able to travel between the two places at the speed of thought (1 John 3:1–3; Luke 24:36–39). The Church (as well as the Old Testament saints) is assigned various leadership roles in the Millennial Kingdom, based upon our faithfulness and works in this life. (Again, we are not saved by works or our own efforts; these are for reward.)

After the nations (the still-surviving physical populations) begin to fill the earth again after the devastation of the Seventieth Week of Daniel; its conclusive battle of Armageddon (Revelation 19); and the sheep and goat judgment (Matthew 25 [the judgment of the nations]), there is a cleansing of the Third Jewish Temple (Daniel 12:11–12). This precludes the necessity for the reestablishment of Third-Temple practices (Ezekiel 40–48).

This is a bit of speculation on our part regarding the purposes for the reinstatement of many of the Old Testament rituals in this coming Third Temple in the Millennial Kingdom.

It is referenced in Ezekiel 40–48 that God reestablishes the Temple practices and rituals, including animal sacrifices. These offerings do not replace what Christ did on the cross or negate His sacrificial atonement for those saved by it. Neither are these animal sacrifices simply conducted as a memorial for the way things used to be done. They represent a very pragmatic form of temporal cleansing for the Millennial Kingdom's population for the daily cleansing of sins so they can even enter the Temple to approach Christ.

Some readers may point to the fact that the book of Hebrews (7:27; 9:12; 10:10) states Christ's sacrifice was *once, for all,* and that is true. However, it is only true for those who live and die before Christ's Second Coming, not for those who are born afterward (i.e., the people born in the Millennial Kingdom with their sinful/unredeemed natures). For them, there still needs to be a process to approach God.

We know people are born in the Millennial Kingdom without redeemed natures (Isaiah 65:20, Revelation 20:7–10). However, these folks can't simply be born again as did believers in the Church Age, because salvation comes by **grace through faith**. For those living in the Millennial Kingdom, what faith do they need when they can already see, feel, speak to, and listen to a ruling and reigning Christ on the throne in Jerusalem? What faith do they need when they can see the New Jerusalem in the sky above? What faith must they have when angels and the glorified saints interact with them on a daily basis? They don't need faith, because they are eyewitnesses to all of it.

According to Scripture, the following is a definition of faith:

Now faith is the substance of things hoped for, the evidence of things not seen. For by it the elders obtained a *good* testimony. By faith we understand that the worlds were framed by the word of God, so that the things which are seen were not made of things which are visible. (Hebrews 11:1–3, emphasis added)

Again, how is faith required when the people born in the Millennium can see with their own eyes, therefore do not need to have hope because they are living in the promised Kingdom? Again, we are not dogmatic about this; we (like you) are trying to put the pieces together in a way that makes the most biblical sense.

This is, in our minds, similar to how we understand salvation in the Old Testament. The Old Testament saints weren't saved in the manner we who are living in the Church Age receive salvation. Those ancient peoples couldn't be born again, sealed by the Holy Spirit, and become heirs/sons and daughters of God in the same way we are, because Christ had not yet come to redeem humankind. The New Testament/New Covenant could not take effect until AFTER He died (Hebrews 9:16–17).

Instead, the Old Testament saints were justified by their faith in God (and received a good testimony) and, when they died, were set aside in "Abraham's bosom"—a place of comfort where they would await the arrival of the promised Christ to Sheol. This visit by the Christ occurred after His crucifixion but before His physical resurrection when He would preach to them His victory over the forces of darkness and deliver them up with Him (Ephesians 4:7–9; 1 Peter 3:19–20). So when He ascended, the Old Testament saints came with Him and He emptied/delivered that Paradise portion of Sheol to Heaven.

Cosmic Changes

At some point during Isaiah's day (circa eighth–seventh century BC), the earth was knocked off its axis by 23.5 degrees. Furthermore, there was, perhaps, so great an earthquake that it knocked the earth out of its normal, 360-day revolution around the sun, which altered the cycle to a 365-day revolution. We know this is possible because it has happened even in our own day.

For instance, back in 2011, a magnitude 9.0 earthquake struck Japan (and the world) so forcefully that it shortened earth's day by 1.8 microseconds after throwing an extra 6.7 inches into the planetary north-south wobble, experts say. It also moved the island nation of Japan up to thirteen feet in certain places. According to the Bible, at least five greater earthquakes will strike the earth with a final, mega-quake, presumably sinking every island and levelling every mountain range (Revelation 6:12; 8:5; 11:13; 11:19; and 16:18).[105]

We know that, throughout the last seven years of the Tribulation, there will be several massive earthquakes unlike any others the world has ever seen (Revelation 6:12; 8:5; 11:13; and 16:18). It stands to reason, given the severity of these quakes, that Revelation 6:12 and 16:18 appear to be well above 10.0 on the Richter scale. If the one in Japan (9.0) could shorten the earth's day by 1.8 microseconds, then one several grades higher could even more significantly alter the number of the earth's revolutions, as well correct the planet by "resetting" it onto its proper axis, bringing back the 360-day year revolution around the sun.

The Short Season

After the thousand-year Millennial Reign is complete, Satan is brought back up from the abyss and set loose for a short season. We aren't told how long this is, but, given our recent experiences and understandings, a season could be a few months or even a few years (for example, the season of the Lord's' return).

Incredibly, Satan is able to amass from the four corners of the world a huge army that marches on the world's capital. This attempted *coup d'état*, much like his very first one, is an abject failure. As the armies surround Jerusalem, Christ calls down fire from Heaven and consumes every last miscreant. These and Satan are then tossed into the lake of fire, where they will remain forever.

Here's the biblical description of those events:

Now when the thousand years have expired, Satan will be released from his prison and will go out to deceive the nations which are in the four corners of the earth, Gog and Magog, to gather them together to battle, whose number is as the sand of the sea. They went up on the breadth of the earth and surrounded the camp of the saints and the beloved city. And fire came down from God out of heaven and devoured them. The devil, who deceived them, was cast into the lake of fire and brimstone where the beast and the false prophet are. And they will be tormented day and night forever and ever. (Revelation 20:7–10)

So, just as soon as it began, it is over.

Those who ignorantly sided with Satan have proved once and for all that the fallen human condition, even if in paradisiacal conditions, will turn wicked if given the opportunity. It is after this point that God calls forth the dreaded great white throne judgment, in which the wicked from all time are summoned to stand before the Creator and give an accounting of their life. Author Lee Brainard puts it like this:

When the ungodly are removed from their temporary prison in hell and ferried to the Great White Throne Judgment, they will be separated from the beauties and glories of the earth and the heavens. They rejected the Creator, so they don't get his creation, not even a glimpse of it. All they will see, is the offended Almighty on his judgment throne. There is nothing else to look at. There is nothing to detract from the awfulness of the moment. And the last light they will ever see, the last beauty they will ever see, before they are cast into the eternal lake of fire in a place of outer and utter darkness, is the face of the God they rejected.[106]

For the redeemed and holy, as amazing as this theocratic Kingdom is, it is not the end. Author Mike Mullin described his perspective on this Kingdom in a recent article:

When I try to envision what the world of the 1000-year kingdom looks like, I always envision an odd mixture of advanced technology coupled with methods of the old world—something like clean, rapid-moving magnetic trains between cities; advanced sea[craft], and airships, yet the continued use of the horse and buggy, fireplaces, and markets. People will live very long lives—centuries—and sickness and disease will be nonexistent. The nations of the world will again be rebuilt, and trade and commerce will flourish again, this time without the motive of primacy being or other selfish motives.

At the end of the 1,000-year period, Satan is allowed out of the holding place in the earth where he has been held. He leads a failed rebellion against the nations…one last vain attempt at getting the entire world to rebel against Christ's rule of the earth. Fire from Heaven burns and relocates the Devil and his followers into the almost unoccupied Lake of Fire. At this point, God also rips Hell itself out of the earth—bloated with the billions of nonbelievers from 6,000 years of human history—into the Lake of Fire.

As the sun sets on the Millennial Kingdom, it really is the end of the Bible. Everything by this point related to saving souls, earthly life, the dominion of man, sin, and separation from God, is effectively over. And, just as how incredible the Millennial Kingdom was, things are about to get a whole lot more interesting.[107]

Thus, the *Apocalypse of Jesus Christ*, as given to the Apostle John on Patmos, was not simply the fantastical foretelling of the end of the world, but of the revelation of Christ's true nature as God-Incarnate.
He is:

~ Messiah
~ The Son of God
~ The Son of Man
~ God in the Flesh

- ~ The Prince of Peace
- ~ The Last Adam
- ~ Our Kinsman Redeemer
- ~ The I AM
- ~ The Alpha and Omega
- ~ The Author and Finisher of our faith
- ~ The Lion of the Tribe of Judah
- ~ The Lion and the Lamb
- ~ The King of kings, and Lord of lords
- ~ Before all, and above all
- ~ The Rock cut without human hands
- ~ The name above all names
- ~ The Almighty

At His First Coming, Jesus came as the prophet. In the interim, during the Mystery Kingdom (the Church Age), He serves as priest (after the order of Melchizedek) and intermediary. In the book of Revelation, chapters 4 and onward, He is the returning King of kings. The book of Revelation does not just reveal all that is to come, but it is the Father's revelation (*apokalupsis*) of Jesus Christ Himself to all of creation, even to a Christ-rejecting world. Thus, this book is God's final, literary *magnus opus* (masterpiece) to a world shrouded in darkness.

> Then I turned to see the voice that spoke with me. And having turned I saw seven golden lampstands, and in the midst of the seven lampstands One like the Son of Man, clothed with a garment down to the feet and girded about the chest with a golden band. His head and hair were white like wool, as white as snow, and His eyes like a flame of fire; His feet were like fine brass, as if refined in a furnace, and His voice as the sound of many waters; He had in His right hand seven stars, out of His mouth went a sharp two-edged sword, and His countenance was like the sun shining in its strength. (Revelation 1:12–16)

Just as Revelation begins with John's mind-shattering encounter with the resurrected and glorified Christ, so too must each of us come to that moment of realization that our world and everything in it is passing away. We have to recognize that we have no hope apart from Christ. When we place our faith (the evidence of things not seen) in His finished and victorious work on the cross (conquering death and Hell), we can be reborn (reconciled) to Him. The God-given spirit within us that was once dead can now be revived and reconnected back to our Creator.

> For with the heart one believes unto righteousness, and with the mouth confession is made unto salvation. For the Scripture says, "Whoever believes on Him will not be put to shame." For there is no distinction between Jew and Greek, for the same Lord over all is rich to all who call upon Him. For "whoever calls on the name of the Lord shall be saved." (Romans 10:10–13)

EIGHTEEN

THE ETERNAL ORDER OF THE AGES

What kingdom will stand forever? The kingdom that the Lord sets up here on earth when He comes in glory. The kingdom that involves the Lord's in-person dominion over the inhabitants of this planet. The kingdom which the saints receive at the second coming of the Lord. These facts speak volumes. If the Lord has eternal dominion over the inhabitants of this planet, then this planet is eternal. If the saints receive an eternal inheritance on this planet, then this planet is eternal. Any other conclusion would empty the passages of all meaning.

LEE BRAINARD, *THE NEW HEAVENS AND EARTH*[108]

For thus says the High and Lofty One who inhabits eternity, whose name is Holy: "I dwell in the high and holy place, with him who has a contrite and humble spirit, to revive the spirit of the humble, and to revive the heart of the contrite ones."

ISAIAH 57:15

ETERNITY IS ONE of those concepts that is virtually impossible for mortals to fully comprehend in our present state. It's impossible because we have only ever lived inside the constructs (and constraint) of time and space. Even the Millennial Kingdom is bound within the limitations of time. However, to understand eternity, one would have to be loosed from the confines of time (this mortal life) through death or Rapture, then be resurrected to even have an inkling of what it means to exist in the realm eternal. Before we continue, let's make sure we understand what "eternity" is:

1: the quality or state of being eternal
2: infinite time lasting throughout *eternity*
3: eternities *plural:* AGE
4: the state after death: IMMORTALITY
5: a seemingly endless or immeasurable time; an *eternity* of delays[109]

Put simply, "eternity" is either the absence of time or time without beginning or end. But "eternal" doesn't necessarily mean the same thing as "immortal." "Immortal" can include those who had a beginning, but then no longer have an ending, such as the case with, say, Enoch or Elijah. "Eternal," however, denotes the existence without beginning or ending. Thus, eternality is one of those qualities exclusively unique to the Triune Godhead of the Bible.

- God the Father is without beginning or end (Deuteronomy 33:27)
- God the Son is without beginning or end (Colossians 1:17)
- God the Holy Spirit is without beginning or end (Hebrews 9:14)
- The Triune Godhead (Father, Son, and Holy Spirit) are one and eternal (Deuteronomy 6:4; Romans 1:20)

Since God is eternal and His plan was to create an eternal world with eternal inhabitants, what does that mean for those of us who are mortal and finite? It means that, once we are raptured (or die) and enter the eternal realm, we will live forever and ever in that state of being. If you're born again, that is amazing. If you are not born again, then it is a fate beyond horror. For those of us who enter eternity with God at the Rapture (or death), time no longer has any hold on us—or even any practical meaning. Just as, to God, a day is as a thousand years, or vice versa (Psalm 90:4; 2 Peter 3:8), we will lose any semblance of how time is or what it means to be in time. For instance, you might be on the other side of the new universe just hanging out with Jonah, sharing about each other's life and experiences. Before you know it, a thousand years might have transpired without you even thinking about it. Then you could visit like that with every person in Heaven (each for a thousand years) and still have all of eternity ahead of you.

So is it a New Heaven and a New Earth, or is it a Heaven and Earth renewed?

> For behold, I create new heavens and a new earth; And the former shall not be remembered or come to mind. (Isaiah 65:17)

> But the day of the Lord will come as a thief in the night, in which the heavens will pass away with a great noise, and the elements will melt with fervent heat; both the earth and the works that are in it will be burned up. Therefore, since all these things will be dissolved, what manner of persons ought you to be in holy conduct and godliness, looking for and hastening the coming of the day of God, because of which the heavens will be dissolved, being on fire, and the elements will melt with fervent heat? Nevertheless we, according to His promise, look for new heavens and a new earth in which righteousness dwells. (2 Peter 3:10–13)

> Now I saw a new heaven and a new earth, for the first heaven and the first earth had passed away. Also there was no more sea. (Revelation 21:1)

We believe, given the entirety of Scripture, which speaks of earth and the heavens as eternal, we cannot take the above-mentioned passages out of context. There are many examples speaking to the eternality of the heavens and the earth (see endnote for a more exhaustive resource).[110] For example, in numerous places, the words of Scripture declare the heavens' eternality:

Praise Him, sun and moon;
Praise Him, all you stars of light!
Praise Him, you heavens of heavens,
And you waters above the heavens!
Let them praise the name of the Lord,
For He commanded and they were created.
He also established them forever and ever;
He made a decree which shall not pass away.
(Psalm 148:3–6, emphasis added)

The same could be said with the earth we currently stand on.

One generation passes away, and another generation comes; *But the earth abides forever.* (Ecclesiastes 1:4, emphasis added)

To strengthen this point, the land and nation of Israel are to be eternal:

Also I give to you and your descendants after you the land in which you are a stranger, all the land of Canaan, as an *everlasting possession*; and I will be their God. (Genesis 17:8, emphasis added)

Either "forever and ever," "forever," and "everlasting" mean what they say or they don't. But they can't mean both. So, perhaps we should put into perspective what "new" means in context of creation and the future eternal state of things. For that, let us go to 2 Corinthians 5:17:

Therefore, if anyone is in Christ, he is a new creation; old things have passed away; behold, all things have become new.

When people become born-again believers, their old bodies aren't shucked into a bin of annihilation never to be seen again, and then they're given new bodies. No! They are renovated into new beings from the old.

Yet, this is the same kind of language we see in Isaiah 65:17 and Revelation 21:1. If God can renovate fallen, sinful, humans into new ones, why can't He do that with a physical, nonsentient creation like the earth, moon, and stars? Author Lee Brainard puts it like this:

> Many prophecy teachers in our day believe that redemption ultimately includes the annihilation of the current heavens and earth and a second *ex nihilo* creation. This is a mistake that actually diminishes the greatness and wisdom of God. Consider the following points:
>
> God's original intention was to enjoy fellowship with Adam, Eve, and their progeny in the paradise that he had created for them here on earth. If the serpent hadn't introduced sin and rebellion into the world, this would have continued for eternity. All agree that God redeemed man from the clutches of the enemy. But according to the recreation theory, God is going to scuttle the earth. This tarnishes the sovereignty of God. If this be true, God will redeem less than he lost in the garden to the serpent.
>
> - God doesn't fix the defilement problem in his moral creation with annihilation. He fixes it with sequestration. He casts the wicked angels and men into the lake of fire forever. The recreation theory introduces a conundrum that challenges the wisdom of God in this regard. If God can fix the problem in the moral creation without the annihilation of the guilty perpetrators, why can't he fix the problem in physical creation, which is an innocent victim, without annihilation? Why would he subject physical creation to a worse fate than moral creation? Physical creation, mind you, has no sin, no wickedness, and no iniquity to remove. It only has scars caused by sinners, both angelic and human.

- When God destroyed the former earth in the flood and introduced the earth that exists now, he did not resort to annihilation. He resorted to resurfacing. The earth did not cease to exist. The earth was radically transformed. Why would God depart from this precedent? He is the God of order and pattern. If this precedent is followed, the earth will be resurfaced by fire and earthquake.

- There is a sanctity about this planet that precludes its non-existence. It absorbed the sweat, tears, and blood of the Lord. He was born here, lived here, died here, buried here, raised here. He walked its dusty surface. It is the scene of many glorious victories he wrought on behalf of his people over the centuries: the ark, the Exodus, the crossing of the Red Sea, the battle of Jericho, and crossing the Jordan on dry ground. Dozens of his prophets and apostles testified here. Millions of his martyrs had their blood mingled with the dust of this planet. To think of God separating himself and his people forever from the scene of all this moral glory is simply unthinkable.

- Time would fail us to mention all the passages and arguments in the Bible which testify to the eternality of the heavens, the earth, the land of Israel, Mt. Zion, Jerusalem, etc. For instance, God pointed the patriarchs to the heavens above their heads and promised them that Israel would endure for as long as the sun and moon endure (Jer. 31:35–36). He didn't misspeak here. This is the eternal truth of the God who cannot lie. If the current heavens ever cease to exist, then Israel will cease to exist. If Israel will never cease to exist, then the current heavens will never cease to exist.[111]

This understanding of renovation vs. recreation is not a new idea. Early Church Fathers like Irenaeus believed this, as well as later saintly theologians such as E. W. Bullinger and Clarence Larkin. In fact, Larkin said this in his commentary on Revelation:

> A surface reading of the above passage (Rev. 21:1) would lead one to believe that the earth as a planet, and the sidereal heavens, are to be destroyed by fire and pass away. But a careful study of the Scriptures will show us that this is not so, that what is to happen is, that this present earth, and the atmosphere surrounding it, is to be Renovated by Fire, so that its exterior surface shall be completely changed, and all that sin has brought into existence, such as thorns and thistles, disease germs, insect pests, etc., shall be destroyed, and the atmosphere purified and forever freed from evil spirits and destructive agencies.[112]

EPILOGUE

WHILE WE TRACK the approaching Tribulation storm, the radar scope that is God's prophetic Word lights up stage-setting issues and events of these troubled end times. Perhaps no such indicator other than Israel being at the center of developments is more compelling than matters involving the World Economic Forum (WEF).

This global gathering is bringing all elements of the developing New World Order into being. Klaus Schwab is founder of the WEF, which is a Swiss nonprofit foundation based in Cologny, Geneva (Switzerland). It describes itself as an independent international organization committed to improving the state of the world by engaging business, political, academic, and other leaders of society to shape global, regional, and industry agendas.

However, we see it as the nucleus around which the coming Antichrist regime might be built. Certainly this organization, or one very similar, will bring about a system of total control over most of the world's populations during the Tribulation—earth's last seven years leading up to the return of Christ at Armageddon.

Developments we are seeing at this time are stunning in terms of numbers and in what they mean. Again, the WEF is indicative of what we find most ominous. Jan Markell, founder and president of Olive Tree ministries, for example, writes the following:

We already see the formation of this coming New World Order through the UN and the World Economic Forum (WEF). Without firing a shot, they have gained the allegiance of most world leaders for their Marxist plans to enslave the people of the world.

The globalists believe they have the means to reshape the world according to their agenda via the influence they have gained over the global leaders of our day. A one-world government will be birthed once the Church vacates! The players are in place.

Further, noted prophecy writer Daymond Duck observes:

America and the world are transitioning from the old normal (as of Jan. 1, 2016) to the satanic New World Order (by 2030 or sooner).

America is in [process of achieving] former Pres. Obama's predicted "fundamental transformation of America" and the UN's "transformation of the world" sustainable development goals.

We are engaged in the end-times battle described by the Apostle Paul. He outlines the formidable evil those who are part of God's forces face while the end of the age swiftly approaches. Here, again, is his assessment:

For we wrestle not against flesh and blood, but against principalities, against powers, against the rulers of the darkness of this world, against spiritual wickedness in high places. (Ephesians 6:12)

Two classes of entities make up the "powers" and "principalities." These are the natural minions and the demonic minions. The natural are the human beings that make up the "rulers of the darkness of this world" and the demonic are the "spiritual wickedness in high places."

Both have as their father the same evil being—the father of lies (John 8:44).

Father of Liars

Jesus said that one of the great signals of His Second Coming and of the end of the age would be deception and deceivers. Paul, in 2 Thessalonians chapter 2, tells us there will be strong delusion in the last days. He prophesied also that there will be "evil men and seducers growing worse and worse, deceiving and being deceived."

God's Word—Jesus Himself—declared that the evil at the core of all the deception is a being full of lies. He said in answer to the Jewish religious zealots who tried to entrap Him:

> Ye are of your father the devil, and the lusts of your father ye will
> do. He was a murderer from the beginning, and abode not in the
> truth, because there is no truth in him. When he speaketh a lie, he
> speaketh of his own: for he is a liar, and the father of it. (John 8:44)

There is scriptural proof, therefore, that the charge is based in God's truth when we say all the lies we see perpetrated in the closing days of this Age of Grace (Church Age) come from the chief minion of Ephesians 6:12 against whom we wrestle. And indeed we have experienced an increase in lies coming at us from many directions.

We remember the explosion of lies following the presidential election of 2016. The accusation of Trump's campaign and election being in cahoots with the Russians—with Vladimir Putin himself—was in our faces for Trump's full four years as president. The lies kept coming and were front and center on every mainstream news outlet and on all left-wing social media every hour of every day for that presidential term.

Then it was proven that that the Russian collusion charge was all lies, based upon a phony, political dirty trick. The opposition presidential campaign paid operatives to concoct and distribute a false dossier involving charges accusing Mr. Trump of paying Russian prostitutes to do salacious things in order to spew vitriol against Barack and Michelle Obama, his predecessor and former first lady.

The same political party concocted lies against a Trump administration Supreme Court candidate. We remember that parade of prevarication. The president was subjected to a daily barrage for weeks and months in impeachment efforts—all based on lies.

Mainstream newscasts and social media blogs and other platforms made up lies about the Black Lives Matter and Antifa destruction of cities across America being peaceful protests rather than riots. The same news and entertainment media, while ignoring those destructive, anti-American insurrections, continued to accuse those of the Trump supporters who protested—mostly peacefully—in Washington, DC, on January 6, 2021, as being insurrectionists. The vice president declared the protest and march to be the evil equivalent of December 7, 1941, and September 11, 2001.

Lies of less magnitude, but progressing geometrically on an hour-by-hour basis in order to maintain the political power they achieved through one of the biggest lies, in our opinion—those involved in the stolen election of 2020—continue to do their destructive work against the republic.

The globalist minions, both human and demonic, are working incessantly to set the stage for the coming Antichrist regime. Two prongs of this evil effort are primary in Satan's blueprint. One is the climate-change mantra, and the other is the globalists' COVID pandemic scam that, it is becoming obvious, is not likely to end anytime soon. Both are built largely on lies generated by the principalities and powers in high places.

The initial effort was the lies of global warming. That morphed into climate change, when the icecap at the North Pole didn't melt and submerge New York City in the waters of the Atlantic after the first prediction of such catastrophe some thirty years ago.

Reports have it that the University of Alabama at Huntsville data set presented from satellite reconnaissance has shown that there has been no global warming at all for the last seven years. Based on the HadCRUT4 data set, there has been no statistically significant global warming for more than nine years—August 2012 to October 2021.

Before the findings, the United Nations-backed Intergovernmental

Panel on Climate Change (IPCC) confidently said in its First Assessment in 1990 that global warming is a great deal and a climate emergency. But, given the succession of long periods without global warning as shown by the HadCRUT4 data set, it is safe to say the IPCC's warning is way off the mark.

One writer renders judgment on the climate-change hoax:

Journalist and blogger Christopher Monckton noted that the West is self-destructing due to its belief in global warming, which has benefited China and Russia....

Monckton noted that totalitarian administrations, such as that of the United Kingdom, is imagining climate emergency—giving as example the situation in rural Cornwall. He predicted that the first political party to find the courage "to oppose the global warming nonsense root and branch" will sweep the board at the next elections.

"There is no more of a climate emergency today than there was in 2012, so the only reason for declaring one now is not that it is true (for it is not) but that it is politically expedient," wrote Monckton.

The political leadership in the West, said Monckton, is committing economic suicide as it allowed high-energy industries to be wasted because of the fear of imagined global warming. "Whole industries have already been or are soon to be laid waste—coal extraction, distribution and generation (and, therefore, steel and aluminum); oil and gas exploration and combustion; internal-combustion vehicles; and a host of downstream industries which will create joblessness and hardship to income earners," he wrote.

With regard to the pandemics that can put the entire world in fear of facing death, the deception is beyond our ability to comprehend at this point. There is good evidence, however, for the conviction that these kinds of fear-inducing lies could be at the center of the prophesied lie that leads to enslavement of the populations of the earth following the Rapture of the Church.

Never has there been such a global effort among national world leaders to bring their peoples into subjection. Demanded compliance in the matter of vaccinations and mask-wearing constitutes a powerful mechanism that could soon force all into the one-world mold Antichrist will impose.

The big lie—the great delusion of 2 Thessalonians chapter 2—might spring from the pandemic delusion that was foisted: that the jab will bring freedom from pestilences, freedom to be an accepted citizen of the new order.

What we have witnessed with the many lies involved with COVID might be a catalyst for Antichrist's underlings—his liars—to bring about control over humanity, which the father of lies has desired for millennia.

Nuclear War Worries

President Dwight D. Eisenhower warned of the global elite's threat. He called them the "military-industrial complex" and warned that these powers, because of the tremendous amounts of money to be made, tend to perpetuate armed conflicts.

Here is how it works in simplest terms. The government of the United States gives money to foreign governments perceived to be threatened by their neighbors or by other nations. The US then discourages the nation of its largesse from coming to diplomatic solutions; rather, it encourages the recipient nation to resist the negotiating table, even to the point of inviting military conflict.

Next, the US military and the arms-production industry receive the money back from the client state for arms sold to them. The US taxpayer, of course, is the one paying the bill. (Can you say "Ukraine"?)

Such has been the way of doing the business of war-making for many decades. To add insult to injury, of course, many young American lives are lost across the months and years when the US military often becomes drawn into the bloody battles.

The New World Order is indeed comprised of minions of the bloodiest of all beings. And we are witnessing as of this writing the buildup to the most horrific time and the bloodiest war of all of human history—Armageddon. Satan is influencing the vilest of all schemers to produce genocide-level warfare, while using media propagandists who put Joseph Goebbels' Nazi liars to shame.

There is a drumbeat for war in all directions we watch. And we are being warned by the media propagandists in cahoots with the military-industrial complex that Russia and its leader are threatening nuclear war. The propagandists have even created ludicrous public-service warnings that New York City residents need to think about steps to take in case of nuclear attack. They are told to go inside their buildings and not come out until the coast is clear—and to stay away from windows.

At least one member of this writing team is old enough to remember the "Duck and Cover" public service announcements of the 1950s. If you were a kid on your bike, you were supposed to jump off and get under a park bench or in a ditch and cover yourself by going into the fetal position.

If there's more ludicrous advice about how to hide from multi-megaton hydrogen bombs, we would like to hear it. We need a good laugh to relieve the tension created by the nuclear war worries.

The military-industrial complex Eisenhower warned of has never gone away, or even lessened in its fervency to use the rest of us for their love-of-money madness. Instead, it is now engaged, under the globalist-elite umbrella of saving the planet from climate change, the threat from pandemics, and nuclear war.

They will protect us by doing away with fossil fuels to stop deadly climate change. They will mask us and force us to take their unproven vaccines to eliminate pestilences, and they will technologically change the way we live through AI technologies that take things out of our human hands and entrust it to AI in the hands of the elites who know what is best for the planet.

They seem to know what's best for us as well as for the planet. Getting rid of most of us is the answer. The recommendation, according to their words engraved upon the recently removed Georgia Guidestones, is that only five hundred million people be allowed to inhabit the earth. That number left to live on the planet, of course, would include them, the New World Order elite.

The New World Order forges ahead, despite the actions of these self-appointed rulers of darkness causing great upheaval. The peoples of the earth are as Jesus Himself prophesied for the end of the age as His return nears. They are the "seas and waves roaring," and, because of food short-ages and other threats to their lives, the nations are in great "perplexity" as to how to deal with the chaos (Luke 21:25).

One of the chief gurus of the globalists elite and the World Economic Forum under the thumb, apparently, of Klaus Schwab, is Yuval Noah Harari.

The enigmatic Harari is an Israeli historian and pop philosopher, considered to be a thinker of first order by the globalist cabal. His book *Sapien* is a bestseller, having sold more than a million copies. His books have consistently made it to number one on the *New York Times* nonfiction list. But, it is often fiction in the guise of nonfiction that he writes—and often is blasphemous.

He writes God out of the picture, calling Jesus Christ and the Christian religion "fake." He proclaims there is no place for such thinking and that humans must begin to learn to become one with AI, if we are to survive and thrive upon a planet doomed without compliance with climate-change regulations and other World Economic Forum demands.

Much of what we've presented in this book is laying out what Satan has planned through the New World Order blueprint he has infused into his human assistants of Ephesians 6:12.

But for those who belong to the Jesus that Mr. Schwab and Mr. Harari mock and blaspheme, the future is the opposite of what the devil will temporarily achieve.

There is coming the "rebirth of liberty," which is the last part of our subtitle. Christ will rule and reign on a newly restored, pristine planet earth for one thousand years from Jerusalem, the capital of all the world.

If you want to be part of that glorious New World Order and live eternally with God, who loves you, here is how:

That if thou shalt confess with thy mouth the Lord Jesus, and shalt believe in thine heart that God hath raised him from the dead, thou shalt be saved. For with the heart man believeth unto righteousness; and with the mouth confession is made unto salvation. (Romans 10:9–10)

HUMAN/GOVERNMENT TIMELINE SUMMATION

Antediluvian/Genesis Patriarch Timeline

ANNO MUNDI - YEAR FROM CREATION CHARTS

MASORETIC TEXT CHART

Patriarch	Life	Birth - AM	Death - AM	Son
Adam	930	0	930	130
Seth	912	130	1042	105
Enosh	905	235	1140	90
Cainan	910	325	1235	70
Mahalalel	895	395	1290	65
Jared	962	460	1422	162
Enoch *	365	622	987	65
Methuselah	969	687	1656	187
Lamech	777	874	1651	182
Noah	950	1056	1954	502
Flood	1 yr.	1656	1657	
Shem	600	1558	2159	100
Arphaxad	438	1658	2097	35
Salah	433	1693	2127	30
Eber	464	1723	2188	34
Peleg	239	1757	1997	30
Reu	239	1787	2027	32
Serug	230	1819	2050	30
Nahor	148	1849	1998	29
Terah	205	1878	2084	130
Abram	175	2008	2184	100
Isaac	180	2108	2289	60
Jacob	147	2168	2316	90

*Enoch was raptured and did not see death.

SEPTUAGINT TEXT CHART

Patriarch	Life	Birth - AM	Death - AM	Son
Adam	930	0	930	230
Seth	912	230	1142	205
Enosh	905	435	1340	190
Cainan *	910	625	1535	170
Mahalalel	895	795	1690	165
Jared	962	960	1922	162
Enoch *	365	1122	1487	165
Methuselah	969	1287	2256	167
Lamech	753	1454	2207	188
Noah	950	1642	2592	502
Flood	1 yr.	2242	2243	
Sem	600	2144	2744	100
Arphaxad	535	2244	2779	135
Cainan	460	2379	2839	130
Salah	460	2509	2969	130
Eber	404	2639	3043	134
Peleg	339	2773	3112	130
Reu	339	2903	3242	132
Serug	330	3035	3365	130
Nahor	304	3165	3469	179
Terah	205	3344	3549	130
Abram	175	3474	3649	100
Isaac	180	3574	3754	60
Jacob	147	3634	3781	90

*Cainan's genealogy is not listed in the Masoretic Text.

*Enoch was raptured and did not see death.

LXX-MT Tables Courtesy of author Randy Nettles

2350 – 2300 BC: Sumer (capital – Erech)

2247 – Global dispersion into seventy families during the days of Peleg (b. 2242)

2300 – 2100 BC: Akkad (Nimrod/Sargon)

2150 – 1450 BC: Minoans (modern-day Crete)

2150 BC – Harrapan civilization (modern-day India)

2100 – 1700 BC: Babylon (modern-day Iraq)

1600 – 350 BC: Phoenicians

1500 – 400 BC: Olmec civilization (modern-day Mexico)

Nation	Dates of Rise and Fall	Time as an Empire	Prophetic Significance
Egypt 1st–24th Dynasty	2109–685 BC	1, 424 years	
Assyria	859–612 BC	247 years	
Babylon	612–538 BC	74 years	Head of Gold/ Lion
Persia	553–330 BC	223 years	Shoulders of Silver/ Bear
Greece	331–00 BC	231 years	Abdomen of Brass/ Leopard
Roman Republic	510–23 BC	487 years	Legs of Iron / Fierce Beast
Imperial Rome	23 BC–430 AD	407 years	Legs of Iron / Fierce Beast
Arab Empire	AD 634–880	246 years	
Holy Roman Empire	AD 753–1806	1, 053 years	Legs of Iron / Fierce Beast
Mameluke Empire	AD 1250–1517	267 years	
Ottoman Empire	AD 1326–1918	592 years	
Spanish Empire	AD 1500–1750	250 years	Legs of Iron / Fierce Beast
Romanov Empire	AD 1682–1916	234 years	Magog
British Empire	AD 1700–1950	250 years	Tarshish
United States	1776–Present	246 years (so far)	Young lions of Tarshish
Revived Roman Empire	1959–Present		Toes of Iron & Clay The Beast (Dan. 70th Week)

The Twentieth–Twenty-First Centuries Countdown

1. From 1897 to 2017: 120 years:

And the Lord said, My Spirit shall not strive with man forever, for he is indeed flesh; yet his days shall be *one hundred and twenty* years. (Genesis 6:3, emphasis added)

This could mean either that a person's life would be no longer than 120 years (which Noah, Shem, Job, and Abraham are all apparent violations of) or that, in 120 years, the judgment would come upon all of humankind via the Flood. We believe the latter explanation fits better with what actually transpired as a converging of events occurred: Methuselah died at the age of 969 years the same year that Noah turned 600, which was the same year the Flood (judgment) came.

2. From 1917 to 2017: 100 years:

Concerning future Israel:

> Now when the sun was going down, a deep sleep fell upon Abram; and behold, horror and great darkness fell upon him. Then He said to Abram: Know certainly that your descendants will be strangers in a land that is not theirs, and will serve them, and they will afflict them *four hundred years*. And also the nation whom they serve I will judge; afterward they shall come out with great possessions. Now as for you, you shall go to your fathers in peace; you shall be buried at a good old age. *But in the fourth generation* they shall return here, for the iniquity of the Amorites is not yet complete. (Genesis 15:12–16, emphasis added)

Here we have God prophesying over an unconscious Abraham that for four hundred years (four generations), his descendants would be in bondage. However, in the fourth generation, they would be delivered. This is the primary passage where we are dealing with a generation being as long as one hundred years in length.

3. From 1947 to 2017: 70 years (from the United Nations legal vote [Resolution 181, November 29, 1947] to allow for the reconstitution of a Jewish state ["70" represents both judgment and fulfillment]):

In relation to the Jews in Judaea:

> And this whole land shall be a desolation and an astonishment, and these nations shall serve the king of Babylon *seventy* years.

"Then it will come to pass, when *seventy* years are completed, that I will punish the king of Babylon and that nation, the land of the Chaldeans, for their iniquity," says the Lord; "and I will make it a perpetual desolation." (Jeremiah 25:11–12, emphasis added)

Their enslavement by the Babylonians lasted for exactly seventy years and was punishment/repayment for idolatry and the seventy Sabbath years they had violated in the land of Israel. (Leviticus 25:1–19; 2 Chronicles 36:20–21; Jeremiah 25:8–12)

To the Jewish people and Jerusalem:

Seventy weeks are determined…For *your people* and for *your holy city.* (Daniel 9:24–27)

We know the Seventy Weeks are weeks of years. Genesis 29:18–28 validates the use of this as a means of measurement, as does Leviticus 25 for a measurement of time (70 x 7 = 490 years). We know God deals with Israel in the form of heptads (groupings of seven); similar to how the Gentile world deals in decades (groupings of ten). We also know that 483 of those years were completed with Christ's death on the cross (Daniel 9:26). His triumphal entry into Jerusalem on Palm Sunday marked the 173,880th day from the commandment given to Nehemiah by the Persian King Artaxerxes in 445 BC (Nehemiah 2).

Since we know nothing historically occurred resembling Daniel 9:27 from AD 33–70, and the Temple ceased to exist after AD 70 until today, this one, final week (9:27) is yet future. This leaves one final week (7 years) to be completed. This week does not begin at the Rapture, but at the confirmation of a covenant between Israel, the Antichrist, and the many nations around Israel (Daniel 9:27). This further develops the idea that Antichrist comes with a deceptive initiative he fully plans to violate at the midpoint of that final week (Matthew 24:15). This Antichrist is the Revelation 6's "rider on the white horse," Daniel 7's "small horn," Daniel 8's "little horn," and Daniel 11's "willful king."

4. From May 14, 1948, to 2018: 70 years:

We are living through a second set of seventy years from the actual proclamation of the birth of the nation of Israel.

Where we see the birth pangs come after the birth:

Before she was in labor, she gave birth; Before her pain came, She delivered a male child. Who has heard such a thing? Who has seen such things? Shall the earth be made to give birth in one day? Or shall a nation be born at once? For as soon as Zion was in labor, She gave birth to her children. (Isaiah 66:7–8).

5. From 1967 to 2017: 50 years:

Fifty equals a Jubilee:

And you shall count seven sabbaths of years for yourself, seven times seven years; and the time of the seven sabbaths of years shall be to you forty-nine years. Then you shall cause the trumpet of the Jubilee to sound on the tenth day of the seventh month; on the Day of Atonement you shall make the trumpet to sound throughout all your land. And you shall *consecrate the fiftieth year*, and proclaim liberty throughout all the land to all its inhabitants. It shall be a Jubilee for you; and each of you shall return to his possession, and each of you shall return to his family. (Leviticus 25:8–12, emphasis added)

6. From 1977 to 2017: 40 years:

For after seven more days I will cause it to rain on the earth forty days and forty nights, and I will destroy from the face of the earth all living things that I have made. (Genesis 7:4)

See also: Exodus 16:35 (Israelites wandered in the desert forty years); 1 Samuel 17:16 (Goliath taunted Israel for forty days); 1 Kings 19:8 (Elijah fasted forty days); Luke 4:1–13 (Jesus' temptation for forty days and nights), etc.

The year 1977 is a unique one that saw the genesis of what would become a forty-year period of testing known as the "Land for Peace" initiatives, which officially began at Camp David after the election of US President Jimmy Carter, Israeli Prime Minister Menachem Begin, and Egyptian President Anwar Sadat.

7. From 1987 to 2017: 30 years:

Thirty years is most commonly associated with the Jewish Temple in terms of age and of measurements (cubits). Men could not enter ministerial duties until they were of age (thirty years), which speaks to why Christ waited until He was "about thirty" before He began His own ministry (Numbers 4; Luke 3:23). In 1987, the Temple Mount Institute was established in Jerusalem with the sole purpose of raising funds, resources, and people to serve in a newly rebuilt third Jewish Temple.

8. December 6, 2017: 0 years:

The leader of the most powerful nation on earth, US President Donald Trump, officially recognizes Jerusalem as the undivided capital of the state of Israel and instructs his administration to begin preparations to move the US Embassy from Tel Aviv to Jerusalem.

He said:

> In 1995, Congress adopted the Jerusalem Embassy Act, urging the federal government to relocate the American embassy to Jerusalem and to recognize that that city—and so importantly—is Israel's capital. This act passed Congress by an overwhelming bipartisan majority and was reaffirmed by a unanimous vote of the Senate only six months ago.
>
> Yet, for over 20 years, every previous American president has exercised the law's waiver, refusing to move the U.S. embassy to Jerusalem or to recognize Jerusalem as Israel's capital city.

Presidents issued these waivers under the belief that delaying the recognition of Jerusalem would advance the cause of peace. Some say they lacked courage, but they made their best judgments based on facts as they understood them at the time. Nevertheless, the record is in. After more than two decades of waivers, we are no closer to a lasting peace agreement between Israel and the Palestinians. It would be folly to assume that repeating the exact same formula would now produce a different or better result.

Therefore, I have determined that it is time to officially recognize Jerusalem as the capital of Israel.

While previous presidents have made this a major campaign promise, they failed to deliver. Today, I am delivering.[113]

9. May 14, 2018: + 5 months:
The US moves its embassy from Tel Aviv to Jerusalem. Other nations have begun to follow suit.

In summary, we see the countdown from the first stirrings of the Jewish people to the final recognition of Jerusalem as Israel's capital. Let us add in the biblical implications.

1897–2017 = 120 years (time-span limits)
1917–2017 = 100 years (outer limits of a generation)
1947–2017 = 70 years (judgment, testing, heptad)
1948–2018 = 70 years (judgment, testing, heptad)
1967–2017 = 50 years (Jubilee, liberation, freedom)
1977–2017 = 40 years (testing)
1987–2017 = 30 years (related to the Temple)
2017 = Year Zero
2018–2028 =10 years (Psalm 90:10; 2 Peter 3:8–9)

HISTORY OF RELIGION

THE ORIGINAL PAGAN RELIGION (or anti-God religion) in the pre-Flood (or Antediluvian world) was Luciferianism. This is a belief system created by the fallen angel Lucifer before his failed heavenly *coup d'état*. Luciferianism is rooted in pride and the false belief that men (and fallen angels) can become like God. From a purely human standpoint, Luciferianism claims to offer those things that were lost in the Garden of Eden—immortality and escape from a future judgment.

Until fairly recently, Luciferianism rarely came in its true form. It was often veiled under the guise of numerous pagan religions and deities. These were/are all works-based religions that claim to grant these two things (immortality and redemption) depending on how faithful you maintain the demands of said pagan religion. Thus, as we go through the numerous pagan religions, remember, all of their roots trace back to the *father of lies*, Lucifer.

Pre Flood Paganism

(Based on Ken Johnson's excellent book, *Ancient Paganism*)

Below is an abbreviated list of some of the commonalities between both pre-Flood and post-Flood pagan religions shared.

1. Practiced idol worship
2. Believed they would evolve into godhood (see Genesis 6:4)

3. Believed God exhausted Himself in creation and would fade away

4. Salvation was not necessary

5. Observed the heavens for signs

6. Used the stars to navigate the future

7. The horoscope did not yet exist (it was created later by the Chaldeans)

8. Ritual use of blood (see Genesis 9:4–6)

9. Luciferianism masked with pantheism

10. Homosexual marriage normalized

Post Flood/Pre-Babel Religions

Noah's sons and daughters-in-law survived the Flood and would go on to help repopulate the planet. The post-Flood planet was vastly different than the world they would come to inherit. They shared with their descendants what the pre-Flood world was like, and idealized and romanticized (as is common with humans) the way things were. The conditions they idealized would include the long life spans, super-human strength, the idyllic natural environment, as well as the common goings-on of the fallen angels masquerading as demigods, intermarrying with human women, and producing human-angel hybrids.

1. Ham's descendants are thought to be largely responsible for carrying the pre-Flood paganism into the new, post-Flood world

2. Ham's descendants were:

- Cush (Nimrod's father)
- Mizraim (Egypt)
- Canaan
- Phut

3. Nimrod would go on to found numerous cities such as Erech, Babel, and other cities in the plains of Shinar. His religion (according to

the extrabiblical book of Jasher 11:19–20) was based on the zodiac, and his death would spawn one of the most prolific religious structures the world has ever seen, the Mother-Child religion.

4. Worship of idols (teraphim) of lesser gods and ancestors

5. Using "high places" to offer their false worship because Satan is the "prince of the power of the air" (Ephesians 2:2)

Post Babel Religions

Although God separated humankind at Babel, the dispersed people would go on to take Babel-based religious ideas with them. This is why ziggurats and other pyramid-like structures, as well as similar pagan religious megalith sites, are found around the world. After God scattered humanity, we can see that, although the names are changed, the same stories emerge from each of these pagan belief systems.

(Based on the *Secrets of Ancient Man* by Don Landis.)

1. Baal and Molech worship—practiced by the Canaanites.

2. Babylonians worshipped Marduk (Nimrod's son Mardon) and created the Mother-Son worship that is later venerated throughout varying pagan cultures under differing names.

	FATHER	MOTHER	SON
Babylonian	Nimrod	Semiramis	Tammuz
Assyria	Nimrod/Sargon	Ishtar/Astarte	Tammuz
Egypt (Mizraim)	Ra	Isis	Horus
Greece	Zeus	Aphrodite	Eros
Rome	Jupiter	Venus	Cupid
Nordic	Odin	Jord	Thor
Hindu	Vishnu	Isi	Aswara
Roman Catholic	God	Virgin Mary	Jesus
Israel		Queen of Heaven	Tammuz
Luciferian	Lucifer	Goddess Diana	Antichrist

From Babylon, by Andy Woods, page 9:

3. Assyrians worshipped Ashur (same as Nimrod's son, just a different name).

4. Although throughout the Shinar valley and Mesopotamia the pagan gods were largely the same, each city-state had its own patron god they prayed to in the Sumerian culture.

5. Various leaders in the post-Babel world claimed godhood.

- Gilgamesh (Sumer) "part god."
- Hammurabi (Babylon) "messenger of the gods."
- Ramses II (Egypt) all pharaohs claimed divine lineage.
- Nebuchadnezzar (Babylon) claimed divine status (Daniel 4:30) but later recanted and repented.
- Qin Shi Huang Di (China) Chinese emperors deified as "sons of heaven" since the Qin Dynasty.
- Alexander the Great (Greece) claimed lineage to Zeus.
- August and Julius Caesar (Rome) Augustus deified Julius, then claimed sonship to him.
- Nero (Rome) claimed godhood.
- Caligula (Rome) claimed godhood.

6. Akkad worshipped Nimrod/Sargon.

7. Minoan culture (Crete) worshipped a form of naturalistic paganism (Mother Earth).

8. Harrapan civilization (India) paganism and polytheism.

9. Babylon covers the Shinar Valley (paganism and ancestor worship).

10. Egyptians worshipped their pharaohs as gods.

11. Olmecs worshipped various pagan gods.

12. Phoenicians (Baal, Molech, etc.).

13. Hebrews/Israelites/Jews were supposed to only worship the one true God, Jehovah. However, many resorted to absorbing or embracing the pagan worship of their neighbors (for example, the golden calf).

Post Exodus through Roman Paganism

(Primary Deity)
1. Sumerians (Enlil)
2. Indus Valley civilizations (origins of Hinduism)
3. Philistines (Dagon)
4. Phoenicians (Baal)
5. Assyrians (Ashur)
6. Chaldeans/Babylonians (Marduk)
7. Medo-Persian (Ahura Mazda)
8. Greeks (Zeus)
9. Romans (Jupiter, Juno, and Minerva)

Common Era Religions and Paganism

1. Judaism
2. Hinduism
3. Buddhism
4. Christianity
5. Gnosticism
6. Roman Catholicism (merging paganism into Christianity)
7. Islam
8. Protestantism (has since splintered into hundreds of separate groups)
9. Pseudo-Christian groups (Mormonism, Jehovah's Witnesses, Christian Science, etc.)
10. New Age (Eastern mysticism and gnosticism)
11. Emergent church (merging Eastern mysticism into the Christianity)
12. Chrislam (merging Islam into Christianity)

MODERN PROGRESSION TECHNOLOGY/PHILOSOPHIES

AD 500–1300: Middle or Dark Ages

- At this point, knowledge (as a whole) was doubling around every five hundred years, until the thirteenth century.
- Religious theocracies (Byzantine and Holy Roman Empires, various Islamic caliphates and sultanates) and dynastic monarchies dominated much of the known world.
- The era was marked by slow academic growth, high illiteracy rates, widespread superstition, and disconnectedness.
- The greatest invention of the era was the mechanical clock (Yi Xing, AD 724).

1300–1600: Renaissance and Reformation

- General knowledge began doubling to about every 250 years.
- The Reformation movements began as the Holy Roman Empire's grip on Europe began to fracture Christendom between Protestants and Catholics.
- The era marked by an explosion of art, scientific theories, astronomy, and naval exploration known as the Renaissance.
- The greatest invention of the era was the printing press (Johannes Gutenberg, circa 1450).

1600–1800: Age of Enlightenment

- General knowledge began doubling every 150 years.
- The era was marked by an explosion of economic and scientific theories.
- Greatest expansion of colonization by European powers.
- The greatest invention of the era was the steam engine (Thomas Newcomen, 1712).

1789–1945: Age of Reason
(Secularization)

- General knowledge began doubling every one hundred years.
- The era was marked by explosions of political conflicts (the American and French revolutions, the American Civil War, and numerous European revolutions) and radical theoretical philosophies (existentialism: Soren Kierkegaard, Friedrich Nietzsche, Jean Paul Sartre, etc.); Marxism (socialism): Karl Marx, Friedrich Engels; Darwinism: Charles Darwin; social Darwinism: Thomas Huxley, Herbert Spencer, Thomas Malthus, Francis Galton, Margaret Sanger, and the Third Reich; and communism/socialism: Vladimir Lenin, Benito Mussolini, Adolf Hitler.

1760–1870 First Industrial Revolution
(Mechanization)

- Technology began doubling every one hundred years.
- Man began to harness the power of steam and fossil fuels.
- The greatest inventions of the era were vaccines (Edward Jenner, 1796), the electric battery (Alessandro Volta, 1800), steam-powered trains (George Stephenson, 1814), and the telegraph (Samuel Morse, 1840–1850).

1870–1969 Second Industrial Revolution
(Mass Production)

- Technological knowledge doubled every twenty-five years.
- Modern warfare was introduced during World War I.
- Electrical grids were developed for urban areas; telephones allowed for instant communication between vast distances.
- The era was marked by the creation of the assembly lines (mass production), automobiles, manned flight, and industrial monopolies (oil, steel, coal, etc.).
- The greatest inventions of the era were the light bulb (Thomas Edison, 1880); the first successful airplane (Wilbur and Orville Wright, 1903); and the atomic bomb (Manhattan Project, 1939).

1969–2000 Third Industrial Revolution
(Automation)

- Technology doubled every fifteen years.
- Atomic warfare was introduced at the end of World War II.
- Information increasingly became digitalized.
- The era was marked by the introduction of automation, electronics, televisions, computers, space travel, and global threats (nuclear war).
- The greatest inventions of the era were the transistor (Bell Laboratories, 1947) and the Internet (ARPANET, 1969).

1980–2000: Post-Industrial Era
(Hybrid/Transition)

- Technology doubled every five to ten years.
- The birth of consumer Internet use and industrial robotization occurred.

- Information was slowly being encoded into separate Internet systems.
- The era was marked by rapid increase of import goods and trades, high consumerism, and distrust in political systems.

2000–Present: Fourth Industrial Revolution
(Digitalization)

- Information processing doubling every twenty-four to thirty-six months.
- Information and processes are increasingly tied to the Internet.
- The era is marked by terrorism, war, economic uncertainty, and rapid technological and scientific breakthroughs.

2010–2020: Industrial Revolution 4.0
(hybrid/transition era)

- Information processing doubling every eighteen to twenty-four months.
- Wireless systems are powered by 3G and 4G networks.
- This period sees the genesis of smart devices, cloud computing, the Internet of Things (IoT), artificial intelligence (AI), quantum computing, cryptocurrencies, and virtual reality, etc.
- Almost all information and processes are now online.
- This era is marked by economic downturns, terrorism, and nationalization.

2020 and beyond
(Virtual/Augmented Reality)

- IBM, Google, Apple, etc., are attempting to get the knowledge-doubling curve down to every twelve hours.

- Goals are to automate everything that can be automated and embed it with artificial intelligence.
- The plan is to transition current information cyber physical systems to nanotechnologies and quantum technologies (for handling massive amounts of data).
- Progress leads to all wireless systems being powered by 5G networks.
- SovereignSky program (space-based blockchain).
- Efforts are being made to implement lethal autonomous (AI) weapons systems (LAWS) to fight wars in the near future (robotic weapon systems [drones], smart bombs, etc.).
- This era is marked by increased uncertainty, deception, violence, and wickedness as "deep-fake" technology, proliferation of hybridized worldviews, and historical revisionism distort all truth.

NOTES

1. https://www.amazon.com/Fourth-Industrial-Revolution-Professor-Dr-Ing-ebook/dp/B01MSJM2TE.
2. https://www.ncbi.nlm.nih.gov/pmc/articles/PMC7577689/.
3. Pentecost, D. *Things to Come* (Grand Rapids, MI: Zondervan, 1958).
4. Cott, J. (1980, December 25). "The Cosmos: An Interview with Carl Sagan." *Rolling Stone*. https://www.rollingstone.com/culture/culture-features/the-cosmos-an-interview-with-carl-sagan-236668/.
5. "Darwin Plagiarism." creation.com. (January 24, 2014). Creation | Creation Ministries International. https://creation.com/darwin-plagiarism.
6. Landis, D. (December 2015). *Secrets of Ancient Man: The Legacy for Rebellion*. Christianbook.com, https://www.christianbook.com/secrets-ancient-the-legacy-for-rebellion/9780890518663/pd/518663.
7. "Cicero Marcus Tullius Cicero." (February 12, 2017). *The Project Gutenberg eBook of the Republic of Cicero, by G. W. Featherstonehaugh*. Free eBooks | Project Gutenberg.
8. Pearce D. "Transhumanism; Nick Bostrom and David Pearce Talk to Andrés Lomeña." (April 26, 2015). *Literal Magazine*. https://literalmagazine.com/transhumanism-nick-bostrom-and-david-pearce-talk-to-andres-lomena/.
9. Evans, D. A. (2021). Meso-Neoproterozoic Rodinia Supercycle. https://www.sciencedirect.com/science/article/pii/B9780128185339000060; https://www.sciencedirect.com/topics/earth-and-planetary-sciences/rodinia.

277

10. The Nephilim, *Grace thru Faith,* (August 6, 2018). https://gracethrufaith.com/end-times-prophecy/the-nephilim/.

11. https://creation.com/nimrod-post-flood-empire-builder.

12. Josephus, F. (1889). *The Works of Flavius Josephus: Antiquities of the Jews,* book XIV to end.

13. "Were the Pyramids Built Before the Flood? (Masoretic Text vs. Original Hebrew)," https://youtu.be/VI1yRTC6kGE).

14. Chaffey, T. *Fallen: The Sons of God and the Nephilim.* (Risen Books, 2019), p. 251.

15. Ibid., p. 233.

16. https://youtu.be/VI1yRTC6kGE.

17. James, T., et al, *Lawless: End-times War against the Spirit of Antichrist* (Crane, MO: Defender, 2020).

18. Page, L. (November 6, 2009). "Something May Come Through" Dimensional "Doors" at LHC." *The Register: Enterprise Technology News and Analysis.* https://www.theregister.com/2009/11/06/lhc_dimensional_portals/

19. Gibbon, E. *The History of the Decline and Fall of the Roman Empire.* (1789).

20. "Third Reich." (n.d.). *Encyclopedia Britannica.* https://www.britannica.com/place/Third-Reich.

21. S. Franklin Logsdon, *Profiles of Prophecy,* (Grand Rapids, MI: Zondervan, 1973), p. 119.

22. Kern, S. (November 7, 2021). "European Army: Rhetoric versus Reality." Gatestone Institute. https://www.gatestoneinstitute.org/17917/european-army.

23. "The Wisdom of Charles Krauthammer." (June 22, 2018). Fox News. https://www.foxnews.com/politics/the-wisdom-of-charles-krauthammer.

24. "Bretton Woods Agreement and System: An Overview." (November 25, 2003). Investopedia. https://www.investopedia.com/terms/b/brettonwoodsagreement.asp.

25. "Marshall Plan." (August 23, 2001,). Wikipedia, the free encyclopedia.

Retrieved August 3, 2022, from https://en.wikipedia.org/wiki/Marshall_ Plan .

26. "From John Adams to Massachusetts Militia." *(October 11, 1798)* (n.d.). Founders Online. https://founders.archives.gov/documents/ Adams/99-02-02-3102.

27. President Ronald Reagan: January 5, 1967: Inaugural address (Public ceremony). Ronald Reagan. https://www.reaganlibrary.gov/archives/speech/ january-5-1967-inaugural-address-public-ceremony.

28. Duca, John V. (n.d.). "Subprime Mortgage Crisis." Federal Reserve History. https://www.federalreservehistory.org/essays/ subprime-mortgage-crisis.

29. Glubb, S. J. (1978). "The Fate of Empires and Search for Survival."

30. Angell, N. (1910). *The Great Illusion.*

31. Kaletsky, A. (June 27, 2014). "World War One: First War Was Impossible, Then Inevitable." U.S. https://www.reuters.com/article/ idUS74746206720140627.

32. "Does China Have an Aging Problem?" (March 19, 2020). ChinaPower Project. https://chinapower.csis.org/aging-problem/.

33. Glubb, S. J. (1978). "The Fate of Empires and Search for Survival."

34. Full text of "Rules for Radicals." (n.d.). Internet Archive: Digital Library of Free & Borrowable Books, Movies, Music & Wayback Machine. https://archive.org/stream/RulesForRadicals/RulesForRadicals_djvu.txt.

35. Luciferianism. (September 26, 2004). Wikipedia, the free encyclopedia. Retrieved August 3, 2022, from https://en.wikipedia.org/wiki/ Luciferianism.

36. https://www.lucistrust.org/about_us/history.

37. Lioness of Judah Ministry. (December 9, 2021). "The occult is the spiritual foundation of the United Nations. The stage is set for the coming one-world government under one world leader." Exposing The Darkness | Lioness of Judah Ministry | Substack. https://lionessofjudah.substack. com/p/the-occult-is-the-spiritual-foundation.

38. Harari, Y. N. (2017). *Homo Deus: A Brief History of Tomorrow.* (New York: HarperCollins, 2017).

39. Franklin, A., and Pearce, T. *EU: Final World Empire*, a video program produced by Hearthstone and distributed in the United States by Southwest Radio Church in Oklahoma City, Oklahoma.

40. Warburg, J. P. Testimony to U.S. Senate Committee on Foreign Relations on 2/27/1950.

41. Rectenwald, M. "The Great Reset, part VI: Plans of a Technocratic Elite, (n.d.). Mises Institute. https://mises.org/wire/great-reset-part-vi-plans-technocratic-elite?fbclid=IwAR3st86DPa2OgIZfCPq5uAIFWRWn C01VYvlh6ZjGeBwpVz300C8iygxhycM.

42. Rhodes, C. "Confession of Faith," 1877. (n.d.). https://pages.uoregon. edu/kimball/Rhodes-Confession.htm.

43. Hodge, S. (n.d.). "Top 10 Obsolete Government Programs." Heritage Foundation. https://www.heritage.org/budget-and-spending/commentary/top-10-obsolete-government-programs.

44. "Elitist Sentiments Threatening Liberties." (n.d.). NOTE: This is a historic archive (2005) using an old HTML. https://www.gwb.com.au/gwb/news/multi/goldwatr.html.

45. The President and the Press: Address before the American Newspaper Publishers Association, April 27, 1961. https://www.jfklibrary.org/archives/other-resources/john-f-kennedy-speeches/american-newspaper-publishers-association-19610427.

46. Schwab, K. (2017). *The Fourth Industrial Revolution*. "Currency."

47. "The Great Reset." (n.d.). World Economic Forum. https://www.weforum.org/great-reset/.

48. Svoboda, M. (n.d.). "Only a Crisis—Actual or Perceived—Produces Real Change." Quotepark.com. https://quotepark.com/quotes/1946283-milton-friedman-only-a-crisis-actual-or-perceived-produces-real-ch/.

49. Johnson, G., Johnson, E., & Johnson, E. (1983). *"Architects of Fear: Conspiracy Theories and Paranoia in American Politics*. (Tarcher, 1983) p. 222.

50. Libertytree.ca. (n.d.). Quotation by Larry P. McDonald. LibertyQuotes. https://libertytree.ca/quotes/Larry.McDonald.Quote.5040.

51. Rockefeller, D. *Memoirs*, (New York: Random House, 2003) p. 406.

52. Teichrib, C. *Game of Gods: The Temple of Man in the Age of Reenchantment.* (Whitemud House, 2018).

53. Schwartz, T. F. (n.d.). "George Soros Warns Trump of Potential Economic Doom before Election." CNBC. https://www.cnbc.com/2020/01/23/george-soros-warns-trump-of-potential-economic-doom-before-election.html.

54. Laudato SI' (24 May 2015) | Francis. (2015, June 18). Vatican. https://www.vatican.va/content/francesco/en/encyclicals/documents/papa-francesco_20150524_enciclica-laudato-si.html.

55. Huxley, A. *Brave New World.* (Vintage Canada, 2007).

56. "False flag," Merriam-Webster, https://www.merriam-webster.com/dictionary/false%20flag.

57. Olsen, H. (May 27, 2022). *Washington Post.* https://www.washingtonpost.com/opinions/2022/05/27/texas-uvalde-shooting-police-we-should-support-law-enforcement-but-they-must-fulfill-their-oaths/.

58. "Sandy Hook Shooting: Active-shooter Drill Confirmed by Law Enforcement Raises Suspicions." (n.d.). Illegal Immigration News & Discussions. https://www.alipac.us/f19/sandy-hook-shooting-active-shooter-drill-confirmed-law-enforcement-raises-suspici-270722/.

59. "Libor Scandal Grows as the Fathers of Two Mass Murderers Were to Testify National Finance Examiner." (June 5, 2018). Las Vegas Criminal Lawyer: Wooldridge Law—LV Criminal Defense. https://www.lvcriminaldefense.com/libor-scandal-grows-fathers-two-mass-murderers-testify-national-finance-examiner/.

60. The LIBOR Scandal was a highly-publicized scheme in which bankers at several major financial institutions colluded with each other to manipulate the London Interbank Offered Rate (LIBOR). The scandal sowed distrust in the financial industry and led to a wave of fines, lawsuits, and regulatory actions. Although the scandal came to light in 2012, there is evidence suggesting that the collusion in question had been ongoing since as early as 2003 (https://www.investopedia.com/terms/l/libor-scandal.asp).

61. https://thenewamerican.com/many-unanswered-questions-about-las-vegas-shooting/.

62. "Bump stocks or bump fire stocks are gun stocks that can be used to assist in bump firing. Bump firing is the act of using the recoil of a semi-automatic firearm to fire ammunition cartridges in rapid succession." (https://en.wikipedia.org/wiki/Bump_stock).

63. History.com editors. (June 16, 2017). MK-Ultra. HISTORY. https://www.history.com/topics/us-government/history-of-mk-ultra.

64. "37 Mass Shooters Who Were on Antidepressants." (September 11, 2019). Thought Catalog. https://thoughtcatalog.com/jeremy-london/2019/09/37-mass-shooters-who-were-on-antidepressants/.

65. Sanford, C. (November 8, 2021). Prince Charles COP26 Climate Summit Glasgow Speech Transcript. Rev. https://www.rev.com/blog/transcripts/prince-charles-cop26-climate-summit-glasgow-speech-transcript.

66. https://www.investopedia.com/terms/k/keynesianeconomics.asp.

67. "Now Is the Time for a 'Great Reset'." (June 3, 2020). World Economic Forum. https://www.weforum.org/agenda/2020/06/now-is-the-time-for-a-great-reset/.

68. "Uniformitarianism." (2001, October 24). Wikipedia, the free encyclopedia. Retrieved August 5, 2022, from https://en.wikipedia.org/wiki/Uniformitarianism.

69. King, A. "The First Global Revolution: A Report." (1992).

70. Maurice Strong, Interview in 1992 concerning the plot of a book he would like to write. https://quotepark.com/authors/maurice-strong/?o=popular.

71. Adams, M. (March 28, 2018). "The United Nations 2030 Agenda Decoded: It's a Blueprint for the Global Enslavement of Humanity under the Boot of Corporate Masters." DC Clothesline (courtesy Natural News). https://www.dcclothesline.com/2018/03/28/the-united-nations-2030-agenda-decoded-its-a-blueprint-for-the-global-enslavement-of-humanity-under-the-boot-of-corporate-masters/.

72. Libertytree.ca. (n.d.). Quotation by Mayer Amschel Rothschild. LibertyQuotes. https://libertytree.ca/quotes/Mayer.Amschel.Rothschild.Quote.8BED.

73. Rectenwald, M. "The Backstory of the Great Reset, or

How to Destroy Classical Liberalism." (June 11, 2022). https://www.michaelrectenwald.com/great-reset-essays-interviews/the-backstory-of-the-great-reset-or-how-to-destroy-classical-liberalism.

74. "A fifth column is any group of people who undermine a larger group from within, usually in favor of an enemy group or nation…. The activities of a fifth column can be overt or clandestine. Forces gathered in secret can mobilize openly to assist an external attack. This term is also extended to organised actions by military personnel. Clandestine fifth column activities can involve acts of sabotage, disinformation, or espionage executed within defense lines by secret sympathizers with an external force." (https://en.wikipedia.org/wiki/Fifth_column).

75. "Five Ways Quantum Computing Will Change the Business World." (October 12, 2021). *Investment Monitor*. https://www.investmentmonitor.ai/tech/five-ways-quantum-computing-will-change-the-world.

76. "What Is Deep Learning?" (May 1, 2020). IBM - United States. https://www.ibm.com/cloud/learn/deep-learning.

77. World Economic Forum. (n.d.). Strategic intelligence https://intelligence.weforum.org/topics/a1Gb0000000LHOUEA4?tab=publications.

78. Hanson, V. D. (February 4, 2005). "The Global Throng." www.nationalreview.com/hanson/hanson200502040750.asp.

79. Inflation. (n.d.). The Economics Network. https://www.economicsnetwork.ac.uk/archive/keynes_persuasion/Inflation.htm.

80. Rectenwald, M. "The Backstory of the Great Reset, or How to Destroy Classical Liberalism." (n.d.). Mises Institute. https://mises.org/wire/backstory-great-reset-or-how-destroy-classical-liberalism.

81. "European Commission Will Launch €1 Billion Quantum Technologies Flagship." (December 2016). Digital Single Market. https://wayback.archive-it.org/12090/20161223175140/https://ec.europa.eu/digital-single-market/en/news/european-commission-will-launch-eu1-billion-quantum-technologies-flagship.

82. https://creation.com/nimrod-post-flood-empire-builder.

83. Read, L. "How to Advance Liberty." (n.d.). Mises Institute. https://

mises.org/library/how-advance-liberty.

84. Conspiracy Fact: https://youtu.be/J0-8ez5exeM.

85. Forbes. (n.d.) https://www.forbes.com/sites/gregsatell/2016/10/02/
heres-how-quantum-computing-will-change-the-
world/?sh=234d7b75ad6d.

86. "Propaganda," definition #2. https://www.merriam-webster.com/
dictionary/propagandaMerriam Webster.

87. "Clausewitz, C. *On War*, pp. 90–123.

88. Source: https://www.gaia.com/article/
oldest-conspiracies-proven-true-project-echelon.

89. From Dr. Tommy Ice. https://www.blueletterbible.org/Comm/ice_
thomas/Mat24-25/Mat24-25_Part07.cfm.

90. "The First Ever Quantum Computer—What Was It Used
For? (October 7, 2019). AZoQuantum.com. https://www.azoquantum.
com/Article.aspx?ArticleID=143.

91. https://expose-news.com/2022/10/27/
drs-find-graph-ene-shed-vax-to-unvax/.

92. https://www.ncbi.nlm.nih.gov/pmc/articles/PMC7577689/.
December18, 2020.

93. "The Return of an Intelligence Code Word with a Storied History."
(July 9, 2014). The Week. https://theweek.com/articles/445540/
return-intelligence-code-word-storied-history.

94. "The Pentagon Finally Admits It Investigates UFOs." (May
22, 2019). *New York Post.* https://nypost.com/2019/05/22/
the-pentagon-finally-admits-it-investigates-ufos/.

95. "Former Intelligence Chief: 'Quite a Few More' UFOs Detected Than
Public Knows." (March 20, 2021). *Washington Examiner.* https://www.
washingtonexaminer.com/news/former-intelligence-chief-quite-a-few-
more-ufos-detected-than-public-knows.

96. https://youtu.be/emn6jozxHxU.

97. *The Encyclopedia of Extraterrestrial Encounters: A Definitive, Illustrated
A-Z Guide to All Things Alien.* (2001).

98. Sprinkle , R. L. *Encyclopedia of Extraterrestrial Encounters.*

99. 116th Congress Second Session. (2021). "Intelligence Authorization Act for Fiscal Year 2021." https://www.govinfo.gov/content/pkg/CRPT-116srpt233/pdf/CRPT-116srpt233.pdf.

100. Cooper, D. L. "Golden Rule of Interpretation," emphasis added. http://www.messianicassociation.org/ezine19-dc.hermeneutics.htm.

101. Kelley, J. "Seven Heads and Ten Horns," Grace thru faith. (August 5, 2011). https://gracethrufaith.com/ask-a-bible-teacher/seven-heads-and-ten-horns/.

102   Koenig, D. https://www.thepropheticyears.com/enddepravity/globalism-will-fail-until-the-beastantichrist.html.

103. Brainard, L. *The New Heavens and Earth: Recreation or Renovation?* (Soothkeep Press, 2022), p. 78.

104. Abbott, J. (n.d.). *John S.C. Abbott, the history of Napoleon Bonaparte,* Ch 38. (Yamaguchy Inc.,Yarmulka Inc.). https://www.yamaguchy.com/library/abbott/bonapart_38.html.

105. Space.com Staff. "*How the Japan Earthquake Shortened Days on Earth.* (March 13, 2011). Space.com. https://www.space.com/11115-japan-earthquake-shortened-earth-days.html.

106. Brainard, *New Heavens and Earth.*

107. Mullin, M. (2022). https://www.rev310.net/post/a-handbook-into-the-terrifying-and-wondrous-realms-of-god-part-ii. (Punctuation edited.)

108. Brainard, L., *New Heavens and Earth*, p. 14.

109. "Eternity." https://www.merriam-webster.com/dictionary/eternityerriam Webster.

110. https://www.ncbi.nlm.nih.gov/pmc/articles/PMC7577689/.

111. Brainard, L., *New Heavens and Earth*, p. 14.

112. Larkin, C. (1919). *The Book of Revelation*, p. 200.

113. U.S. Mission Israel. (January 20, 2021). Statement by former President Trump on Jerusalem.

CPSIA information can be obtained
at www.ICGtesting.com
Printed in the USA
BVHW072104140323
660158BV00012B/24